THE LANGUAGE OF
FRENCH SYMBOLISM

The Language of French Symbolism

BY JAMES R. LAWLER

PRINCETON UNIVERSITY PRESS

PRINCETON, NEW JERSEY

1969

Publication of this book has been
aided by the Whitney Darrow Publication Reserve Fund
of Princeton University Press

This book has been composed in Linotype Caledonia

Printed in the United States of America
by Princeton University Press, Princeton, New Jersey

For Christiane

Preface

THIS BOOK is a contribution to the study of six French poets whose principal works span the half-century between 1870 and 1920. I take the term "Symbolism" primarily in a historical sense, as applying to a group of writers who brought rare intensity to the practice of their art. They had no common doctrine or exclusive techniques but a profound acquaintance with the Romantics, above all Lamartine and Hugo, and with Charles Baudelaire, who stands by their side, having opened the path. To such predecessors each in his way provided an answer.

It will be evident that I owe much to the numerous scholarly essays on Symbolism, in particular those of the last decade, which have led us further than ever before into its secrets. I have also drawn on the critical writings of the authors themselves, deeply concerned as they were with their art, carrying linguistic consciousness to a point unknown in poetry, sensitive to the accomplishments of their peers. I consider myself especially fortunate in this respect to have been able to consult certain unpublished papers of two figures who are at the heart of this analysis. Yet despite such obvious indebtedness I trust that the approach adopted has a focus of its own: I have centered my remarks on what I take to be important compositions of the period; I have tried to combine linguistic and formal study with reference to other parts of each author's work, so that details can be seen in the light of an individual quest; and I have suggested, in the terms of each, that although the poem contains its author as nothing else can—bearing the name of "Beauty," "Naïveté," "Love," "the Abyss," or "Purity," or "Music"—it opens out onto a pattern greater than any personal myth.

Mallarmé appeared to be an invaluable point of departure. He may be said to sound the keynote for the variety of poetic experiences contained in these pages by his pursuit of a "purer meaning" which was in essence the utilization to the full of the resources of language. He divorced poetry from the particular, wrung the neck of eloquence and sought a controlled ambiguity which would give the initiative to words themselves. The delicacy and determination with which he strove toward that end by way of the concept of an unwritten and doubtless unwritable Book, and the many poems he published "en vue de mieux," are the subject of my chapter on him. In the case of Verlaine, the project, if more intuitive, was carried out with comparable integrity. His work aspires to an ideal of ingenuousness which he summoned the ruses of language to attain; it reveals a concerted art dedicated to reason's overthrow. My third poet is Rimbaud, who, of the six authors chosen, has received the most contradictory critical estimates. However, instead of tackling the Rimbaud "problem" directly, I have examined in detail one of his most remarkable prose-poems in order to show the rhetoric of vision it demonstrates; I have also suggested that his exhaustive appraisal of words, and the reliance on diverse rhetorical principles we discover in "Génie," may help us to read other obscure pieces and to understand more keenly the nature of his originality. This is not the art of a mystic, I take it, but of an eminently able stylist for whom language became the means of "changing the world."

The fourth chapter is intended to serve as a bridge between my reading of the first and second generations of Symbolists. It attempts to explore the relationship between two poets on whom Mallarmé had a profound influence and who remained closely attached to his work and personality throughout their later lives; who wrote perceptively of Verlaine; who found Rimbaud to be a heady mixture. Yet the works they left are of a very different kind and allow us, by a summary confrontation, to measure the vast ambitions of Symbolist poetry that could reach toward both "magic" and "movement," exultant immobility and joyful progression beyond the self. After this preliminary approach I have proceeded to consider the two poets in turn: Claudel first of all, as he goes about the writing of perhaps his greatest work and gradually elucidates a total meaning that emerges from the form, in proportion as three attitudes are explored with respect to the absent lover. "The words I use are everyday words," but they are part of the dialectical pattern that reveals presence in absence, transcendence in an isolated moment, the drama of Christian sacrifice in a resolutely concrete language. Valéry, on the other hand, explored the drama of the mind in the 26,000-odd pages of notes he kept from 1894 to 1945, and attempted to find a rigorous way of defining it. At the same time his central preoccupation was consigned in the series of great poems written mainly during the First World War, in which he traced out privileged moments of the intellectual sensibility and the ceaseless quest for a crystal of self-contained thought. The manuscripts of one such piece, together with the final text, enable us to appreciate his endeavor and the importance he accorded to possessing the exact and euphonious elements of a "language of the gods."

The volume concludes with an essay on Apollinaire, who, for all the unevenness of his work, caught some of the most moving accents of Symbolism. In an attempt to show the impulses that animate his writings I have sought to delve into his ambition to make of language a continuum, to transmute the "alcohol" of experience into a "new reality." No doubt, I suppose, some critics would contest his inclusion alongside the five other poets; it is clear that he is a marginal case and that, expressing as he did the tension between tradition and invention, order and adventure, he owes no small amount of his appeal to this very marginality; but he partakes of Symbolism chronologically, just as he develops the Symbolist idea of the constructed poem, whether in "La Chanson du Mal-aimé" or later pieces like "Zone," and by poetic self-awareness. When he died in 1918 another theory and practice would prevail.

I have pleasure in expressing my gratitude to the Australian Research Grants Committee, which supported this project; to the Myer Foundation, which enabled me to spend a short term of study leave in France; and to Madame Paul Valéry and Monsieur Pierre Claudel for their gen-

Preface

erosity in allowing me to consult various unpublished man-
uscripts. I also wish to thank the editors of several reviews
in which essays that appear in this book, often in modified
form, were first published: "Mallarmé and the *Monstre
d'or*" is reprinted by permission of *The Romanic Review*,
Columbia University, New York, N.Y.; "The Serpent, the
Tree and the Crystal," by permission of *L'Esprit créateur*;
"A la fontaine de Psyché," *Livres de France*; "Music in Apol-
linaire," *French Studies* (Oxford); "Apollinaire et *La
Chanson du Mal-aimé*," the *Australian Journal of French
Studies*. Both "Verlaine's 'Naïveté'" and "'Magic' and
'Movement' in Claudel and Valéry" originally appeared in
Essays in French Literature, which is issued by the Univer-
sity of Western Australia Press. The texts of Claudel, Valéry,
and Apollinaire are reproduced by kind permission of the
copyright holders, Librairie Gallimard, Paris.

J.R.L.

Perth, Western Australia
December 1968

Contents

THE LANGUAGE OF
FRENCH SYMBOLISM

Chapter I

Mallarmé and the "Monstre d'or"

ORE clearly perhaps than any other writer, Mallarmé has long divided the ranks of literary criticism in France into two uneasy groups. The first, predominantly academic in origin, concerns itself with the exegesis of the most hermetic of the great French poets. The second, on the other hand, is apt to ignore such attempts and, instead of a meaning, to seek to define the obscure experience of the author as found, as it were, beyond the sense, in his work seen primarily as a sign and not an object complete in itself, as an act and not an expression. We pass, then, abruptly from one critical language to another, from the subtleties of textual analysis to the often tendentious, but no doubt more exciting discourse of psychological description as practiced notably by Blanchot and Poulet. A recent publication is the highest achievement of this latter approach; indeed, by dedicating *L'Univers imaginaire de Mallarmé* to Georges Poulet, Jean-Pierre Richard underlines for us his own critical parentage. In a thesis whose thought is as brilliant as its style, he studies the phenomenology of the poet's perception, scrutinizes the mirrors, fires, foam of Mallarmé's language, the fountains, ballet dancers, diamonds, and fans, with the skill of an admirable literary psychoanalyst: "Car l'objet décrit l'esprit qui le possède. . . ."[1] It follows, however, that the individual poems hardly interest Richard as such and are treated less as works of art than as documents that record a vital pursuit, an "existential project," an inner drama.[2]

[1] *L'Univers imaginaire de Mallarmé* (Paris: Le Seuil, 1961), p. 20.
[2] See Pierre Missac, "Tel que jamais en lui le temps ne le change," *Critique*, XVII, 675-690, who writes: "Si l'on n'y prend garde, l'oscillation se poursuivra longtemps encore entre les deux extrêmes: entre la biographie et la désincarnation, le mot à mot et l'ontologie, la trivialité et la quintessence, la grammaire et la philosophie; entre ceux qui croient démarquer un polisson et ceux qui révèrent un saint;

The Language of French Symbolism

The observer, faced with this apparent "dialogue de sourds," may suspect that there is some intrinsic dichotomy in Mallarmé's attitude and work; but it may well be that in reality he is an ideal example of the meeting of a poetic system and a fundamental stance in life and art, which was both intuitively attained and consciously developed. If his poems most certainly present an ornamental beauty, and the precious charm of a language whose delight is self-sufficient, they also coincide with deeper layers of meaning that Mallarmé had lucidly considered. A single form, we suggest, can be the epitome of abstract reason and the imagination, like the essential pattern of a reflective mind. (We recall that a phrase from the essay on Wagner gives a striking definition of Mallarmé's concept of the poetic: "strictement imaginatif et abstrait, donc poétique").[3] In the hope of pointing to a pervasive symbolism of this kind, I would like to examine a motif that is found in one of his best-known poems and, by a review of parallel texts, to make some tentative observations about his language and thought as a whole. This motif we shall call the "monstre d'or."

The phrase we have chosen is taken from "Toast funèbre," the poem written in 1873 as an homage to Théophile Gautier, who had recently died. The dead poet is paradoxically a symbol, as necessary as fate, of men's happiness, of the glorious triumph of poetry; and Mallarmé offers him a toast that itself is poetry, the demential act that we yet know to be our salvation.

> O de notre bonheur, toi, le fatal emblème!
> Salut de la démence et libation blême,

---

entre M. Jacques Scherer, chez qui l'on ne trouve pas Mallarmé et M. Maurice Blanchot, avec qui on le perd un peu de vue" (p. 677). Cf. also J.-P. Richard (op.cit.), p. 13: "Bref, entre Mallarmé sorcier de l'expression et Mallarmé métaphysicien de 'l'absolu,' semblent aujourd'hui s'être créés une distance, un hiatus, que l'effort immédiat de la lecture parvient assez mal à réparer."

[3] "Richard Wagner: rêverie d'un poète français," Œuvres complètes, ed. Henri Mondor and G. Jean-Aubry (Paris: Gallimard, Pléiade, 1945), p. 544. Mallarmé is here characterizing the spirit of France.

4

Mallarmé and the "Monstre d'or"

Ne crois pas qu'au magique espoir du corridor
J'offre ma coupe vide où souffre un monstre d'or!

His toast, Mallarmé proclaims, is no attempt to recall Gautier in some magical hope of a spiritualistic reappearance. It is not for this that he raises his glass—"J'offre ma coupe vide où souffre un monstre d'or!" This last verse is harmonious in movement, ample in its evocation, and mysterious. How, we may ask, are we to interpret it? Suggestions are not lacking in the numerous articles that have been written on the poem, and I shall return to them in a moment. But first we may like to refer to an anecdote that seems to bear the stamp of truth and that brings into question Mallarmé's own reaction to this particular line; here it is, as recounted by a friend of the poet and a highly competent sonneteer in his own right, José-Maria de Heredia:

> L'autre jour, dès l'aurore, j'ai vu accourir notre énigmatique Mallarmé. Sans préambule, il me dit: "Je viens de faire une pièce superbe, mais je n'en comprends pas bien le sens et je viens vous trouver pour que vous me l'expliquiez." Il me lut sa pièce. Il y avait entre autres mystérieux alexandrins celui-ci:
>
> J'offre ma coupe vide où souffre un monstre d'or.
>
> Cela rimait avec un sombre corridor. Pour répondre à sa confiance en mes facultés de devin, je lui donnai l'explication que voici: "C'est très clair; il s'agit d'une coupe ancienne où un artiste, Benvenuto Cellini, si vous voulez, a gravé dans l'or massif un monstre d'or qui se tord, avec une expression de souffrance." Stéphane, en m'écoutant, a bondi et s'est écrié: "Que c'est beau! Que c'est émouvant!" et il m'a quitté rayonnant et reconnaissant, en me disant: "J'ai monté dans ma propre estime, et vous, mon cher, du même coup!"[4]

[4] Virginie Dumont-Breton, *Les Maisons que j'ai connues. Nos amis artistes*, quoted by Henri Mondor, *Vie de Mallarmé* (Paris: Gallimard, 1942), p. 347.

5

If we take this anecdote to be substantially true, are we to assume that Mallarmé was trying out on a fellow poet a new system of expression; that, having an ulterior aim in view such as might concern the structural integration of his language, he rejoiced to see that his image retained also for a sensitive reader an immediate and satisfying impact? It is impossible for us to judge with any sureness. What we must note, however, is that the majority of the exegetical critics have themselves adopted by and large Heredia's reading, even though his tone as reproduced in these lines appears to be far from serious. Thus Madame Noulet, in 1948, wrote in her commentary on the poem: "allusion, soit à une ciselure que présente la coupe que le poète tient en mains, soit, et l'on préfère ceci, au reflet concave et mouvant du fond de la coupe."[5] Two years later, Gardner Davies came down on the side of the former of these alternatives, which was Heredia's choice also: "il est peut-être préférable cette fois-ci de prendre Mallarmé au mot et de croire à une coupe portant réellement un monstre gravé et doré."[6] Later still, Guy Delfel, in his annotated *Pages choisies* of Mallarmé, agreed that "la coupe est ornée de quelque motif baroque";[7] while in *Mallarmé et la morte qui parle*, published in 1959, Léon Cellier reverted to Madame Noulet's second conjecture and surmised that the monster was a reflection: "Dans la coupe vide grimace, en ce jour funeste, le reflet du soleil."[8]

Now, the assumption behind all these interpretations is

[5] *Dix poèmes de Stéphane Mallarmé* (Geneva: Droz, 1948), p. 12; cf. also the same author's remarks in *L'Œuvre poétique de Stéphane Mallarmé* (Geneva: Droz, 1940), p. 379.

[6] *Les "Tombeaux" de Mallarmé* (Paris: José Corti, 1950), p. 19.

[7] *Pages choisies* (Paris: Classiques illustrés Vaubourdolle, 1954), p. 56.

[8] *Mallarmé et la morte qui parle* (Paris: Presses Universitaires de France, 1959), p. 138. J.-P. Richard (*op.cit.*, p. 246) also interprets the monster as the reflection of the sun: "A la disparition du mort derrière les dures murailles du tombeau—porphyre et fer—à l'extinction sacrificatoire de la torche humaine, reflet de la torche solaire qui se tord elle aussi et agonise sous les espèces d'un 'monstre d'or' dans une coupe brûlante, succède alors une première résurrection brûlante."

that Mallarmé's image is basically a plastic one; that, as an ornamental poet, he is describing with intricate art an ideal glass, an elegant decorative design, which might be compared to the fans and bracelets, the mirrors and diadems of his other poems. It seems impossible to deny that this reading is valid, backed as it is by some of the most perceptive of Mallarméan scholars, and, indeed, despite the variations of detail, beautiful as such. Yet it may well be that to interpret the image exclusively in this way is to form too limited an idea of the poetic vision of Mallarmé, who confessed that he had never been able to compose a poem of isolated lines of verse or isolated metaphors. It is perhaps a tenable hypothesis that his line may signify more than critics have proposed, and have an organic role in the poem's inner development. Several things tend to support this view as we pursue our analysis of "Toast funèbre," and I shall discuss them later; but particularly important seems to me a trait that is sure to strike the reader on reflection. For is it not true that the magnificent glass the poet is offering in a gesture of libation is nothing but the tributary poem we are reading? Indeed, the very ambiguity of the word "coupe" already evokes both its ordinary sense, as champagne glass, and its technical use in poetry. I shall therefore venture to submit that the "monstre d'or" may well be taken not merely as a plastic image but, more especially, as a symbol of poetry itself; and that, if we admit this point of view, our reading will be greatly enriched, and the whole idea of art as Mallarmé conceived it will be brought into the focus of the poem.

ONE POSSIBLE symbolic reading will no doubt immediately suggest itself to the reader of Mallarmé. This glass that is both empty and not empty, both inanimate and writhing, both funereal and crowned with gold, is the symbol of the poet's memory. Mallarmé recalls to the vacant sphere of thought the resplendent image of Gautier's career. To write a threnody is in a sense to destroy the present and discover the true sign of the past as a glorious form. Memory,

7

Mallarmé says, is agony and desire, the "désir et mal de mes vertèbres" as we read in one of his most moving sonnets, the "affres du passé nécessaires" of another, these "maux, dragons qu'il a choyés." In a letter of 1867 we come upon a similar, but more explicit statement concerning the process of remembering: "Toute naissance est une destruction, et toute vie d'un moment l'agonie dans laquelle on ressuscite ce qu'on a perdu, on l'ignorait avant."[9] It seems, then, most significant that Mallarmé constantly develops the curious polarity of suffering and desire, birth and destruction, when he evokes poetic memory. The finest handling of this theme in his work is to be found in "L'Après-midi d'un faune," in which he composed the myth of the poet's act of recollection. Just as in the "coupe vide" of "Toast funèbre," so in the poem, and so in the empty grapeskins, the faun finds his remembered source of exultation:

> Ainsi, quand des raisins, j'ai sucé la clarté,
> Pour bannir un regret par ma feinte écarté,
> Rieur, j'élève au ciel d'été la grappe vide
> Et, soufflant dans ses peaux lumineuses, avide
> D'ivresse, jusqu'au soir je regarde au travers.

In the same way, the faun's breast is untouched, empty of proof ("vierge de preuve"), and yet it bears unmistakable witness, like the golden monster, to the strange and noble suffering that his dream has left and that the poetic imagination contains.

> Mon sein, vierge de preuve, atteste une morsure
> Mystérieuse, due à quelque auguste dent.

But, as we know, the drama of the faun is that memory for him is not enough, since he seeks to transform the past into the present, image into reality, sign into human flesh; to separate twin forms, even to violate the goddess of imagination. The mythical eclogue shows that the forms we

[9] *Correspondance* (1862-1871), ed. Henri Mondor and J.-P. Richard (Paris: Gallimard, 1960), p. 249.

8

desire cannot be extracted from the ideal past in which they must live and dwell, the "grappe vide" and "sein vierge" of the faun, the "coupe vide" of "Toast funèbre." As Mallarmé himself prescribes in his essay on Villiers de l'Isle-Adam: "Un à un, chacun de nos orgueils, les susciter, *dans leur antériorité* et voir."[10]

Yet if he finds that poetic recollection conforms to the pattern of suffering and desire, empty glass and golden monster, it is also true that he sees a similar tension in the rhetoric of the ideal poem itself, in the verbal action of the poetic form. The role of language, as he sees it, becomes itself a drama, for it is by interaction of the individual words that a series of tensions (or, as he says, *torsions*) is built up which presents to us, before and beyond any precise sense, a particular figure, a pattern. Once again, in remarkable fashion, we find that Mallarmé's formal imagination is fertile in describing the inner structure of the ideal poem; and once again it is important for us to observe that he has recourse to the image of the golden monster whose writhing is circumscribed by a pure line: "Quelle agonie [. . .] qu'agite la Chimère versant par ses blessures d'or l'évidence de tout l'être pareil, nulle torsion vaincue ne fausse ni ne transgresse l'omniprésente Ligne espacée de tout point à tout autre pour instituer l'idée."[11] We may well ask ourselves what Mallarmé means. Is it not, prosaically speaking, that no image in the unity of the poem can be allowed to exist in its own right but, by the interplay of symmetry, complementarity, and contrast, must be modified, transformed until it undergoes a kind of alchemical change? In one letter to a friend, Mallarmé translates this same notion into less metaphorical language; yet, as we can see, the image of the monster suffering, gnawed at, is even here implicit. "Tout le mystère," he writes, "est là: établir les identités secrètes par un deux à deux qui ronge et use les objets au nom d'une centrale pureté."[12] Similarly, in one

[10] *Œuvres complètes*, p. 481. (Italics mine).
[11] "La Musique et les lettres," *Œuvres complètes*, p. 648.
[12] *Propos sur la poésie*, ed. Henri Mondor (Monaco: Editions du Rocher, 1946), p. 174.

of his most delicate octosyllabic sonnets, he speaks of the act of composition as a kind of murder by which a cry is stifled; as a woman's head of hair, superbly sensuous, radiant like some constellation ("la considérable touffe"), that becomes by language a finely wrought diamond.

> Non! La bouche ne sera sûre
> De rien goûter à sa morsure,
> S'il ne fait, ton princier amant,
>
> Dans la considérable touffe
> Expirer, comme un diamant,
> Le cri des Gloires qu'il étouffe.

It would not be difficult to add to these examples by quoting other passages in which language is conceived as a glorious death, both agony and triumph. Thus, in the homage to Wagner, the consecration of the dead composer consists of his musical scores themselves, whose dark signs, like so many sobs, are at the same time a golden affirmation spread out on the manuscripts ("Trompettes tout haut d'or pâmé sur les vélins"). But it is in "Ses purs ongles . . . ," a sonnet of 1868, that we discover one of the most brilliant illustrations of the pattern we are discussing. It will be recalled that, in a letter to Cazalis, Mallarmé described his poem as being taken from a study on language: "J'extrais ce sonnet, auquel j'avais une fois songé, d'une étude projetée sur *la Parole*";[13] but he significantly entitled the first version "Sonnet allégorique de moi-même." This allegory, then, which links the self and poetic language, composes for us, by the negation of all presences, all objects in the nocturnal room, a singular agony of creation. The poem is written, as it were, without the intrusion of any individual emotion, by means of internal consonance and a system of reflection. Yet in this closed room of night and negation where all things are sacrificed to absolute purity, a positive image suddenly imposes itself: a golden

---

[13] *Correspondance* (1862-1871), p. 278.

form is in the throes of suffering, and the development will show that it possesses cosmic dimensions.

> Mais proche la croisée au nord vacante, un or
> Agonise selon peut-être le décor
> Des licornes ruant du feu contre une nixe,
>
> Elle, défunte nue en le miroir, encor
> Que, dans l'oubli formé par le cadre, se fixe
> De scintillations sitôt le septuor.

The poem has no message, and the object chosen as its theme is not important; but beauty is created out of the interplay and mutual destruction of a system of images. The world is denied, and no word has a simple referential value; but from this apparent act of negation the form will compose and contain a pure ideal, like the golden monster in the empty glass.

There is also, I suggest, a third important plane on which we find the same pattern reproduced. Mallarmé declared on many occasions that it is by his own agony and ultimate death that the poet himself achieves beauty. In this sense his life is a kind of ascesis which is destined to display the triadic rhythm—suffering, passion, redemption—of Christian martyrdom. "Pour moi, le cas d'un poète, en cette société qui ne lui permet pas de vivre, c'est le cas d'un homme qui s'isole pour sculpter son propre tombeau."[14] He thus creates his own tomb, which, by a mystic oxymoron, will also be his substantial immortality, the eternity of his art: "un fond de grotte précieuse demeurée le beau sépulcre pour y vivre avec une enchanteresse idée."[15] This concept furnishes the argument of *Un Coup de dés*; it also finds an admirable expression in the opening poem of Mallarmé's collected verse, "Salut." The ternary rhythm of the first line ("Rien, cette écume, vierge vers") is echoed by the three words of the last tercet ("Solitude, récif, étoile"); while the drowning of the sirens in the nothingness that is

[14] "Réponse à l'enquête de Jules Huret," *Œuvres complètes*, p. 869.
[15] *Propos sur la poésie*, p. 149.

11

the glass of champagne ("Telle loin se noie une troupe/ De sirènes mainte à l'envers") adumbrates and justifies in advance the poet's solitary sacrifice, which is crowned with glory. We also remember that another octosyllabic sonnet, in very much the same way, compares the long journey of the poet in search of a new world to Vasco da Gama's rounding of the Cape. He follows unswervingly a bird announcing the presence of a land which is not rich in gold but useless—"un inutile gisement"—for the beauty that poets must ever seek offers no treasures, no mines to exploit. What he pursues is his own death, under the triadic sign of his guiding faith: night, agony, and the consolation of artistic achievement—"Nuit, désespoir, pierrerie."

But it is in *Igitur* that Mallarmé achieved the most remarkable mythical expression of the theme of self-immolation. As its title implies, this prose-poem is a demonstration of the logic that controls the poet's experience, the logic of poetic madness. An absolute moment of consciousness is evoked, in which Igitur at midnight descends the staircase of the human mind, meditates, discovers his own *necessity* in time and space. He then lies down in the tomb of his ancestors and, it would seem, commits suicide; but what he has created by his genius will remain as "le château de la pureté," where in the empty room the monsters that decorate the furniture have suffered their last agonies: "jusqu'à ce qu'enfin les meubles, leurs monstres ayant succombé avec leurs anneaux convulsifs, fussent morts dans une attitude isolée et sévère, projetant leurs lignes dures dans l'absence d'atmosphère, les monstres figés dans leur effort dernier, et que les rideaux cessant d'être inquiets tombassent, avec une attitude qu'ils devaient conserver à jamais."[16] Such was the dream of Igitur, which required that he should wholly sacrifice himself in the dark room of his mind so as to attain the pure idea of the world, which is poetry; like the golden monster, or like the swan that, undergoing its icy martyrdom, yet triumphs over past, present,

[16] *Œuvres complètes*, p. 441.

and future, transcends its "blanche agonie" in the eternal form of Cycnus:

> Fantôme qu'à ce lieu son pur éclat assigne,
> Il s'immobilise au songe froid de mépris
> Que vêt parmi l'exil inutile le Cygne.

We see, then, that the "monstre d'or," when looked at in the dialectical system of Mallarmé's aesthetics, represents poetic memory, poetic language, the poet's destiny itself. It is possible however, I believe, to discover still another echo, a final illustration of the same central pattern—this time perhaps the basic one which served to evoke the rest. Or, to use Vigny's comparison, here was, it would appear, the grain of sand around which the diverse layers of the pearl were to grow. For at the heart of Mallarmé's approach to the act of writing there was, as we know, a philosophical experience which divided his life in two as decisively as Valéry's "nuit de Gênes": an experience which seems almost literally to have reformed his whole attitude between the ages of twenty-three and twenty-six. Of those tormented years spent in the provinces at Tournon, Besançon, and Avignon, the correspondence that has been recently brought together gives us a striking picture, albeit an incomplete one, which links up with, and helps explain, many obscure references in his published work. If we had to resume his experience in one sentence we might choose the well-known words of a letter of 1866 to Cazalis: "après avoir trouvé le Néant, j'ai trouvé le Beau."[17] Beauty, he believes, can only be a lie, a glorious lie ("le Glorieux Mensonge," "la Gloire du Mensonge")[18] that we utter in the face of cosmic immensity and eternal void, but a lie that is still man's supreme joy, since it is a heroic, an ideal act. It is the world seen through a sensibility that endows objects with high splendor despite the nothingness Mallarmé found once Christianity was rejected: "les douer de resplendissement, à travers l'espace vacant, en des fêtes

---

[17] *Correspondance* (1862-1871), p. 220.
[18] *Ibid.*, p. 208.

à volonté et solitaires."[19] The truth one cannot deny is non-being, death, silence; but man's glory is to impose on the void—this "coupe vide"—an articulate image of his dream of beauty.

Yet why should the golden monster be shown as suffering? In an intricate and intriguing way Mallarmé conceived ideal beauty as bearing within itself the knowledge of its own secret, which poetry discovers in an awesome violation ("la Beauté ayant été mordue au cœur depuis le christianisme par la Chimère, et douloureusement renaissant avec un sourire rempli de mystère, mais de mystère forcé et qu'elle *sent* être la condition de son être").[20] Venus de Milo, the Mona Lisa were for the poet the two great types of beauty so far created—the former calm and joyful, the latter smiling as if through the experience of pain; yet their smiles had to be transcended in an image of happiness and calm as complete as the Venus de Milo's, a joyful image that would at last embrace the full knowledge of the philosophical cause and nature of suffering: "La Beauté, enfin, ayant par la science de l'homme, retrouvé dans l'Univers entier ses phases corrélatives, ayant eu le suprême mot d'elle, s'étant rappelé l'horreur secrète qui la forçait à sourire—du temps du Vinci, et à sourire mystérieusement—souriant mystérieusement maintenant, mais de bonheur et avec la quiétude éternelle de la *Vénus de Milo* retrouvée ayant su l'idée du mystère dont *La Joconde* ne savait que la sensation fatale."[21] And so poetry is a tragic struggle carried on in full consciousness against the nothingness which we know to be the truth about the universe—"le rien qui est la vérité."

---

[19] "La Musique et les lettres," *Œuvres complètes*, p. 647.

[20] *Correspondance* (1862-1871), p. 246; cf. *Œuvres complètes*, p. 860: "l'éternelle blessure glorieuse qu'a la poésie, ou mystère, de se trouver exprimée déjà, même si près du silence."

[21] *Correspondance* (1862-1871), p. 246. Robert Greer Cohn has briefly alluded to the tragic aspect of the image of the monster (*L'Œuvre de Mallarmé: "Un Coup de dés"* [Paris: Librairie "Les Lettres," 1951] pp. 234-235; *Towards the Poems of Mallarmé* [Berkeley: University of California Press, 1965], p. 98).

Now, if this theory was the sufficient and necessary condition for Mallarmé's work as planned and carried out over thirty years, it is important to observe that it is regularly expressed in explicit terms in individual poems. Thus we find the combat of beauty and the void, glass and golden monster, in one of his finest and best-known sonnets, "La chevelure vol d'une flamme . . . ," in which the woman's head of hair appears as a dazzling affirmation in the face of philosophical doubt:

> Une nudité de héros tendre diffame
> Celle qui ne mouvant astre ni feux au doigt
> Rien qu'à simplifier avec gloire la femme
> Accomplit par son chef fulgurante l'exploit
>
> De semer de rubis le doute qu'elle écorche
> Ainsi qu'une joyeuse et tutélaire torche.

Rubies are sown on skepticism like the monster on the void. Several other poems reproduce the same pattern, in similar terms, but it is in *Les Noces d'Hérodiade* that Mallarmé sought to give an extended aesthetic and philosophical development to the drama of beauty. Only one part of the poem, the "Scène," was published during the poet's lifetime, but two other sections which are reasonably complete have come down to us, as well as numerous fragments that were made known by Gardner Davies in 1959. It is clear, as Mallarmé himself indicates, that his figure of Hérodiade is not the traditional one; for him she represents, like the Venus de Milo, virgin beauty unconscious of its future—"La splendeur ignorée et le mystère vain."[22] Yet, in the breaking day, she is disturbed and annoyed by the Nurse's words, which are, as it were, a premonition of her coming violation. The violator himself will soon appear: St. John is the symbol of the artist who kneels before the vision of Hérodiade's naked form; but having done this he will die, since the language of poetic genius is a double-edged sword: "Ces mots

[22] *Les Noces d'Hérodiade (Mystère)*, ed. Gardner Davies (Paris: Gallimard, 1959), p. 67.

rigides comme une épée" (p. 128), which cuts off the poet's own head at the same time as it violates beauty, whose secrets it painfully reveals. As Hérodiade says: "Le glaive qui trancha ta tête a déchiré mon voile"(p. 136). There is, then, a kind of mystic marriage between the virgin ideal and poetic genius, "l'affreux génie," the poet impersonal; and from this contact results the poem, by which beauty at last knows itself. "C'est toi, cruel," Hérodiade says to the dead St. John "qui m'as blessée en dessous par la tête—heurtant l'au-delà—par le bond de la pensée" (p. 125). She will in turn die too, but she has become humanly beautiful, meaningful for herself and for all—"belle," as she says, "mais par ta mort douée de le savoir"(p. 135). The golden monster of beauty writhes in its agony of self-knowledge, yet at the same time finds its name written on the void.

IF WE now return to "Toast funèbre," we can see that the multiple layers of meaning suggested by one image are not only implicit, and therefore presumably known only to Mallarmé and his initiates, but explicitly developed in the rest of the poem. Here, I submit, the golden monster and the empty glass are no mere ornament, but a keynote that suggests the semantic complex of this particular composition. It will, for instance, be evident to the reader that an image in the second verse-paragraph reproduces the same central pattern when, evoking the death of Gautier and of poets in general, Mallarmé speaks of "le blason des deuils épars sur de vains murs." Grief is turned into an emblazoned sign spread out on purple draperies, which denies by its very presence the void that is beyond. The empty glass has been transformed into the emptiness of walls, the monster into a bold figure that conveys to us the notion of art as an *anti-destin*. In the last section of the poem this same notion is expressed even more fully when the dead poet, "le poète pur," becomes himself the heroic figure whose gesture, both modest and magnificent, wards off the inroads of encompassing fate:

16

C'est de nos vrais bosquets déjà tout le séjour
Où le poète pur a pour geste humble et large
De l'interdire au rêve, ennemi de sa charge. . . .

We recognize, then, that the conflict of beauty and the void forms an essential theme of "Toast funèbre." Yet a further reflection of the pattern we have examined will be found with the reference to poetic language which requires the death of the object, the creation of a void, and, at the same time, the discovery in language itself of the object's essence:

Le Maître, par un œil profond, a, sur ses pas,
Apaisé de l'éden l'inquiète merveille
Dont le frisson final, dans sa voix seule, éveille
Pour la Rose et le Lys le mystère d'un nom.

In like manner the theme of memory will be expressed in terms that are familiar to us. The poet, in comparison with the void which has no past, is the "souvenirs d'horizons," he who remembers earth's horizons, where, on the point of disappearance, the object merges with the ideal. Mallarmé imagines vast space calling out to the dead poet: "Souvenirs d'horizons, qu'est-ce, ô toi, que la Terre?" Yet Gautier must reply in a resonant shout that traverses space: "Je ne sais pas!" For like the faun, he who remembers is not concerned with the earth as it is, but with the world destroyed and recreated by his own imagination—the fullness we create to fill precisely a realized absence.

Finally, a last echo of Mallarmé's pattern becomes apparent at the end of the poem, where the poet's tomb rises in some Christ-like resurrection as the substantial form which, by death, triumphs over death: the glorious silence and potential voice of the poem contain the forces of fate which are hostile to the poet, yet essential to his highest achievement.

Afin que le matin de son repos altier,
Quand la mort ancienne est comme pour Gautier
De n'ouvrir pas les yeux sacrés et de se taire,

Surgisse, de l'allée ornement tributaire,
Le sépulcre solide où gît tout ce qui nuit,
Et l'avare silence et la massive nuit.

We have no need to emphasize in conclusion the original use of imagery that our study of one line of Mallarmé's work has revealed. Naturally he is not unique in developing the multivalent properties of language, its "plurisignificance," for that might almost be the definition of a good poet. Where he is perhaps unique is in the intense and necessary relationship he establishes between an apparently plastic image and his own complex theory of poetry.[23] A single alexandrine calls into question not only the immediate scene depicted but the very means and end of writing the poem; it becomes indeed an act of faith accomplished in full consciousness and almost Pascalian anguish. Mallarmé realizes that the only subject which poetry must forever express is the conflict between man's dreams and his destiny: "Il n'est point d'autre sujet, sachez bien: l'antagonisme de rêve chez l'homme avec les fatalités à son existence départies par le malheur."[24]

The reader may well ask himself whether this conflict, and the ever-changing image Mallarmé found to express it, was in any sense a literary borrowing; if, for example, Mallarmé owed anything to Baudelaire, who knew, as he wrote

[23] Cf. Teodor de Wyzewa: "A chacun de ses vers il s'est efforcé d'attacher plusieurs sens superposés. Chacun de ses vers, dans son intention, devait être à la fois une image plastique, l'expression d'une pensée, l'énoncé d'un sentiment et un symbole philosophique" (quoted by Henri Mondor, *Vie de Mallarmé*, p. 657).

[24] "Hamlet," *Œuvres complètes*, p. 300. It is clear that we could have begun our inquiry with a poem other than "Toast funèbre" and still have been led to the same conclusions. Thus, the "monstre d'or" corresponds to the design of a fabulous tapestry: "Quelle soie aux baumes de temps / Où la Chimère s'exténue" (p. 75), or a woman's dress: "Pour les changer en soie Méry / De nos chimères se décore" (p. 115), or, more dramatically, the constellations in their death-throes against the ebony of night: "Luxe, ô salle d'ébène où, pour séduire un roi / Se tordent dans leur mort des guirlandes célèbres" (p. 67). J.-P. Richard (*op.cit.*, pp. 213-218) quotes a number of such parallel passages when discussing *Igitur*, but does not develop the imaginative and philosophical complexity the motif resumes.

in the *Petits poèmes en prose,* that "l'étude du Beau est un duel où l'artiste crie de frayeur avant d'être vaincu." On the contrary, we are struck by the fact that adumbrations of this image are already to be noted in Mallarmé's earliest poems.[25] But it was not until 1866 or 1867 that he came to realize that this struggle must be for him the only struggle, the supreme sacrifice which he conceived as a task undertaken, like some redeemer's, in the name of all men: "ce moment de la jeunesse dans lequel fulgure le destin entier, non le sien, mais celui de l'Homme! La scintillation mentale qui désigne le buste à jamais du diamant d'un ordre solitaire. . . ."[26] His evolution must be seen against the background of his rejection of Christianity, a personal event which could not but serve as a condition for his poetics; yet poetry was envisaged as no mere desperate flight from the world, but rather as the world's justification, and man's pride. Death of the self, death of objects, death of the world must be attained by the poet so as to create a pure sign, the essence of things. This is the golden monster and

---

[25] Cf. "Oh! qu'il est beau ton corps / Quand d'amour tu te tords!" (*Mallarmé lycéen,* ed. Henri Mondor [Paris: Gallimard, 1954], p. 140); "Souffles-y qu'il se torde! une ardente fanfare" (*Œuvres complètes,* p. 39). Nevertheless I am particularly struck by the parallel of cup, agitated monster, chimeras, and accomplished beauty that I note in Théophile Gautier's "Le Thé" (*Rondels*). Do not Gautier's metaphors and verbal music point in pregnant fashion to poems such as "Quelle soie aux baumes de temps . . ."?

> Miss Ellen, versez-moi le Thé
> Dans la belle tasse chinoise,
> Où des poissons d'or cherchent noise
> Au monstre rose épouvanté.
>
> J'aime la folle cruauté
> Des chimères qu'on apprivoise:
> Miss Ellen, versez-moi le Thé
> Dans la belle tasse chinoise.
>
> Là sous un ciel rouge irrité,
> Une dame fière et sournoise
> Montre en ses longs yeux de turquoise
> L'extase et la naïveté:
> Miss Ellen, versez-moi le Thé.

[26] "Villiers de l'Isle-Adam," *Œuvres complètes,* p. 489.

this the void: poetry as affirmation, as joy, which bears with it the knowledge of its own precariousness. The simplest themes can be selected by the poet—a console-table, a vase, a head of hair, an empty room—and yet, by conformity to one underlying structure, they will have a philosophical sense as well as purely plastic ones. The pattern was thus woven and rewoven throughout his poetry by a mind that was both imaginative and abstract, and bound inexorably to its own logic. It is not surprising that on a few occasions Mallarmé should have failed to weld the poetry of forms and the poetry of ideas into a compelling unity; but although his "Grand Œuvre" was left unfinished, he did succeed in his attempts remarkably often—often enough to leave us a series of poems more exquisitely mannered than a seventeenth-century verse "énigme" and yet as daring as a primal act of faith.

Chapter II

Verlaine's "Naïveté"

A T THE beginning of the last World War, in one of the
first of a score of books he devoted to aspects of
French Symbolism, the late Henri Mondor published
a moving tribute to the friendship of Verlaine and Mal-
larmé.[1] Critics had hitherto indulged in the scholastic game
of contrasting the lives they led, the works they composed,
their literary posterity, but Mondor took pains to show the
mutual warmth and, especially, the sympathetic insight into
each other's writings that for thirty years linked the two
leading poets of their generation. One could no longer
easily forget that Verlaine was instrumental in bringing
Mallarmé wide notice by his essay in the series of *Les
Poètes maudits*; on the other hand, Mallarmé also left many
a penetrating comment on his friend, characterizing him as
the great reformer of French versification ("lui qui a le
premier réagi contre l'impeccabilité et l'impassibilité par-
nassiennes"),[2] as a master of the language ("cher gram-
mairien"),[3] as a writer to whom was henceforth reserved an
indisputable place of his own ("par exemple, entre Lamar-
tine et La Fontaine").[4] But his most beautiful homage

---

[1] *L'Amitié de Verlaine et Mallarmé* (Paris: Gallimard, 1939; 272
pp.). In the *Lettres inédites à Charles Morice*, ed. Georges Zayed
(Geneva: Droz, 1964) we find the trace of a brief period of friction
in 1887 (pp. 110-111); but their long friendship seems on the whole
to have been remarkably cordial.

[2] "Réponse à l'enquête de Jules Huret," *Œuvres complètes*, p. 870.

[3] Letter to P. Verlaine, 23 July 1895, reproduced in H. Mondor,
L'Amitié de Verlaine et Mallarmé, p. 237. Mallarmé was well aware
of his friend's exquisite artistry. Referring to *Jadis et naguère* he
wrote: "Au fond [. . .] rien ne ressemble moins à un caprice que votre
art agile et certain de guitariste" (*Correspondance*, II, ed. Henri
Mondor and Lloyd J. Austin [Paris: Gallimard, 1965], p. 276). In the
same vein Valéry's comment is characteristically incisive: "Jamais art
plus subtil que cet art, qui suppose qu'on en fuit un autre, et non
point qu'on le précède" ("Villon et Verlaine," *Œuvres*, ed. Jean Hy-
tier [2 vols.; Paris: Gallimard, Pléiade, 1957-1960], I, 442).

[4] "Discours au bout de l'an Verlaine," *Œuvres complètes*, p. 865.

Mallarmé kept for the sonnet that he wrote in 1896 on the death of his friend. The "tombeau de Verlaine" tenderly affirms that the poet who recently disappeared is victorious over the grave, for in death he is like a rivulet that is hidden in the grass, present yet unseen, flowing, freshly redolent, yet essentially elusive:

> Qui cherche, parcourant le solitaire bond
> Tantôt extérieur de notre vagabond—
> Verlaine? Il est caché parmi l'herbe, Verlaine
>
> A ne surprendre que naïvement d'accord
> La lèvre sans y boire ou tarir son haleine
> Un peu profond ruisseau calomnié la mort.

His death signifies, in fact, the triumph of his work, which will continue to run crystal-clear, heard, says Mallarmé, by those who possess a corresponding ingenuousness of heart.

It is the word "naïvement" in the last tercet of the sonnet to which I should like to draw particular attention. The highly sophisticated Mallarmé—he who was, in Claudel's phrase, "la fleur suprême de Paris, le résumé exquis d'une race urbaine et d'une société courtoise en qui de tout ne passait que *l'esprit*"[5]—singled out in Verlaine a native rural note of inimitable simplicity which was to be valued on its own terms. We would presume that long acquaintance with each successive collection of verse as it appeared would have guided Mallarmé in the choice of his word had he been able to consult nothing else; but he was not ignorant of the fact that Verlaine had constantly made reference to this same quality throughout his work, having written of himself in 1866 in his very first letter to Mallarmé: "J'ose espérer que ces essais vous intéresseront et que vous y reconnaîtrez, sinon le moindre talent, du moins un effort vers l'Expression, vers la Sensation rendue, si je puis ainsi parler, dont l'Auteur qui est *naïf*—il a 22 ans!—est tenté de se savoir gré."[6] We note in particular that the word

[5] "Notes sur Mallarmé," *Œuvres complètes* (26 vols.; Paris: Gallimard, 1950-1967), XVIII, 126.
[6] Quoted by H. Mondor, *L'Amitié de Verlaine et Mallarmé*, p. 18.

"naïf," here used, one suspects, in a primarily literal sense, has its meaning extended in the next lines of Verlaine's letter to include quite specifically the idea of childlike, even aggressive, candor: "pour que vous ne souriiez pas trop de cette franchise d'enfant terrible." Yet it is possible to refer to a host of other instances in his writings, many of them doubtless completely familiar to Mallarmé, in which one finds precise echoes of the same notion. Indeed, I would go so far as to suggest that "naïveté" offers an important key to the understanding of Verlaine, since it contains for him a central and complex pattern of meaning. In this regard I believe it to be comparable, in the language of Valéry, to "pureté," or to "musique" in Apollinaire. Did he not in fact consider "naïveté" to be the "mère et nourrice de toutes les perfections grandes et petites"?[7] The semantic field has been greatly enlarged the better to express a personal vision, and thereby to invest a relatively neutral term with uncustomary power.

It is important to indicate—if we are unable succinctly to define—the associations the word held for Verlaine as they are outlined in his work, above all in the prose writings, which, despite their singular interest, have been largely neglected. The high frequency of "naïf" and "naïveté" is at once striking and in itself significant. Yet although we shall enlarge on the positive values attached to these words, we might emphasize from the start that they can also bear a strongly pejorative nuance. Thus he will use "naïf" to point the finger of scorn at his own lack of sincerity ("parfois des airs naïfs et faux de bon apôtre")[8] as well as at the self-importance of the bourgeois ("sobre et naïf homme de bien"),[9] at certain Catholic writers who produce but feeble literature and feeble thoughts ("un peu ternes, étroits, mesquins, ignorants et naïfs dans le

---

[7] "La Décoration et l'art industriel," *Œuvres posthumes* (Paris: Messein, 1929; henceforth designated *OP*), II, 329.

[8] "Gabriel Vicaire," *Œuvres complètes* (Paris: Messein, 1926; henceforth designated *OC*), V, 450.

[9] "Georges Lafenestre," *OC*, V, 430.

gris"),[10] at those whose ideal of art is grossly emotional ("Irriter les passionnistes, en bon français les naïfs, n'est-ce pas au moins tout un côté de l'art?"),[11] at stupid ignorance ("des critiques naïfs assez jusqu'à flétrir ce Décadent d'Adoré").[12] We could multiply such examples were it necessary, but I take our observation to have been sufficiently illustrated: Verlaine does not innocently wield terms to which he ascribes a virtue he favors beyond all else; he also perceives the other side of the coin and is able to protect himself from the wiles of gullibility. One realizes that "naïveté" has not become his linguistic master, since, clearly, its use is studied and controlled.

Nevertheless, in what is by far the majority of cases, he gives a distinctly meliorative value to the term, combining it with the images and concepts he most cherishes. It is first of all, as one might expect, the quality he finds in children and which he delights in evoking ("une naïveté, comme de la candeur enfantine et de la gentillesse tout plein," "quelque joie naïve et pétulante d'écolier en vacances," "le meilleur des garçons, [. . .] un [. . .] des plus fins et des plus naïfs dans le meilleur sens du mot");[13] and, by a simple transfer, it can also serve to describe the objects a child possesses, such as a hat ("rond, naïf, celui d'un enfant de l'Auvergne et de la Savoie")[14] or even a small girl's language that is graciously simple as though heard in a fairy tale ("elle a des mots naïfs, telle une jeune fille de conte").[15] One might also mention in this respect the humorous way in which the National Guard is transformed into a troop of toy soldiers parading resplendently as for children ("de naïfs gardes nationaux, tambours battant, clairons sonnant, d'ailleurs que peu mili-

[10] "Jules Barbey d'Aurevilly," *OC*, V, 325.
[11] "Charles Baudelaire," *OP*, II, 20.
[12] "Au bois joli," *OP*, II, 275.
[13] "Deux mots à une fille," *OP*, I, 324; "Chroniques de l'hôpital," *OC*, IV, 336; "Gosses," *OP*, I, 263.
[14] "Chroniques de l'hôpital," *OC*, IV, 338.
[15] "Gosses," *OP*, I, 266.

tairement! mais enfin!").[16] We recall, moreover, that a part of one of his prose collections is given over to a series of portraits of children ("Gosses") in whom the presence of "naïveté" is underlined; that frequent allusion is made to children throughout his work; that Lucien Létinois was loved by Verlaine for his childlike quality (at twenty, "cet âge natal," his letters were written in a style Verlaine found to be "naïf et chaste");[17] and that for him children's rounds could take on the beauty and the kind of mystical resonance that is heard in the last haunting line of *Parsifal*: "Et ô ces voix d'enfants chantant sous la coupole!" It is thus evident that "naïveté" calls up a whole atmosphere in conformity with the poet's romanticism of childhood, which, if it does not "trail clouds of glory," implies ingenuousness, an unpretentious charm. An extension of this scheme will allow him to encompass references to the nameless crowd ("l'esprit naïf de désintéressement"),[18] their public meetings ("des réunions publiques, et naïves d'ailleurs, des temps tout proches de l'Empire"),[19] even their credulous dreams ("Il est bon, n'est-ce pas? d'avoir de tels héros d'humanité, toute ronde et comme naïve dans notre pauvre tête harassée de paradoxes");[20] while it also serves to describe the exchanges between refreshingly young lovers like Verlaine himself and Mathilde ("correspondance innocente et confidences naïves sous la surveillance des bonnes gens de beaux-parents").[21]

Yet it is when Verlaine is referring to himself and, either in poems or in prose, describing his own childhood that the notion is alluded to most often and most liberally. "Etant né très naïf avec un cœur très droit" he proclaims,[22] with designedly gauche repetition and a touching, all but pleo-

[16] "Mon 18 mars 1871," *OP*, II, 145.
[17] "Lucien Létinois," *Œuvres poétiques complètes*, ed. Y.-G. Le Dantec (Paris: Gallimard, Pléiade, 1948; henceforth designated *OPC*), p. 321.
[18] "Chroniques de l'hôpital," *OC*, IV, 349.
[19] "Mes souvenirs de la Commune," *OP*, I, 296.
[20] "Croquis de Belgique," *OP*, II, 124-125.
[21] "Pierre Duchatelet," *OC*, IV, 135-136.
[22] "Etant né très naïf . . . ," *OPC*, p. 775.

nastic use of "naïf." In the same way, when he looks back on the boy he was, he emphasizes his lack of guile—"des oreilles comme de souris, dressées naïves aux côtés de mon innocente tête,"[23] and his candor—"l'air foncièrement naïf et bon."[24] However, he feels that the years have not basically changed him and that "naïveté" is still his principal quality: "Ai-je tant changé que ça? En laid, oui; en mal? je ne crois pas."[25] His "œil naïf" has survived, so that he can envisage the act of faith as firmly as before:

> Ma conviction, que tous les problèmes
> Etalés en vain à mon œil naïf
> N'ont point mise à mal, séducteurs suprêmes,
> T'affirme à nouveau, dogme primitif.[26]

Such underlining does not blind him to his present adulthood: he recognizes his own complexity, his tergiversations, for, if he has a "cœur naïf," his mind is "à la ventvole";[27] and his inner waywardness he expresses in a suggestive manner: "moi, naïf aux cent replis."[28] He could not again be the lost child, but perhaps he might manage to rediscover his own past, however briefly, and to achieve an attitude of complete "naïveté" by virtue of the act of artistic composition. Did not Baudelaire ally poetry and childhood and define his effort, simply as "l'enfance retrouvée à volonté"? Was it not also natural that Verlaine, with his idealization of children, should have held a similar view and spoken of the awakening of his own gift as of a child whose coming had required no birth pangs on the part of its parent: "son génie sortit, et ne naquit pas, sortit, ne fut pas conçu de ses malheurs, de ses joies, n'en fut pas conçu, en sortit, naïf et *genuine*, suivant l'intraduisible expression anglaise."[29]

[23] "A propos du dernier livre posthume de Victor Hugo," *OP*, I, 285.
[24] "Confessions," *OC*, V, 8.
[25] *Ibid.*
[26] "Acte de foi," *OP*, I, 86.
[27] "Confessions," *OC*, V, 92.
[28] "Odes en son honneur," *OPC*, p. 587.
[29] "Fragment . . . ," *OP*, II, 161.

Other uses of the noun and adjective enrich the notion and add to it different dimensions: thus "naïveté" can describe both the candor of the child and the violent sensuality of an adolescent such as we find in "Louise Leclercq," Verlaine's transposition of his meeting with Rimbaud: "sa modestie un peu hautaine et l'habitude chaste de toute sa démarche ne disait rien aux sens naïfs de cet adolescent trivial";[30] or else the heady atmosphere of a bar in which he was to find his future mistress Philomène:

> Oui, c'était par un soir joyeux de cabaret,
> Un de ces soirs plutôt chauds où l'on dirait
> Que le gaz du plafond conspire à notre perte
> Avec le vin du zinc, saveur naïve et verte.[31]

Or once again, in a daring combination of terms, it can serve to evoke a dancer in a ballet: "L'innocent sourit, rit, baise les garçons sur la joue, les filles sur la nuque—voyez-vous ça—et s'élance, premier sujet mâle, fort plein de naïvetés grivoises, en tête avec le premier sujet de l'autre sexe, dans un ballet où toute la troupe donne."[32] Candor is placed alongside erotic desire and display in a manner that might seem to us perverse if it did not, as I submit, form an integral part of the poet's singularly broad concept of "naïveté."

A further important category of words to which the term is attached concerns the countryside. Claudel once remarked incisively: "Verlaine, par ce qu'il a de meilleur, est resté un rural";[33] and it is true that his finest work, whether written in France, Belgium, or England, has an intimate feeling for the gentleness of certain landscapes, a manner of caressing their slopes and valleys and typical small de-

---

[30] "Louise Leclercq," *OC*, IV, 110.
[31] "Elégies, II," *OPC*, p. 598.
[32] "Scénario pour ballet," *OC*, IV, 246.
[33] "Paul Verlaine: poète de la nature et poète chrétien," *OC*, XVIII, 113. Cf. "Mémoires d'un veuf," *OC*, IV, 185: "Mon idée a toujours été d'habiter dans la vraie campagne, dans un village 'en plein champ,' une maison d'exploitation, une ferme dont je fusse le propriétaire et l'un des travailleurs, l'un des plus humbles, vu ma faiblesse et ma paresse."

tails with sensuous delicacy. At times he does so by direct description (as in "Bournemouth"), at others, obliquely (as in the final stanzas of "Crimen amoris"), but it is apparent in either case that the atmosphere of the country is that in which Verlaine is most plainly at ease. He will, then, attach his term to the appearance of farmhouses ("des naïves masures et des bâtisses à la bonne franquette")[34] or, perhaps, regret the absence of this same quality in a suburban scene ("cette physionomie qu'on voudrait croire provinciale, n'étaient telle lacune dans la bonhomie, tel manque de naïveté forte").[35] As for the inhabitants themselves, "naïveté" is their prime quality ("Les paysans sont naïfs et de province," "C'est l'instant / Où l'on songe aux récits des aïeules naïves . . .").[36] although this for him is very far from implying banality or brutishness. He evokes peasant merriment in the following way: "La gaieté [. . .] sans fiel, quelque malice, ô l'innocente malice, toute spirituelle et naïve tant!";[37] such "naïveté" contains a twinkle of humor and wit which is at the other extreme from ignorance. Similarly, when he wishes to describe Belgian French and compares it to a provincial patois, he maintains in his analysis a dosage of good-natured irony: "le belge ne serait-il pas bonnement un français de terroir, non sans ses saveurs particulières et ses tours très souvent, pour ne pas dire plus, gentiment naïf ou joliment narquois?"[38]

One privileged term has taken us, then, into three major areas that Verlaine elects to validate. Yet there are two central semantic clusters that must still be mentioned: those of religion and art. No doubt the domain of religion may appear at first a surprising association for "naïf," but it is a coherent extension of the uses we have seen. Thus, it will be used to qualify a vicar ("un jeune curé de village, bon,

[34] "Croquis de Belgique," *OP*, II, 136.
[35] "Louise Leclercq," *OC*, IV, 93.
[36] "Le Charme du vendredi saint," *OP*, I, 23; "Dans les bois," *OPC*, p. 67.
[37] "Croquis de Belgique," *OP*, II, 123.
[38] "Quinze jours en Hollande," *OC*, V, 201.

naïf"),[39] the sacred pictures in a country church ("comme une église de village [. . .] garnie de deux ou trois naïfs tableaux"),[40] or a Christian narration ("l'histoire de ce beau miracle [. . .] ce chef-d'œuvre naïf et fin").[41] Most significantly of all, it serves to suggest the consolation of Christianity itself:

> O la foi, la naïve et bonne certitude . . . ,[42]

or firm belief in the teachings of the Christian church:

> Exemple de vertus joyeuses, la franchise,
> La chasteté, la foi naïve dans l'Eglise . . . ,[43]

or the unquestioning expression of faith that is made through traditional hymns:

> "Esprit-Saint, descendez en" ceux
> Qui raillent l'antique cantique
> Où les simples mettent leurs vœux
> Sur la plus naïve musique.[44]

As for the field of art, Verlaine had recourse to "naïf" and "naïveté" on numerous occasions when he wished to praise a text, a painting, or a piece of sculpture. Among the clearest statements he made in this regard is his draft preface for the second printing of his early collection of poetry, when he was looking back on thirty years' work. After describing his "Art poétique" as no theory, nothing but a song —"JE N'AURAI PAS FAIT DE THÉORIE"—he continued: "C'est peut-être naïf, ce que je dis là, mais la naïveté me paraît être un des plus chers attributs du poète, dont il doit se prévaloir à défaut d'autres."[45] With wry humor rather than disingenuousness ("C'est peut-être naïf"), he makes it clear he is speaking of one of the basic and most endearing quali-

---

[39] "Voyage en France par un Français," *OP*, II, 97.
[40] "Enfance chrétienne," *OP*, I, 205.
[41] "Vieille ville," *OP*, I, 212.
[42] "Meliora," *OP*, II, 220.
[43] "Amour," XV, *OPC*, p. 328.
[44] "Veni, sancte . . . ," *OPC*, p. 557.
[45] "Projet de préface . . . ," *OP*, II, 231.

ties of the poet and of poetry as a whole. We do not have to search long in his writings to discover ample confirmation of this; and he will even say (and here we return directly to the twelfth line of Mallarmé's sonnet) that "naïveté" is as essential to the reader as it is to the poet, and will refer to the negligible number of Parisians who are "naïfs assez pour lire encore des vers":[46] that is to say, unprejudiced and unaffected as the melody of poetry itself, ready to respond to a flow freed from the conventions of intellectual discourse.

> Ou,—le trouver ou pas, le mériter ou pas,
> Le conserver ou pas!—l'assentiment d'un être
> Simple, naïf et bon, sans même le connaître
> Que par ce seul lien comme immatériel?[47]

Whereas Mallarmé, we remember, required of his readers that they should remain conscious of literature as at one and the same time an enchantment and a lie, a pure fiction ("un subtil mensonge") as well as a speculative pattern of abstract thought, Verlaine speaks out in favor of those who first of all are capable of innocent acceptance.

In his critical essays he will relish the "naïveté" he perceives in the work of Albert Glatigny, whose licentious themes might at first seem to preclude such a quality: "les strophes envolées toutes de verve et d'une si jolie et forte et saine, en dépit des 'sujets,' 'naïveté' ";[48] but in fact, just as the ingenuous child and the sensual adolescent can both be described as "naïfs," so Verlaine uses the word here in a similarly inclusive manner. Such examples lead us to observe that a most revealing aspect of Verlaine's use of "naïf" and "naïveté" with reference to art is the frequency with which he combines them with words of an apparently opposite nature: of the now-forgotten "Adoré Floupette" he will say: "ce, je le répète, bon, excellent poète, à la fois naïf et raffiné, primitif et 'fin-de-siècle,' pour

---

[46] "Charles Baudelaire," *OP*, II, 3.
[47] "Bonheur," XXII, *OPC*, p. 506.
[48] "Confessions," *OC*, V, 93.

parler l'affreux langage contemporain";[49] the same alliance of "naïveté" and refinement will appear in his description of a poem ("sa forme encore naïve et déjà un peu raf-finée"),[50] a love story of Francis Poictevin is described as a "simple histoire d'amour [. . .] naïve et subtile et même compliquée comme l'Homme et peut-être comme la Femme";[51] while, in like manner, two religious statues are felt to be "enluminées d'un effort savamment naïf."[52] Rather than wilful paradox, I believe such linguistic cou-plings reflect an essential tension in the attitude of Ver-laine between his themes, manner, tone on the one hand, and his hidden artistry on the other; between the candor that is proposed to us and the control, the poetic ruses by which it is achieved. "Quant à la question de forme," he writes of one of his own works, "l'auteur a procédé, comme il fait toujours, naïvement non sans prudence."[53] He started his career as a Parnassian whose aim was to be as ostenta-tious in form and subject, as distant from his own emo-tions, as possible; but his brilliantly rapid evolution showed he had learnt that the greatest art was to conceal art behind the most tenuous, and simple, and childlike of manners. Sur-rendering none of his rights as a poet in the process, he found, in a transcended Parnassianism, the self-conscious "naïveté" that is characteristic of his work. He would sing with an innocence that would not preclude sensuality, with a charm that would evoke the countryside he loved to-gether with the maternal consolation and solemn calm he remembered nostalgically. Into a poetry which is at the other extreme from pre-critical artlessness, he would put his vital aspirations, not motifs borrowed from exotic liter-atures. Well might he, then, when writing in 1893 of the young poets who were forced to choose between his poetry and that of Mallarmé, employ "naïveté" as the term that

[49] "Gabriel Vicaire," *OC*, V, 448.
[50] "Confessions," *OC*, V, 80.
[51] "Francis Poictevin," *OC*, V, 468.
[52] "Vieille ville," *OP*, I, 236.
[53] Preface to "Liturgies intimes," *OPC*, p. 547.

indicated a personal theory and practice, or, as it were, Verlainian poetics in little: "D'aucuns, parmi ces jeunes gens, voulaient plus de profondeur, d'intellectualité, dans la poésie, et ceux-là relevaient surtout de Stéphane Mallarmé, l'esprit pur dans la forme impeccable, d'autres s'avisèrent d'admettre la naïveté, l'humble expansion de l'artiste qui vous parle."[54]

IT IS POSSIBLE to say in retrospect that such "naïveté" was in a sense peculiarly attuned to his generation's notion of lyricism. For the reading public of the 1890's there was little doubt that Verlaine was one of the great French writers, and his election in 1894 as Prince of Poets consecrated the widely held estimation that, more than Mallarmé, and certainly more than any other of his contemporaries, it was he who produced the most significant work. On his death in 1896 the literary reviews were full of tributes that lingered over his achievement; and it was quite evident that this vogue was not soon destined to wane. The mass of poetry that appeared between 1900 and 1920 contains a rich heritage of Verlaine techniques: typical repetition of words and phrases, the suspended thought at the end of the poem, the indeterminate word and image, rhymes rare rather than rich, frequent use of assonance within the body of the line. Nevertheless, the reaction came quite brutally after 1918. First there was the attack launched by the Surrealists: "La surestimation de Verlaine a été la grande erreur de l'époque symboliste," wrote André Breton. The ideal of the young became Rimbaud and Lautréamont, and not the fluid suggestion of Verlaine. At the same time he was subjected to the unsympathetic hands of certain biographers who revealed details of the life he led—as if this

[54] "Notes sur la poésie contemporaine," *OP*, II, 340. In a sonnet addressed to Gustave Le Rouge (*OPC*, p. 443) we find the words "expansion" and "naïve" once again linked to describe a particular kind of poetry:

> Bah! faites comme moi, dussent trouver naïve
> Votre ample expansion ceux forts que vous fallait
> Aimer sans fin ni loi. Et qui m'aime me suive!

somehow cast doubt on the depth of his writing. And Verlaine was left almost wholly to such commentators; for while Mallarmé had the great good fortune to find in Albert Thibaudet a perspicacious reader, Verlaine's work was not given the attention it deserved.

This dearth of worthwhile criticism undoubtedly reflects the distance separating the new generation from a non-intellectual, if far from unintelligent, poet. Yet over the last ten years there have been signs of a reaction in taste, no doubt wholly welcome, that became apparent for one thing in academic circles with the publication in 1959 of J.-H. Bornecque's edition of *Fêtes galantes*, a work of precise scholarship and incisive sympathy. Even more significant were two long essays that analyzed the poetry from original points of view. I refer to Jean-Pierre Richard's article "Fadeur de Verlaine"[55] and to the preface by Octave Nadal to a new edition of the poet's writings.[56] Neither of these critics sought to redeem from oblivion the whole of Verlaine, but each brought his critical acuteness to the analysis of the early works in an attempt to assess their importance.

Nadal and Richard have in common the virtue of asking two fundamental questions: firstly, what is the essential attitude of Verlaine as revealed in his poetry, and secondly, how is it that his conversion to Catholicism seems to coincide with a loss of his poetic gift? Here, as in other articles and books, Richard pursues a dual endeavor to define the pattern of sensation of the author he is scrutinizing and to evaluate his "authenticity"; and he comes to the conclusion that the vital experience Verlaine expressed in his early work concerned the provocative *insipidity* of the world— its "fadeur," or "le mystère inquiétant de l'indétermination sensible." After 1873, however, there came a rejection of this experience, in favor, Richard says, of an ordered categorical universe: "La sensation fanée, il tâche de s'en dé-

[55] *Poésie et profondeur* (Paris: Le Seuil, 1955), pp. 163-185.
[56] Introduction to *Œuvres complètes de Verlaine* (Paris: Club du meilleur livre, 1959); later, in expanded form, in *Paul Verlaine* (Paris: Mercure de France, 1961; 164 pp.).

livrer en la laissant, ou en la faisant mourir."[57] And so the work of Verlaine constitutes an implicit tragedy in the eyes of his critic, because the poet rejected the call of his authentic self in favor of conventional ideas and feelings; "tragédie d'un être," he concludes, "qui, à partir d'un certain moment, a refusé l'expérience sensible, et qui savait pourtant très bien que tout le reste est littérature."[58] The weakness of this approach is certainly not due to a failure of style (Richard's expression is brilliantly evocative) nor of sensibility, but rather, we feel, to a lack of rigorousness which gives him free license to range over the poet's work and establish intuitively a pattern and order of development. In his study of Mallarmé, Richard follows the poems one by one and makes of them a scheme that is convincing; the much shorter essay on Verlaine tends, on the other hand, to leave an impression of gratuitousness because it fails to maintain constant touch with individual poems as organic unities, and conceives the author more as a delicate sounding board that submits to sensation than as the true poet of his experience.

Nadal's analysis differs markedly, although he too does not attempt to defend the later work and, like Richard, stops before *Sagesse*. Instead of speaking of a central experience in phenomenological style, he finds in Verlaine an exploration of the dream that implies a positive rejection of the world similar to Rimbaud's. From this point of view Verlaine becomes a landmark in the tradition of the "poètes du pur songe," the "poètes démiurgiques du songe": "Son œuvre demeure un des plus importants relais dans cette aventure de notre poésie du XIXe et XXe siècles à la recherche de son ordre véritable et de son authenticité."[59] All this, however, finishes early, in 1873, to which year Nadal limits practically the entire achievement of Verlaine. His conversion in the prison of Mons was fatal to his poetry: "La conversion de Verlaine, du point de vue de son art, a donc opéré un véritable retourne-

---

[57] *Poésie et profondeur*, p. 182.
[58] *Ibid.*, p. 185.　　　　[59] *Paul Verlaine*, p. 19.

34

ment de l'expression vitale du rêve ainsi que des valeurs formelles qui en marquaient jusque-là le style. Elle l'a tiré de l'exode du rêve."[60] The crucial point is Nadal's central notion of the dream: he calls it "l'acte suprême de la connaissance," "l'unique outil qui pourrait avoir raison de la mort"; however, to reduce it to a common denominator such as hostility to life is surely to bandy words and to confuse the intrinsic nature of the dream as Nerval expressed it, or the Surrealists, or Supervielle. Although this does not of course detract from the valuable emphasis Nadal places on Verlaine's refusal to allow poetry to be the simple mirror of events (an error that has plagued French criticism long enough), he appears to us to have blurred by his very vagueness the visionary character of the work under discussion. Might he not have sought a term less plainly subject to misunderstanding than "rêve"?

From a brief outline of these divergent explanations we should observe in particular, I feel, that there is no hesitancy in the minds of the critics as to Verlaine's early greatness. If Richard condemns his evolution according to existentialist values, and Nadal judges in terms of oneiric power, both would claim that Verlaine's poetry is one of the most estimable of the nineteenth century, since it provides, in the same way as *Les Fleurs du mal*, to which it owes so much, a dramatic expression of disquietudes and aspirations that move us by their plaintive voice, their noble charm, their wholly distinctive purity of tone. The aim of the present chapter is, similarly, to examine his work from an initial attitude of admiration but to take as focus the "naïveté" we consider to be fundamental. As already indicated, this notion enjoys singular favor with Verlaine and serves to call forth the motifs that are especially close to his heart. Above all, we believe that it enables him to express his search for newborn innocence like that of a renewed first communion. Writing to his "muse" he says in "Les Limbes":

[60] *Ibid.*, p. 68.

Quant à ta bonté, c'est ma vie et c'est mon être,
Sans elle je languis dans ma fade ironie.
Par elle je retrouve en une aube bénie,
Toutes naïvetés où le jour va renaître,
Le beau jour baptismal de mon adolescence![61]

Nevertheless, instead of attempting a global discussion
which would necessitate an essay of major length, we have
chosen to examine one page that was written in 1873 and
published in the collection Mallarmé rightly described in
these terms: "l'unique livre: là, en un instant principal,
ayant écho par tout Verlaine, le doigt a été mis sur la touche
inouïe qui résonnera solitairement, séculairement."[62] *Sa-
gesse* is in our eyes Verlaine's central attainment that offers
the vital expression of his genius; and the poem we are to
study appears not only as a work beautiful in itself, but a
testimony that allows us better to grasp the creative act as
conceived and characteristically practiced by its author.

L'espoir luit comme un brin de paille dans l'étable.
Que crains-tu de la guêpe ivre de son vol fou?
Vois, le soleil toujours poudroie à quelque trou.
Que ne t'endormais-tu, le coude sur la table?

Pauvre âme pâle, au moins cette eau du puits glacé,
Bois-la. Puis dors après. Allons, tu vois, je reste,
Et je dorloterai les rêves de ta sieste,
Et tu chantonneras comme un enfant bercé.

Midi sonne. De grâce, éloignez-vous, madame.
Il dort. C'est étonnant comme les pas de femme
Résonnent au cerveau des pauvres malheureux.

Midi sonne. J'ai fait arroser dans la chambre.
Va, dors! L'espoir luit comme un caillou dans un creux.
Ah! quand refleuriront les roses de septembre!

[61] "Dans les limbes," XII, *OPC*, p. 632. Cf. "There," *OPC*, p. 289:
> C'est la Grâce qui passe aimable et nous fait signe.
> O la simplicité primitive, elle encor!
> Cher recommencement bien humble! Fuite insigne
> De l'heure vers l'azur mûrisseur de fruits d'or!

[62] "Enquête sur Verlaine," *Œuvres complètes*, p. 873.

The third piece in the final section of *Sagesse*, "L'espoir luit . . . ," has long been favored by readers of Verlaine, who have devoted many articles to its interpretation. Indeed, one can have little uncertainty in stating that it is, by a considerable margin, the most extensively discussed of any of Verlaine's writings, concerning which each year rarely fails to produce a new article. But if there is virtual unanimity as to its worth ("le plus beau poème peut-être de Verlaine"), the meaning to be ascribed to it is not at all clear ("le plus mystérieux aussi").[63] Mystery there certainly is in the foreshortened presentation, in the details of the scene, in the relationship between speaker and silent listener, so that one Verlaine scholar after another has sought the key to this mystery in a conjectured episode of the poet's life which might explain away the shadows. For them it is as if the sonnet were an elliptical transposition of reality. Thus, in a commentary to end all commentaries,[64] Antoine Fongaro in 1955 made an exhaustive review of the various critiques of the poem and concluded that the melancholy it expresses was induced by the memory of Verlaine's cousin Elisa Moncomble, who had died several years before; that "les pas de femme" evoked in the first tercet were those of the innkeeper's wife; and that the maternal voice of consolation speaking in the poem was Rimbaud in one of his gentler moods. Fongaro's article is rich in erudition and lucid in argument, but it is, I take it, beset by the

---

[63] A. Fongaro, "L'espoir luit . . . ," *Revue des Sciences humaines*, Nos. 77-78 (1955), p. 227. Y.-G. Le Dantec (*OPC*, p. 960) writes: "Ce mystérieux poème a fait couler beaucoup d'encre, dont celle, aigre-douce, de Jules Lemaître, mais, ce jour-là, 'sympathique'; toutes les explications sont plausibles: présence de Rimbaud ou de Mathilde, ou intervention de la Vierge."

[64] *Ibid.*, p. 227. In a subsequent review published in *Studi francesi*, No. 20 (May-August 1963), p. 316, Fongaro explained his position in slightly modified terms: "je me suis efforcé de montrer que la situation dans laquelle se trouve Verlaine lors de *l'inspiration* [. . .] de ce sonnet, situation matérielle (décor de l'auberge, fatigue physique, etc. . . .) et morale (accablement, désespoir, etc. . . .) fait revivre en lui le souvenir (probablement *sub*conscient) de sa cousine Elisa, concrétisé dans le besoin enfantin d'être dorloté et dans le thème de la rose."

assumption that Verlaine imitated an event of his life rather than a figure of the imagination; he thereby ends up by rearranging the terms of an anecdote, as Jules Lemaître and others did before him. One might perhaps have thought, however, that his exhaustive reading had carried to its limits this particular approach had not, two years later, an English critic felt impelled to launch upon a new study, in which he stated that the scene of the poem was a prison cell and not a rustic shelter ("étable" being attracted by the prisoner's "paille"!), that the wasp was not real but the symbol of the prisoner's fears and anxieties, and that the speaker might be "his prison warden metamorphosed by the poet into a guardian angel who endeavors to console him by insisting on the ray of hope which has not yet been extinguished."[65] We had not realized jailers could show such understanding!

It is no doubt unnecessary to describe at length other commentaries that have appeared over the past decade. One of the most recent, published at the end of 1964, adopts by and large the conclusions of Fongaro regarding the anecdote that inspired the poem and the individual protagonists of the action ("il s'agit de 'l'ami' compréhensif, qui console le désespéré des cruautés de la femme. Celle qu'interpelle l'ami est sans doute la patronne ou une servante d'auberge . . ."), reserving its original remarks for questions of literary background and prosody, to both of which we shall return.[66] An interpretation that is briefer but, we

[65] C. Chadwick, "Two Obscure Sonnets by Verlaine," *Modern Language Review*, Vol. LII, No. 3 (July 1957), p. 353.

[66] Eléonore Zimmermann, "Verlaine: *Vieux et nouveaux Coppées.* Une analyse de *L'espoir luit* . . . ," *Studi francesi*, No. 24 (Sept.-Dec. 1964), pp. 482-488. After A. Fongaro, Miss Zimmermann compares "L'espoir luit . . ." to an early sonnet of François Coppée, "Le Cabaret," which by any fair standards, I think, is banality itself in expression and theme. One finds it difficult to imagine that such a poem would be stored in his memory and later adapted by him to form a masterpiece; it may perhaps be considered even less acceptable to have Coppée used to unravel the secrets of "L'espoir luit . . . ," as when Miss Zimmermann writes (p. 485): "Nous voyons que Verlaine avait bien à l'esprit un cabaret ou une auberge, ce qu'il ne

find, more searching, is given by Claude Cuénot in his monumental thesis entitled *Le Style de Verlaine.*[67] Cuénot considers that the atmosphere of the poem corresponds to the moment when sleep triumphs over consciousness and the self becomes strangely double: "Il s'endort et rêve, et en même temps se regarde dormir, prend pitié de lui-même et cherche à écarter de lui le fantôme qui pourrait troubler son sommeil—l'image de Mathilde irritée."[68] He does not, however, wholly forego the anecdotal approach, since he refers to the scene as being constituted by elements of Verlaine's prison cell and the memory of a country inn at Jehonville, where, as we know, the poet had been in the summer of 1873; while he takes the image of "les roses de septembre" in the last line as the recollection of personal experience ("le vers final [. . .] raisonnablement, ne peut être qu'une allusion à la lune de miel avec Mathilde").[69] The argument is perhaps "reasonably" correct if we are obliged to assume that Verlaine was incapable of universal metaphor and forever tied down to retelling particular events, but this is surely not consonant with the writings of the author of *Fêtes galantes* and would unjustifiably prejudice his significance as a poet. Yet if, in this regard, Cuénot seems to be mistaken, he has, by his emphasis on the poet's duality in the poem ("fait courant dans les états de demi-sommeil"), provided a valuable suggestion as to what we may take to be the proper theme.

For us it is the song of an inner drama in which encouragement and solace are offered to the troubled soul. Not an allegorical transposition, it states in humbly intimate terms that hope is present, that nature can be trusted, that nothing must deter the recourse to refreshing sleep. With a mother's intuition the poet senses the hesitations, the

---

mentionne pas expressément dans le poème." This analysis is taken up in the author's more recent book, *Magies de Verlaine* (Paris: José Corti, 1967), pp. 94-100.

[67] *Le Style de Verlaine* (Paris: Centre de Documentation Universitaire, 1962), *passim*, esp. pp. 243-245, 270, 470, 492.

[68] *Ibid.*, p. 470.   [69] *Ibid.*, p. 270.

agitated reluctance of his listener and allays them by words that conjure away care. And yet the final line of the sonnet resolves itself into a sigh toward a future that will restore past happiness, toward the full flowering of hope in the form of September roses that mean an end to the fevers of summer: it is the moment when the voice most movingly reveals the very tenuousness with which it has sung.

Whose is this voice? I have suggested that it is the poet's; but more precisely, it is that of "naïveté" itself, or his own poetry at its most personal, which Verlaine instinctively associates with candor, innocence, trust, rural charm. Cuénot neglects to say that the phenomenon of "dédoublement" is characteristic of Verlaine and not of this example alone, and that what makes his work so unmistakable is the manner in which the fluid voice of "naïveté" is "heard," incorporated in the poem. His ambition is to recapture the sweetness of an idyllic source and to submit to it, to be both subject and object, creator and consoled. Hence the technique of duality; hence the constancy with which throughout his finest work one typical metaphoric pattern recurs. We need no recourse to the Romantic arguments of Schiller and Schlegel to explain the notion and its stylistic consequences: I believe that it is peculiar to Verlaine, that he gives it a wholly personal interpretation, and that it may well be traced back, as I shall suggest, to a determining experience of his childhood. In an effort to illustrate this process, I would like, then, in examining the most celebrated sonnet of *Sagesse*, to trace as best I can the poetic originality that marries tenderness and control, art and inspiration. If a text be allowed to provide our keynote we might perhaps recall a stanza from a piece that suggests the poet's prevailing ideal, and whose place in *Sagesse* is immediately alongside "L'espoir luit . . .":

> Ah! surtout, surtout,
> Douceur, patience,
> Mi-voix et nuance,

Verlaine's "Naïveté"

Et paix jusqu'au bout!
Aussi bon que sage,
Simple autant que bon,
Soumets ta raison

Au plus pauvre adage,
Naïf et discret,
Heureux en secret![70]

As regards the circumstances of the poem's composition, we know something if not all. From the prison of Mons, to which he had been transferred in October 1873, Verlaine sent his friend Lepelletier a letter containing four poems ("Printemps," "Eté," "Automne," "Hiver") under the title *Mon almanach pour 1874*. Looking into the coming year, imagining scenes that depict each of the seasons, it was a tour de force, a planned and executed poetic exercise which, by its very presentation, divested his poetry of the show of spontaneous generation. The sequence reappears in the manuscript of *Cellulairement*, dated 1875, but it has been given a new name (*Almanach pour l'année passée*), while the individual titles have been suppressed. Yet this was not the form in which the four compositions finally were published: the first of them, an irregular sonnet, was lengthened by six lines and included in *Sagesse*, where it became a new hymn to hope's burgeoning—"Va, mon âme, à l'espoir immense"; the third, in lines of nine syllables on the theme of autumn, found a place in *Jadis et naguère*, where it was called "Vendanges" ("Les choses qui chantent dans la tête"); the fourth also was published in the same collection, where its title, "Sonnet boiteux," now served to emphasize the strange and hypnotic effect of its thirteen-syllable line ("Ah! vraiment! c'est triste, ah! vraiment ça finit trop mal . . .") rather than the howling of London's wintry images. Our present main concern is with the second of the sequence, originally called "Eté," which bears no title either in *Cellulairement* or *Sagesse*. It may

[70] "Sagesse," III, 2, *OPC*, p. 182.

have been revised in prison—Verlaine dates the sequence "Br[uxelles] septembre 1873"—although in the copy of *Sagesse* which the poet gave Count Kessler it bears the annotation "Jehonville, Belgique, été 1873." We know that he left Jehonville in Belgian Luxembourg in late spring of that year, so that the note cannot strictly be exact; what seems certain, however, is that he conceived and perhaps wrote the first version of "L'espoir luit . . ." at that time. Further corroboration of this is to be found in the comment he made to Lepelletier about "Eté," "Automne," and "Hiver": "C'est le système dont je te parlais de Jehonville, les trois derniers sonnets, mais ce n'est qu'un *essai*, ceci."[71] It is appropriate therefore that a letter sent to Lepelletier from Jehonville in the previous May should receive our attention. It shows Verlaine aspiring to a system, a kind of poetry that offered exciting possibilities for his work. "Je caresse l'idée de faire," he writes:

> Je caresse l'idée de faire,—dès que ma tête sera bien reconquise,—un livre de poèmes (dans le sens *suivi* du mot), poèmes didactiques si tu veux, d'où l'homme sera complètement banni. Des paysages, des choses, malice des choses, bonté, etc., etc., des choses.—Voici quelques titres: *La Vie du Grenier.—Sous l'eau.—L'Ile.—* Chaque poème serait de 300 ou 400 vers.—Les vers seront d'après un système auquel je vais arriver. Ce sera très musical, sans puérilités à la Poë (quel naïf ce "malin"! Je t'en causerai un autre jour, car je l'ai tout lu en english) et aussi pittoresque que possible. La vie du *Grenier* de Rembrandt. *Sous l'eau*, une vraie chanson d'Ondine; *L'Ile*, un grand tableau de fleurs, etc., etc. Ne ris pas

[71] Letter to E. Lepelletier, dated "Mons, fin 1873," *Correspondance*, I (Paris: Messein, 1922), p. 130. The Pléiade edition (*OPC*, p. 960) indicates the variants to be found in the letter to Lepelletier and the two manuscripts of *Cellulairement*; while C. Cuénot (*op.cit.*, p. 243) discusses at some length the early and late texts. He observes (p. 243): "Voici un exemple où les variantes témoignent d'un effort pour rendre le réseau des refrains plus dense, moins volatil, ce qui ne lui enlève rien de sa subtilité."

avant de connaître mon système: c'est peut-être une idée chouette que j'ai là.[72]

His ambitious conception was never fulfilled; yet, just as Mallarmé was guided and sustained by his idea of the "Book," so Verlaine found in his theorizing, admittedly to a much lesser degree, a secret orientation that served many of his later compositions and significantly, "L'espoir luit. . . ." Let us recapitulate the main points of the poet's statement: firstly, the sonnet appears to have been part of a draft ("ce n'est qu'un *essai*, ceci") of a sequence of long poems, each to comprise three to four hundred lines; secondly, Verlaine's intention was didactic in that he would eliminate man from the center of the poem, where the Romantics had previously put him, so that the lyrical movement would not be the effusion of an "écho sonore," but a landscape, or objects, speaking in their own right. Yet Verlaine was too much of a poet not to know that "things" do not contain an intrinsic interest unless they say something that is coherent and compelling, unless for example they are made to express a theme—such as, in his own words, their "malice" or their "bonté." This takes us back directly to "L'espoir luit . . . ," concerning which we can say that the voice is not so much that of the poet as of "naïveté," which tells the pale and troubled soul of the goodness of things and reconciles it to simplicity, repose. Thereby the poet can be absent from himself, from his troubled hours of waking, and wholly surrender to the comfort of a natural presence that is imbued with hope.

Yet we need also to consider Verlaine's reference to the themes he intended to develop in his series of poems. When he speaks of a composition to be entitled "*Sous l'eau, une vraie chanson d'Ondine*," we recall that among his first adolescent writings were, in his own words, "d'étranges nouvelles sous-marines à la façon, plutôt, d'Edgar Poë,"[73] and that much of his subsequent poetry is comparable to

[72] Letter to E. Lepelletier, 16 May 1873, *Correspondance*, I, 98.
[73] "Confessions," *OC*, V, 78.

a reverie which blurs the outlines of objects, "drowns" them
in his own particular atmosphere ("Ferme tes yeux à demi /
Croise tes bras sur ton sein, / Et de ton cœur endormi /
Chasse à jamais tout dessein"; or again: "Combien, ô
voyageur, ce paysage blême / Te mira blême toi-même, /
Et que tristes pleuraient dans les hautes feuillées / Tes
espérances noyées").[74] As for *"L'Ile . . .* un grand tableau
de fleurs," one would be mistaken if one were to seek a kind
of Mallarméan garden, a *Prose pour des Esseintes,* among
Verlaine's compositions: nothing could be less characteris-
tic; but to know that he was capable of strongly sensuous
verse, of "islands" of exotic gratification, we have only to
think of "Le Dahlia" in the *Poèmes saturniens,* or "Green"
in *Romances sans paroles,* or else the whole collection of
the *Fêtes galantes* with its idyllic depiction of his soul in
the guise of a bittersweet game of love:

> Votre âme est un paysage choisi
> Que vont charmant masques et bergamasques. . . .[75]

On the other hand, the reference to Rembrandt may per-
haps appear unexpected. We know, however, that Verlaine
was very sensitive to the visual arts and that *Fêtes galantes*
in particular provides evidence both in themes and treat-
ment of the attraction held for him by painting of the eight-
eenth century. Yet if we read his prose it is not so much
a predilection for Watteau, Fragonard, and others that we
remark, but the singular importance he attached to the
works of Rembrandt. Proportionally, no doubt, such obser-
vations are to some extent unduly emphasized because of
the presence of an essay *Quinze jours en Hollande* writ-
ten in the eighties, where his very subject almost de-
manded an evocation of the Dutch master. But the letter
of 1873 from which we have quoted indicates that even
then he was far from ignorant of Rembrandt's paintings
and that his appreciation was in fact already firmly
established.

---

[74] "Romances sans paroles," IX, *OPC,* p. 126.
[75] "Clair de lune," *OPC,* p. 83.

A few words in *Quinze jours en Hollande* indicate the quality of his enthusiasm: "que dire encore de Rembrandt, sinon ce que Voltaire disait d'*Athalie*: beau, admirable, sublime"; or again: "tout le génie, toute la haute franchise du Maître."[76] Such pronouncements allow us to glean the evident attraction the painter held for him, and his deep admiration; yet other statements are even more revealing. Thus we find that he appears to have associated Rembrandt with the artistic and conscious creation of a grandiose magic: "les *Syndics* de Rembrandt, toile magnifique, magique! Les beaux personnages si bien, si logiquement campés."[77] The "magic" he designates is not just a rhetorical flourish but undoubtedly synonymous with the "mystery" he mentions when describing the *Nightwatch* ("chef-d'œuvre mystérieux"), which leads him to adopt De Amicis' formula: "Rembrandt est un spectre." An unreal and ghostly figure amid mundane reality, the painter, by the supernatural power of his art, bears witness to a world beyond our own. But we have to turn to the poem which concludes the article on his Dutch journey to discover the fullest expression of his attitude toward Rembrandt, who is evoked at the end of a long description in such a way as to provide in one word its résumé:

> Gens de la paisible Hollande
> Qu'un instant ma voix vint troubler,
> Sans trop, j'espère, d'ire grande
>
> De votre part, voulant parler
> A vos esprits que la nature
> Fit calmes pour mieux y mêler
>
> L'enthousiasme et la foi pure
> En l'idéal fou de réel,
> Et l'idéal et l'aventure
>
> De sorte équitable,—ô le ciel
> Non plus brumeux, mais de par l'ombre
> Même et l'éclat essentiel,

[76] "Quinze jours en Hollande," *OC*, V, 235; *ibid.*, p. 266.
[77] *Ibid.*, p. 265.

O le ciel aux teintes sans nombre
Qu'opalisent l'ombre et l'éclat
De votre art clair ensemble et sombre.

Ciel dont il fallait que parlât
Aussi ce vieux siècle au-then-tique,
Et dont il fallait que perlât

Cette douceur vraiment mystique
Et crue aussi vraiment, qui rend
Rêveuse notre âpre critique,

O votre ciel, fils de Rembrandt![78]

Like "L'espoir luit . . . ," Verlaine's *terza rima* composes a
tableau of realized calm within variety, an equation of
diverse images. The leitmotif is given by the words
"paisible" and "calmes," after which comes a striking inter-
play of elements in the third stanza that is resolved by the
phrase "de sorte équitable"; then contrast is again under-
lined as shadow is thrice placed alongside brightness;
finally a new synthesis is established in the last four lines,
in a mood of peace and mystical gentleness to which the
soul responds ("et crue aussi vraiment"). The evocation
of Holland is thus obtained by means of a pattern that
plainly recalls the sky of such a canvas as the painter's
Landscape with a Castle.

Is it possible to go further and ask ourselves to which
painting in particular Verlaine was referring when he spoke
to Lepelletier of "Le Grenier"? Critics—and one might
point, for instance, to Octave Nadal—appear to have pro-
ceeded on the assumption that a work bearing that title exists,
but this is not the case. We must therefore assume, I be-
lieve, that Verlaine was recalling the atmosphere and motif
of a painting officially known under another name, and if

---

[78] "A mes amis de là-bas," *OPC*, p. 412. We must also refer to the
evocation of the *Nightwatch* in "Epigrammes" (*OPC*, pp. 660-661):
"Cette *Ronde de nuit* qui du reste est *de jour*, / De *quel* jour de
mystère avec *quelle* ombre autour?" The final line expresses the
complex emotions Rembrandt's painting produces: "On s'égaie, on
s'étonne, on frissonne, on admire."

we do this, we shall find a picture which corresponds to his poem in the marvelous *Adoration of the Shepherds* (1646), which he might have viewed at the National Gallery. Without doubt one of Rembrandt's masterpieces, it was done in his maturity: the Child is bathed in a bright light reflected on the circle of faces around Him, while another group of shepherds, one carrying a lamp, stands in the dim right background. The room is a high-roofed barn; cattle are glimpsed behind the main group of characters; and a number of simple details go to compose a movingly realistic portrayal. Yet no attempt is made to create a grandiose impression, for everything is patently modest. We have no difficulty in seeing how Verlaine could not but appreciate the painter's restraint, his "naïveté" let us say, in which a mystical gentleness emerges from precise representation. As in "L'espoir luit . . . ," promise shines forth amid the humblest surroundings.

Art, and specifically a Rembrandt canvas, thus may well have served as a kind of catalyst in the origin of "L'espoir luit . . ."; but we must turn to literature, to the poets that went before, if we would pursue our search for possible sources of Verlaine's sonnet. In poetry much more than in painting he was manifestly a sophisticated connoisseur. Nothing meant so much to him as the indulgence of his literary taste ("nous, si curieux de bons et beaux vers," he once described himself).[79] Now, the study of his debt to his predecessors has received generous attention of late from Georges Zayed, in a book that endeavors to run all influences to ground by means of a battery of comparative texts, from schoolboy readings to chance contacts with contemporaries. In his conclusion Zayed states his belief that Verlaine was a poet only when, swayed by artistic influences, he was unable to yield to an innate penchant for facility.[80] Such a thesis is understandable when it comes from the pen of a scholar who has fixed his attention on

[79] "Marceline Desbordes-Valmore," *OC*, IV, 49.
[80] Georges Zayed, *La Formation littéraire de Verlaine* (Geneva: Droz, 1963), p. 377.

verbal parallels and neglected to take full account of the whole; but after all, it is only the whole that matters, and that shows us whether the parallel is fortuitous, or else truly seminal. If I wish here to submit that Verlaine owes not a little to two poetic masters, my real intention is to allow us to measure how irreducibly personal the common elements become: despite his astonishing receptiveness he could not fail to transform others into a substance of his own fashioning.

One poet we know to have been foremost in Verlaine's thoughts at the time of the composition of "L'espoir luit . . ." is Marceline Desbordes-Valmore, whose work had just been republished under the collective title *Poésies*. No doubt, as his friend Lepelletier emphasized, he had long known examples of her poetry and had savored them; but until Rimbaud forced him (perhaps in London in the spring of 1873) to read her writings as a whole, he had taken it for granted that the best-known pieces were rather exceptional. Nevertheless, when he finally gave them the reading they deserved, it came as something of a revelation: "Notre étonnement fut grand."[81] He was enchanted by the command of prosody, the subtleties of rhythm, the use of the *vers impair* which he himself handled with consummate skill. He could not but be sensitive also to the gentle warmth of her themes, which lose none of their effect for being femininely openhearted. Here was an unknown but secretly intimate spirit whose praise he would choose to sing more than once:

> Un large fleuve harmonieux de confiances
> Vives et de désespoirs lents. . . .[82]

---

[81] "Marceline Desbordes-Valmore," *OC*, IV, 50. Evidence of Verlaine's early acquaintance with at least some of Desbordes-Valmore's work seems to be firmly established: the most recent discussions of the relationship between the two poets have been conducted by G. Zayed (*op.cit.*, pp. 338-345), Eliane Jasenas (*Marceline Desbordes-Valmore devant la critique* [Geneva: Droz, 1962], pp. 108-121) and A. Fongaro ("Sur Verlaine et Marceline Desbordes-Valmore," *Studi francesi*, No. 23 [May-August 1964], pp. 288-289).

[82] "Marceline Desbordes-Valmore," *OPC*, p. 468.

Yet what interests us especially with regard to "L'espoir luit . . ." is a letter Verlaine sent to Emile Blémont from London in June 1873, in which he urged his friend to acquaint himself with Desbordes-Valmore. In so doing, the reference he makes to one of her poems must surely strike in us a familiar chord. "Lisez donc," he writes:

> Lisez donc *Pleurs et Pauvres Fleurs* de Desbordes-Valmore; il y a une *Berceuse* ainsi:
> > Si l'enfant sommeille,
> > Il verra l'abeille,
> > Quand elle aura fait son miel,
> > Danser entre terre et ciel . . .
>
> Est-ce assez une chambre d'enfant au berceau, en été? Tous les vers de cette femme sont pareils, larges, subtils aussi,—mais si vraiment touchants,—et un art inouï![83]

We cannot fail to draw a parallel between the lines quoted and "L'espoir luit. . . ." Both poems are an invitation to sleep, to surrender to nature's care; and, while the bee, or wasp, murmurs in the dreamlike atmosphere, a calm voice allays disquietude. It will be noted, moreover, that Verlaine in his letter alludes specifically to the summer setting of Desbordes-Valmore's poem—although she herself is not so precise—so that we are not surprised when we recall that the original title of his cradle song in the form of a sonnet was "Eté."

Now it would go beyond my thought to assert that Desbordes-Valmore's poem is the direct ancestor of "L'espoir luit . . .": other influences, both poetic and pictural, must be considered, as I shall endeavor to show. But I wish to submit that this "berceuse" perhaps played a hidden role in the formation of Verlaine's sonnet, recalling and renewing a vital pattern of summer warmth, country simplicity, childhood innocence, maternal tenderness that he felt was his own. It is not without relevance to observe that during the very same summer of 1873 he composed a short

[83] Letter to Emile Blémont, 21 June 1873, *Correspondance*, I, 318-319.

piece entitled "Berceuse," which was, so to speak, the despairing counterpart of Desbordes-Valmore's lullaby.

> Un grand sommeil noir
> Tombe sur ma vie:
> Dormez, tout espoir,
> Dormez, toute envie!
>
> Je ne vois plus rien,
> Je perds la mémoire
> Du mal et du bien . . .
> O la triste histoire!
>
> Je suis un berceau
> Qu'une main balance
> Au creux d'un caveau:
> Silence, silence!

The Romantic poetess is even here present, although, so to speak, antithetically. Inspiration has turned brackish, nature offers no reassurance; instead, while maintaining the technique of a maternal crooning ("Dormez . . . Dormez . . . Silence, silence!"), the poet shows that the night of his sensibility has obscured in him all hope.

I feel we are on sure ground in emphasizing the importance of Desbordes-Valmore. Yet "L'espoir luit . . ." offers, I believe, an example of the workings of an even more decisive literary influence, in that it constitutes a tribute, none the less real for being implicit, to a poet whom he never failed to praise in his essays and conversations. "Mon plus cher fanatisme" is the phrase he used to describe Charles Baudelaire, who, he said, first awakened his sense of poetry and whose *Fleurs du mal* became the *vade mecum* of the schoolboy versifier.[84] This was indeed no mere passing fancy, even though his initial attachment was largely uncomprehending ("J'étais fermement persuadé que le livre s'appelait tout bonnement: *Les Fleurs de mai*");[85] for, with the passage of time, he recognized more and more

[84] Letter to Léon Deschamps, 23 August 1892.
[85] *Ibid.*, p. 74.

clearly that much of his own genius appeared to him as an inevitable development that had drawn preeminently on one source. There are, I think, few more generous acknowledgments by one poet of another than those we find in Verlaine's *Confessions*: "Baudelaire eut à ce moment, sur moi, une influence tout au moins d'imitation enfantine et tout ce que vous voudrez dans cette gamme, mais une influence réelle et qui ne pouvait que grandir et, alors, s'élucider, se logifier avec le temps. . . ."[86] Sensuality and mysticism, nervous tension and intoxication, allegory and modernism, intimacy and broad suggestiveness: all these interacting qualities Verlaine cherished in Baudelaire, and they found their way after a chemical change into his own work. It is even possible to suppose that Verlaine may well have adopted "naïveté" as a key word in his own vocabulary, especially as concerns its role in art, from his reading of Baudelaire's critical articles. Thus we are surely struck to find in the *Salon de 1846*: "Delacroix est, comme tous les grands maîtres, un mélange admirable de science,—c'est-à-dire un peintre complet,—et de naïveté, c'est-à-dire un homme complet";[87] and even more emphatically: "la naïveté, qui est la domination du tempérament dans la manière, est un privilège divin dont presque tous sont privés."[88] I believe that such importance given to a term by near-contemporaries can hardly be fortuitous and that Verlaine may well have been developing what he divined in Baudelaire. However that may be, we could, of course, approach the general question of the affinity of these two poets from many angles, chronologically, thematically, or otherwise, but I shall suggest that this affinity marks in a subtly effective way the sonnet we have in hand.

For me the page that served as a kind of hidden resource in Verlaine's composition is "Recueillement," which was published for the first time in 1861 and included in the

[86] *Ibid.*, p. 74.
[87] Baudelaire, "Salon de 1846," *Œuvres complètes* (Paris: Gallimard, Pléiade, 1951), p. 616.
[88] *Ibid.*, p. 667.

third edition of the *Fleurs du mal*. Nowhere else in Baude-
laire do we find a more satisfying calm, such a complete
resolution of inner torment. The hangman, always present
or just offstage in the *Fleurs*, tries to impose new penitence
and remorse, yet this time he is exorcised by an all-embrac-
ing peace.

> Sois sage, ô ma Douleur, et tiens-toi plus tranquille.
> Tu réclamais le Soir; il descend; le voici:
> Une atmosphère obscure enveloppe la ville,
> Aux uns portant la paix, aux autres le souci.
>
> Pendant que des mortels la multitude vile,
> Sous le fouet du Plaisir, ce bourreau sans merci,
> Va cueillir des remords dans la fête servile,
> Ma Douleur, donne-moi la main; viens par ici,
>
> Loin d'eux. Vois se pencher les défuntes Années,
> Sur les balcons du ciel, en robes surannées;
> Surgir du fond des eaux le Regret souriant;
>
> Le Soleil moribond s'endormir sous une arche,
> Et, comme un long linceul traînant à l'Orient,
> Entends, ma chère, entends la douce Nuit qui marche.

The parallels that may be drawn between the two poems
are apparent: both Baudelaire and Verlaine present dis-
ciplined sonnets that contain the voice of hope, a con-
soling promise in the midst of agitation; both are suffused
with a profoundly tender atmosphere, the intimate tone of
which is established from the beginning by the use of the
second person singular; both contain a mixture of allegory
and natural imagery, abstraction and precise allusion; both
have protagonists who are strangely alike, the person spoken
to in each case being a child, or at least someone child-
like in his ways, while the speaker who brings comfort and
maternal solicitude remains unnamed. Finally, we may
note at the beginning of "Recueillement" the expression
"Sois sage," which recalls the title of Verlaine's collection
from which "L'espoir luit . . ." is taken, and the similar al-

liance of ingenuous attitudes and religious overtones this title designates there. The resemblances are therefore striking, and strongly suggestive, I believe, of Verlaine's seminal reading of "Recueillement." Besides, how could he fail to discover, one may ask, the affinities between himself and this theme and poetic technique that had been so masterfully demonstrated? Yet it is obvious that he was no mere untutored beginner exploiting a proven recipe. My contention is rather that by comparing these two admirable sonnets, one of which we may take to be the furtive ancestor of the other, we are the better able to measure their essential differences and to understand the way in which Verlaine, while he continued to proclaim his indebtedness to Baudelaire, had unsealed a fresh and vital spring of the poetic imagination.

Baudelaire's atmosphere, as we know, is that of the modern city and the immense sky above it, while the time is the coming of night, appropriate to tragic meditation. Against this background his poem attains two rhythmic and emotional climaxes that constitute equal halves despite the traditional typographical divisions. The movement rises to the end of line seven in proportion as the stern and moralistic tone unfolds; then, after a transition that runs for over a line, a new development takes place which has its complete resolution in the last words. It is clear that the wondrously tender quality of the sonnet comes from the contrast that is created between these halves, each of which represents the approach of death. In the second quatrain the effect is bitter as "fête" is linked with "servile," "cueillir" with "remords," "plaisir" with "bourreau": this is the vain agitation of the nameless crowd driven to the death to which it is doomed by its very being ("Pendant que des mortels"). The tercets, however, show that the self has become, as it were, coextensive with the universe: the dead Years, Regret, the Sun, Night are seen and felt by the poet as both within him and without, intimately meaningful and yet universal. Are these Years—both dead and alive, absent and present—a cloud formation, or rather the charming forms of the poet's memory? Baudelaire does not distinguish but proposes to us a richly ambiguous image (whereas, when he treats a parallel passage in prose, he is forced into explanation). In the same way, the smiling figure that rises from the waters is both the moon and the poet's own nostalgia for the past; the Sun that curls up, tramplike, in its last sleep under a bridge is, more than daylight, the solitary soul that at last finds peace; while Night, wearing its apparel of mourning, forms the perfect counterpoise to the conventional hangman, for she is also motherly Death that advances in majestic triumph to embrace and comfort her own. Thus we find that Baudelaire creates a magnificent duality of the self and the movement of nature by which all things in the poet's soul and all things outside are placed in strange correspondence, and bathed in a single solemn harmony that contains the acceptance of what is seen and felt.

The poet's voice is remarkable for its exquisite control of rhythm as well as variety of pitch. The first quatrain is gravely calm and balanced, introducing the two "postulations" around which the poem will center; on the other hand, if lines 5 to 7 are intense and purposely raucous, Baudelaire reminds us that they do not bear equal weight or emphasis, since they make up a subordinate clause that prepares the main proposition; then in line 8 he slackens his pace and lowers his tone before giving rein to a full and deep continuity, wholly comparable to the motion of those slow-moving rivers to which he compares true poetry—"qui s'avancent vers la mer, leur mort et leur infini."[89] The last line, so apt in its sound (we observe the impression of vast suggestiveness produced by the succession of nasal "a" sounds), falls into dissyllabic groups with a rising iambic surge. Such are the admirable prosodic means of stating the final confidence of the poet that coincides with tragic awareness.

For the author of "Recueillement" the acceptance of

[89] "Théophile Gautier," *ibid.*, p. 1035.

death signifies, then, the redemption of life, and he pro-
claims a lesson of wisdom, of knowledge he does not
doubt. He aims to console, but above all to convince, and
to this end his death wish is a solemn sermon. His poetry
is that of a preacher, both moralist and visionary, who util-
izes and weds these divergent strains. To the service of his
reasoned unreasonableness he brings the figures of tradi-
tional allegory, as in the second quatrain, as well as others
highly personal, that draw strength from the controlled
ambivalence we have noted. In this manner he is able on
the one hand to distance the hangman Pleasure; on the
other he gives us the sense of all space transformed by a
single and immediate act of grace, his internal monologue
having become the narration of a miracle that enraptures
wayward Grief.

Verlaine's sonnet, on the other hand, is not at all gran-
diose nor somber. Instead of night, the time is noon on a
hot summer's day; instead of the broad canvas of sunset,
clouds, moon, and approaching darkness, the scene is a
country inn or perhaps a cottage—a limited space with the
dim outline of a bedroom beyond. Throughout the poem
we are reminded of this rural setting by a number of con-
crete details ("la guêpe ivre de son vol fou," "le soleil tou-
jours poudroie à quelque trou," "cette eau du puits glacé")
and, in an indirect but deeply moving way, by the two
similes used to describe the allegorical image of consola-
tion ("comme un brin de paille dans l'étable," "comme un
caillou dans un creux"). Heat and freshness, activity and
drowsiness, dust and cool water are evoked in a painterly
chiaroscuro that composes a scene of simple and familiar
calm. From the first words the mood is one of gentle mur-
mur as the self affirms, and again reaffirms, the presence,
however tenuous, of its hope.

Thus we must begin by observing that although their
themes are very close to one another, "Recueillement" and
"L'espoir luit . . ." move in a wholly dissimilar atmosphere.
Verlaine's voice is muted and uses a scheme of reference
and a tone that are intimate and tender, yet never verge on

mawkishness. It accommodates its speech to the soul of an unsophisticated listener, plays on the gamut of childhood innocence, rustic simplicity, and consolation. These varied notes, however, compose a single pattern of meaning which we may summarize by saying that, if Baudelaire's consolation consists in the image of maternal death, that of Verlaine wells up from an overriding sense of the "goodness" of things natural.

It is certain that Verlaine paid particular attention to the mode as distinct from the theme; in fact this no doubt is at the heart of the "system" he spoke of with regard to "L'espoir luit. . . ." In referring to "Automne" and "Hiver," the two other pieces he considered to have derived from the same ambition, we note that there is in each a similar fundamental effort to write "impersonal" poetry, the song that man hears despite himself; no longer the Romantic visionary, he is a humble recipient of grace. Poetry thus appears as the record of another "voice" that rejects reason and control; and although prosody and language lose not a jot of their refinement, the impression is one of fidelity to the inflections of a natural diction.

From this viewpoint it will be seen that "L'espoir luit . . ." offers first and foremost a dramatic monologue, peculiar insofar as it plunges us *in medias res* with no explanation as to whose this voice is, the details of the scene, the setting, the person addressed; and yet it is precisely this vagueness, which we have called the foreshortened description, that establishes poetic immediacy. Verlaine followed a strictly regulated prosodic form of which he had been a master since his Parnassian days, and of whose "superbly French" tradition[90] he was fully aware; but he used it to compose a light, completely unrhetorical poem whose law is discontinuity and whose effect is to evoke the gratuitous bounty of traditional lullabies. It is, as it were, the almost unthinkable alliance—unthinkable if Verlaine had

---

[90] "A la louange de Laure et de Pétrarque," *OPC*, p. 200: "Chose italienne où Shakespeare a passé / Mais que Ronsard fit superbement française."

not written—between Baudelaire at his most reconciled and
Marceline Desbordes-Valmore, whereby formal and spir-
itual discipline is invested with extraordinary freedom of
movement.

> L'espoir luit comme un brin de paille dans l'étable,
> Que crains-tu de la guêpe ivre de son vol fou?
> Vois, le soleil toujours poudroie à quelque trou.
> Que ne t'endormais-tu, le coude sur la table?

The first line establishes for us an atmosphere of grace
that is marvelously tender, if frail. We might have expected
a grandiose image to fill out the allegorical suggestions of
"l'espoir," as would almost certainly have occurred in Bau-
delaire, but Verlaine compares the abstract word that
gives orientation to his whole poem with a concrete de-
tail, familiar, precise, minute, while his verb underlines
the tenuous quality of the moment. We are struck also by
the particularity of the simile that refers us to "l'étable,"
as if speaker and listener shared a common experience. Is
it the manger of the Virgin and Child? Or is it the place
where the monologue we are listening to is situated (so
that the line may have its origin in the reversal of a much
more conventional image, for example: "Un brin de paille,
tel l'espoir, luit dans l'étable")? It is impossible to say
with any certainty; on the contrary, Verlaine achieves po-
etic power in an admirably discreet way by the very am-
biguity he maintains between Christian overtones and rustic
description.

After such an original opening the poet proceeds to em-
ploy a technique of discontinuous development, interrupt-
ing all emphasis and extended metaphor in favor of the
short periods of typically unelevated speech. A question
framed in the intimate mode of address that follows the first
statement will in turn be followed by a second affirmation,
and finally by a second question, which now has the force
of an injunction. Thus, with tone and pitch being constantly
modified, the reader cannot anticipate the line of discourse
and must of necessity put his trust in the "voice" of the

poem to lead him through apparent disorder to the dis-
covery of a pattern.

One characteristic of such poetry is that, freed from an
evident scheme of reference, proceeding by small touches,
rejecting the anecdotal sequence, it is open to a multiplicity
of interpretations. Yet such richness is surely not a disad-
vantage when it extends the resonance of the imagery. In
this regard the second line may signify for us primarily the
disquieting murmur of the wasp, with its threatened sting
—which is here exorcised, since the speaker can assure his
childlike companion that nothing is to be feared. It may
also recall to us other summer scenes in Verlaine ("Comme
la guêpe vole au lis épanoui!"; "L'été dans l'herbe, au bruit
moiré d'un vol d'abeille") in which wasp or bee are in-
cluded in an ideal composition that abolishes every ill. May
we not even go so far as to think of it in terms of an obsessive
thought that cannot be forgotten, some *idée fixe* that is re-
ferred to, and simultaneously banished by the message
of consolation ("Que crains-tu")?

In the third line the presence of natural goodness sur-
rounding and comforting man is reaffirmed by means of
an image of light; once again, however, the statement is
tentative, for brightness is glimpsed only impressionistically
as if it were a small stirring cloud of dust ("poudroie"),
the exact location of which is uncertain ("à quelque trou").
Verlaine's description, then, is exquisitely precise in point-
ing to a detail whilst still maintaining an aura of vague-
ness (we are asked to *look at* an object that is *evaporating*
—and the assonance of "vois" and "poudroie" emphasizes
the tension between the words). In this way he manages
to reflect, and reinforce on a second level, the initial image
of glimmering hope.

The last words capture a tone of reproach that is charged
with maternal gentleness: the self must eliminate fear and
entertain firm confidence in the present and future; there
is now no cause for disquietude, nor—as can plainly be
seen—was there any in the past. The "voice" calls up the
purpose of its song, which is to compose a lullaby, to console

and lead to refreshing rest. It tenderly imagines the posture the listener might have adopted, a physical attitude of surrender: despite the heat, within this simple shelter invaded by sunlight, his head should already be bowed in sleep.

It is perhaps appropriate for us to notice here, before turning to the remaining sections, the mixture of simplicity and sophistication in the language of the first quatrain. The references are familiar, not to say common, the rhythms purposely hostile to Romantic and Baudelairian eloquence, but Verlaine couches them in terms that constantly deviate from the obvious ("Il faut aussi que tu n'ailles point / Choisir tes mots sans quelque méprise").[91] In the fourth line, for example, we would expect to find in colloquial French: "Pourquoi ne t'es-tu pas endormi," whereas the poet employs a literary interrogative ("que" in the sense of "pourquoi") and an imperfect that is most unexpected (it conveys, as the *passé composé* could not have done, a gentle transition from wakefulness). One might also mention in line 3 the position of "toujours" in front of the verb, indicating to us the speaker's nicety of style; it admirably expresses the lingering heat by placing the rhythmic emphasis on "poudroie." Likewise "ivre" and "fou," which conjure up the wasp "drunk with its own mad flight," surprise us by their unusual alliance suggestive of visual and auditory activity. We may also hark back to the first two words of the poem, which bring striking particularity to an abstract noun, even if the use of "luit" reminds the reader of the timidity with which the poet proposes his image. Thus it is that in his handling of the ordinary elements of the language, in the control of syntax, in the union of divergent terms, Verlaine displays, I believe, supreme taste and virtuosity.

> Pauvre âme pâle, au moins cette eau du puits glacé,
> Bois-la. Puis dors après. Allons, tu vois, je reste,
> Et je dorloterai les rêves de ta sieste,
> Et tu chantonneras comme un enfant bercé.

[91] "Art poétique," *OPC*, p. 206.

While maintaining the closed structure of the quatrains, the poet does not aim to achieve the immobility of the traditional sonnet form. His poem is composed on seven rhymes (instead of five) which, by means of a modified pattern in the second quatrain, facilitate a change of harmony and tone. The "voice," as it were, now begins again, adopting new tactics as it calls directly on its childlike companion to drink, to agree to accept this simplest of offerings. Nothing could be less demanding, and it is precisely for this reason that the speaker makes his proposal ("au moins"), the words of comfort becoming suddenly concrete. Here cool refreshment is nature's gift in the warmth of day; in addition we cannot fail to interpret Verlaine's image, in the context of *Sagesse*, as being imbued with associations from the Gospel. Moreover, we note that this extension of meaning is strengthened in our minds by the terms in which the listener is addressed: "pauvre âme pâle," although primarily an expression of sympathetic affection and solicitude, suggests a religious background. Yet instead of developing this and underlining the allegory, the speaker returns in his next brief sentence to an injunction to sleep, then gives an assurance of continued presence: "Puis dors après. Allons, tu vois, je reste." What poetry could be less ambitious in its language? These rhythms are touching by their very absence of grandeur as they call on memories of the voice that once quieted with two or three words our own obscure cares. But a new rhythm in lines 7 and 8 rises and expands, momentarily capturing the symmetry of the classical alexandrine and swelling the wave of promise, an ideal portrait of lulling tranquillity. "Dorloter" takes up the echo of "endormir" and "dormir," but tells of the caresses that will be bestowed like a mother's on her child. We note that the poet gives a personal slant, a "méprise," to his use of "dorloter" by making it govern an abstract entity rather than a person (one says "dorloter un enfant qui rêve," not "dorloter des rêves"), thereby imparting to the word an original accent. The tenderness is not so much for a child as for a man who is treated as a child; in particular the comparison "comme un enfant bercé" is a firm sign that the listener is indeed no longer of an age for the speaker to cradle him. Sleep will come ("sieste"), the listener will be wholly at one with the soothing voice he hears and will respond to it by his own soft humming, like the wholly confident and contented breathing of a child asleep. Thus the two future tenses, which make use of characteristically modest verbs, have opened up an unclouded ideal that is close at hand.

> Midi sonne. De grâce, éloignez-vous, madame.
> Il dort. C'est étonnant comme les pas de femme
> Résonnent au cerveau des pauvres malheureux.

The first tercet begins with a series of short rhythmic groups which turn our eyes forcibly away from the future to the present, at the same time breaking the tone of gentle murmur. A persistent assonance suggests the feeling of wearisome monotony ("sonne," "étonnant," "résonnent") and coincides with the speaker's sudden shift of attitude. The stroke of midday galvanizes him, as he becomes aware of a third person disturbing the calm. Immediately he assumes the role of the guardian he had promised to be ("je reste") in order to protect his "soul," and the "voice" is raised to a pitch of agitation. We are not told the nature of the woman mentioned: at first she is courteously but directly ordered aside ("de grâce, éloignez-vous"), then the speaker pursues his meditation within himself. It is certain, however, that she is all women—"l'éternel féminin"—not merely one figure which it would be unjustifiable to identify with Verlaine's wife Mathilde. She is woman the unloving, the provoker of discordant despair, that is to say, the opposite of the speaker's desire. Thus everything in these three lines echoes with the rhythm of a new disturbance and, particularly, with the sound of the clock and the echoing footsteps of the woman, heard not so much in the ears as in the mind, that obsess those who, through women, have pitifully learnt the meaning of unhappiness ("au cerveau des pauvres malheureux"). The reader is once again struck by the discontinuity of rhythm that makes a tercet of four sentences, the last of which is expanded by enjambment to constitute a long, sinuous group of twenty-two syllables. For the third time "comme" is repeated (it is found in each of the four parts), gaining strength from preceding uses, but on this occasion carrying the force of dismayed wonder.

> Midi sonne. J'ai fait arroser dans la chambre.
> Va, dors! L'espoir luit comme un caillou dans un creux.
> Ah! quand refleuriront les roses de septembre!

At first an anapestic meter, similar to those of the first quatrain and the first tercet, offers the reproduction of the rhythmic pattern of the one and the very words of the other. This is the beginning of the complete reassurance that is proposed in the last three lines as the "voice," having lost its own agitation, is once more attentive and tender. Indeed, the nature of the sonnet as a lullaby becomes apparent with these words, as well as with the repetition of "dors" and the kind of refrain in line thirteen that repeats the opening. The periods are colloquial, short (the tercet is composed of no fewer than five sentences), as fleeting and varied as the different elements of an Impressionist landscape; but it is essential for us not to confuse Verlaine with the ambitions of the Impressionists (as some critics have done), since his characteristic concern is with the world of feelings—nostalgia and desire—and not sight.

The country atmosphere is caught by allusions to roses, the stone, and the bedroom (a room *beyond*, as in Rembrandt), the floor of which has been watered to cool it and keep down the dust. As in line 5, water is evoked with the traditional suggestions of physical and spiritual renewal. On the other hand, the simile by which hope is compared to a stone in a hollow must attract the reader's attention by its originality: opening up to us a vision of nature such as we have not had before, it may make us think of a Hugolian perspective (for instance: "J'ai cueilli cette fleur pour toi sur la colline. / Dans l'âpre escarpement qui sur le flot s'incline"), but the possibilities it offers for dramatic antithesis are naturally not developed in Verlaine. In this way the image of hope is not so much meaningful in itself (a stone) as in its very smallness—humbleness being a quality the poet fixes upon—and in the fleeting light that seems to emanate from it; the landscape, like the shed, is illuminated and transformed by the most modest of objects.

Yet Verlaine does not end on this note of promise: the last line contains two exclamations that translate the intermingling of nostalgia and desire. What the speaker seeks is no vague and gratuitous vision but something which he has already known and experienced, and must rediscover. Although hope has been affirmed and conjured up, we now realize that it has not been grasped, and is porous with uncertainty. Is this a personal memory (roses associated with Elisa, or Mathilde)? Is it a literary allusion (the refashioning of a line of d'Aubigné, for example)? I should prefer to suggest that its poetic efficacy in no way depends on references extraneous to the poem. Expressed in universal terms, it is the aspiration toward an idealized past, as well as the Proust-like desire to change linear time into a circle ("refleuriront"). The voice itself pines for rebirth in sympathy with the soul it strives to inspire, but its goal is not desperate, and the need to recover the past is not presented in some tragically impossible way. Here the answer is known: September roses will bloom again *in September*, at summer's end, when at last hope will be grasped, time redeemed, and nostalgia and desire resolved into a satisfying presence.

IN CONSIDERING in detail one sonnet of Verlaine I have endeavored to show the attainment of an unique expression. "L'espoir luit . . ." composes the poem of "naïveté" that is plaintively touching in language and tone, disciplined in form while adopting a freely associative manner, richly ambiguous in imagery. We have no hesitation in saying that it constitutes for us a kind of summum of Verlaine's work, which it crystallizes at a point that appears most universal. On the other hand, I also believe it to be typical inasmuch as it expresses a scheme that constantly informs Verlaine's writings and to which he gave varied treatment. Does it not, in its particularity, offer a paradigm of the whole? In this regard, if we return for a moment to the metaphor of the stream as proposed in Mallarmé's tribute to him, we may recall these suggestive words of Verlaine himself: "Il serait des plus facile, à quelqu'un qui croirait que cela en valût la peine, de retracer les pentes d'habitude devenues le lit, profond ou non, clair ou bourbeux, où s'écoulent mon style et ma manière actuels."[92] The new poem was less a sudden departure, and the fruit of an influence or event, than a language configuring the poet's pattern of imagination.

Throughout his work, in poetry and prose, one hears echoes of "L'espoir luit . . . ," as we have already suggested by our study of the notion of "naïveté," the constituents of which draw deeply on the vital springs of his lyricism. Countryside, childhood, sensuousness, the dream of consolation are the abiding images of his poetry. Nevertheless, we also observe in his earliest pieces precise developments that prepare us in no uncertain way for the atmosphere and action of the later composition. Thus we need look no further than his first book of verse to discover, in the collection's "Epilogue," an immediate harbinger. For although it is considered to be one of his peculiarly Parnassian writings, the opening stanzas encompass the combination of feverish warmth and cool ("La Nature . . . daigne essuyer les moiteurs de nos fronts"), tender cradling ("L'atmosphère ambiante a des baisers de sœur"), above all the sense of the natural goodness of things that delivers the poet from perversity and brings him long-sought solace:

> Le frais balancement des ramures chenues,
> L'horizon élargi plein de vagues chansons,
> Tout, jusqu'au vol joyeux des oiseaux et des nues,
> Tout aujourd'hui console et délivre.—Pensons.[93]

[92] "Critique des *Poèmes saturniens*," *OPC*, p. 901.
[93] "Epilogue," *OPC*, p. 78. We recall that Verlaine placed a favorite quotation of his from Homer (*Iliad*, viii, 502; ix, 65) at the top of his manuscript copy of the "Almanach pour l'année passée," included

In like manner, if we turn further on in Verlaine's career to *Jadis et naguère*, we shall find a sonnet that is held by the best known of Verlaine's editors to be the "type du poème conçu selon la recette parnassienne";[94] yet its echoes of Leconte de Lisle being once again merely superficial, it stands in reality as a kind of companion piece to "L'espoir luit. . . ." Verlaine creates a midsummer atmosphere in which everything is subject to the dominion of sun, silence, and an immobility pregnant with movement. Man has found calm at the breast of a benign countryside. We should perhaps draw particular attention to the title "Allégorie," which shows us that the poet has sought to present an imaginative realization and not a mimetic one, channeling intimate forces he fostered with the greatest care.

> Despotique, pesant, incolore, l'Eté
> Comme un roi fainéant présidant un supplice,
> S'étire par l'ardeur blanche du ciel complice
> Et bâille. L'homme dort loin du travail quitté.
>
> L'alouette au matin, lasse, n'a pas chanté,
> Pas un nuage, pas un souffle, rien qui plisse
> Ou ride cet azur implacablement lisse
> Où le silence bout dans l'immobilité.
>
> L'âpre engourdissement a gagné les cigales
> Et sur leur lit étroit de pierres inégales
> Les ruisseaux à moitié taris ne sautent plus.
>
> Une rotation incessante de moires
> Lumineuses étend ses flux et ses reflux . . .
> Des guêpes, çà et là, volent, jaunes et noires.[95]

---

in *Cellulairement*; it suggests the desire to be at one with nature and obey familiar routine: "But let us be persuaded by dark night, and make ready our meal."

[94] Y.-G. Le Dantec, *OPC*, p. 977.

[95] *OPC*, p. 208. We might also quote these wonderful lines from the "Prière du matin," composed at Juniville in the Ardennes in 1880:

> La paisible oraison comme la fraîche étable
> Où cet agneau s'ébatte et broute dans les coins
> D'ombre et d'or quand sévit le midi redoutable
> Et que juin fait crier l'insecte dans les foins.

Like "Epilogue" and "L'espoir luit . . . ," "Allégorie" repre-
sents a fundamental attempt to transform poetry into a
kind of lullaby. Again inspired no doubt in part by Des-
bordes-Valmore, the self strives to become a vague con-
sciousness ("pur pivot de tout ce tournoiement")[96] in
which senses, soul, reason, an ingenuous setting will be
drowned ("une immense pâmoison").[97] Hence the allied
pleasures of the intoxicating merry-go-round, or drunken-
ness, that blot out the world as it is and substitute a non-
intellectual order. Verlaine discovers, after Baudelaire, an
intimate correspondence between such a state and that of
the poet:

> Etre saoul, vous ne savez pas quelle victoire
> C'est qu'on remporte sur la vie, et quel don c'est![98]

His victory is the discovery of a kind of grace sufficient unto
itself, a euphoria of the sensibility that has rejected reason.
And nothing will later hinder the direct transfer of these
terms in *Sagesse* from the profane to the religious level, as
Christianity becomes the supreme consolation, the manifest
answer the poet has pursued in other forms:

> . . . un doux vide, un grand renoncement,
> Quelqu'un en nous qui sent la paix immensément,
> Une candeur d'une fraîcheur délicieuse. . . .[99]

Is it possible to ascribe an origin to his yearning? Can we
go beyond the close affinity with Desbordes-Valmore and
Baudelaire? Speculation of this kind holds its dangers, but
Verlaine has provided an illuminating comment in his *Con-
fessions* that seems to have escaped the attention of critics.
"Un soir donc," he writes in his recollections of childhood:

> Un soir donc, je me sentis pris de fièvre: rien de délicieux
> comme un commencement de fièvre; c'est volatil, les
> idées (de pensée, on n'en a plus et quel bon débarras!)

[96] "La Bonne Chanson," *OPC*, p. 106.
[97] "Crépuscule du soir mystique," *OPC*, p. 54.
[98] "Amoureuse du diable," *OPC*, p. 274.
[99] "Sagesse," I, vi, *OPC*, p. 151.

tourbillonnent en s'entrelaçant sans cesse et toujours. On ne sait plus *où* on *en* est, sinon qu'on s'y en trouve bien et mieux. C'est un peu comme certain moment de l'ivresse où l'on croit se rappeler qu'on a vécu le moment où l'on est, et le vivre, ce moment-là. Seulement, ici, la sensation est si vague qu'elle n'est plus sensation, mais caresse indéfinie, jouissance de néant meilleure que toute plénitude. Je remplirais un chapitre et un volume à vouloir analyser cette sorte d'état que je n'ai jamais éprouvé autant qu'à ce moment de ma vie.[100]

For Verlaine, the feverish mind is an elect condition that exercises a special attraction; in fact, as the last sentence affirms so revealingly, it evokes a desire to analyze and examine that is disproportionate to its content, since it possesses for the poet the infinite power of a charm. Ideas in their isolation replace the continuity of thought, and perform each with each a dance of constantly changing motifs. Nothing is precise apart from delight in the gracious interweaving of forms, so that the poet can speak of a condition of vacancy ("jouissance de néant meilleure que toute plénitude"). But he makes it clear that the self is not absent, for it enjoys a kind of second sight, being both vacant and conscious of its own vacancy, both alive in the present and yet looking at the present with the distance and understanding we might have if we had already lived it. The passage provides, I believe, an acute and suggestive description; but it also enables us to place in a wider context the will that prevails in Verlaine to achieve a particular state we have called *conscious naïveté* ("Ce sera comme quand on a déjà vécu / Un instant à la fois très vague et très aigu," as he says in "Kaléidoscope").[101] Most importantly, it also offers the poet's implicit justification of the technique of duality in "L'espoir luit . . ." and elsewhere, by which he becomes the creator and his own creature.

Indeed, a centrally significant part of Verlaine's work

[100] "Confessions," *OC*, V, 39.   [101] *OPC*, p. 201.

appears to us to be inherent in the use of dramatic mono-
logue, as we saw in "L'espoir luit. . . ." My contention has
been that, at the other extreme from autobiography and
anecdote, Verlaine's finest poetry is constantly endeavoring
to capture the reassuring tone and words of another voice
that is dimly felt and, as it were, already recognized.
Everywhere one perceives the awareness of a presence
which is not simply the poet's mother, or Mathilde, or
Rimbaud, but an imagined source. From his earliest poems
he attempts to describe it, to define both its closeness and
distance, its tenderness and inaccessibility, that brings less
a message than a known inflection, like the tone of dead
ones we love and now miraculously hear again.

> Et pour sa voix, lointaine, et calme, et grave, elle a
> L'inflexion des voix chères qui se sont tues.[102]

Rising up to surprise first of all him who hears them, the
words bring a melodious swaying whose consolation re-
calls our remotest memories.

> Qu'est-ce que c'est que ce berceau soudain
> Qui lentement dorlotte mon pauvre être?
> Que voudrais-tu de moi, doux chant badin?[103]

As to the voice which, like that of "L'espoir luit . . . ," is
light and slumberous in intent, the poet recognizes it as
the one he has always sought because it allays his every
care.

> Elle dit, la voix reconnue,
> Que la bonté, c'est notre vie.[104]

He must accept the grace that tells of innocence, that offers
it to him anew in an alliance of the soul with its secret
"naïveté":

> Accueillez la voix qui persiste
> Dans son naïf épithalame.[105]

---

[102] "Mon rêve familier," *OPC*, p. 48.
[103] "Ariettes oubliées," V, *OPC*, p. 123.
[104] "Sagesse," I, xvi, *OPC*, p. 160. [105] *Ibid.*

In the prison of Mons this voice can only seem a long re-proach to the erring poet, an insistent plea to realize that his youth has been misspent: "Dis, qu'as-tu fait, toi que voilà / De ta jeunesse?";[106] but it finally imposes itself despite pride, hatred, the flesh, that cry out and seek to pass themselves off as his true expression:

> J'entends, je vois toujours! Voix des bonnes pensées!
> Innocence, avenir! . . .[107]

Poems like "Crimen amoris" and "Bournemouth" shimmer-ingly stand forth from the dross of much of the later writ-ings, the action of the poem being constituted by an inter-change of voices that resolves itself into an ultimate purity.

> Voici trois tintements comme trois coups de flûte,
> Trois encor! Trois encor! L'*angelus* oublié
> Se souvient, le voici qui dit: Paix à ces luttes!
> Le Verbe s'est fait chair pour relever tes chutes,
> Une Vierge a conçu, le monde est délié![108]

Now it is clear that the voice which recurs in these poems as in "L'espoir luit . . ." is not simply that of a particular state of somnolence (as suggested by Cuénot), nor, prop-erly, of dream (Nadal), nor of "l'indétermination sensible" (Richard). It is the voice he knew in a state like fever and drunkenness, an answered aspiration, the magical re-demption of the gulf between the self and its source. An-other voice speaks, but it is through this mask that Verlaine is reconciled with himself and discovers his truth. We re-member Claudel's words: "C'est *vrai*! il y a des moments dans la vie, où nous sommes bien forcés d'écouter quelqu'un qui prend la parole [. . .]. L'inconnu, le refoulé, le séquestré, à la fin c'est son tour!"[109] In this sense, we might say that Verlaine's work is one of the most "spiritual" in French poetry, since it entails the sacrifice of the self, of declama-

---

[106] "Sagesse," III, vi, *OPC*, p. 184.
[107] "Sagesse," I, xix, *OPC*, p. 162.
[108] "Bournemouth," *OPC*, p. 288.
[109] Letter of Paul Claudel to J.-L. Barrault, 10 August 1948, *Œuvres complètes*, XI, 314.

tory or lyrical affirmation; but unlike Mallarmé's ambition, it involves no angelism, for the visiting presence is none other than the candid child within, whose images compose the world Verlaine called "naïveté."

Such poetry is far from the passive outpouring of an inspired author. It is very exactly an achievement, wrought in refined modes and forms, by a man who became the poet of his ideal. There was here no question of *being naïf* but rather of *making oneself naïf*, in the same way as Rimbaud spoke of the need to "make oneself a visionary." I would not wish to dispute the fact that Verlaine's efforts were less and less successful after *Sagesse*: he was destined sadly to confuse the simple and the sincere with banal chatting ("L'art, mes enfants, c'est d'être absolument soi-même"),[110] while he lost the true poetic humbleness, the technique of distanced language, which was implied by his quest. But we must conclude that in his finest poems like "L'espoir luit . . ." Verlaine provides a privileged example of the ambition to represent an essential pattern of which he made, because he could be both spokesman and listener for his fugitive desire, his durable monument.

[110] "Bonheur," XVIII, *OPC*, p. 500. Speaking of the technique of "distant emotions" in Verlaine, Philip Stephan suggests that the poet can treat love humorously, ironically, and thereby dissociate himself from it; but after *Fêtes galantes* "he no longer feels the need to attenuate poetic expression of emotion, to mask his sentiments by the element of distance" ("Verlaine's Distant Emotions," *Romantic Review*, LII [1961], 208). However, as we have indicated, the process of distancing in Verlaine is coexistent with his genius; when it is abandoned for a univocal approach, poetry dies. We think of a passage in one of Philippe Jaccottet's recent meditations (*La Promenade sous les arbres* [Lausanne: Mermod, 1961], p. 148): "La poésie est donc ce chant que l'on ne saisit pas, cet espace où l'on ne peut demeurer, cette clef qu'il faut toujours reperdre. Cessant d'être insaisissable, cessant d'être ailleurs (faut-il dire: cessant de n'être pas?), elle s'abîme, elle n'est plus."

Chapter III

Rimbaud As Rhetorician

To Mallarmé he was merely a "passant considérable,"[1] but no Symbolist has held as much fascination for the poets that followed, and for his readers, as Arthur Rimbaud; and now, nearly a century after his wonderful adolescence, his work still provides more than ample scope for further probing. One of the most detailed critical bibliographies we have of any French author is Etiemble's *Le Mythe de Rimbaud*, the central volume of which appeared in 1952: if one might say that the author did not submit a convincing solution of his own, he did show on a vast scale just how many keys have been proposed—from the Symbolist "myth" to Surrealist, Catholic, totalitarian, bourgeois and antibourgeois ones—and with what justice he could deride extravagant critics.[2] Nevertheless, despite the wide notice that greeted his analysis, the past fifteen years have not seen a diminution in writings on the poet, or indeed less audaciousness in their theses. One recalls, for instance, the recent sexual interpretation proposed by Robert Faurisson, who found in the letter E of "Voyelles" a woman's breasts, and in the title of the sonnet a pun: "Vois-Elles."[3] Other critics, however, have sought to learn from Etiemble's lesson by concentrating first and foremost on the texts, and no admirer of Rimbaud can fail to profit from the commentaries we owe to Yves Bonnefoy, W. H. Frohock, and John Porter Houston, to name but three.[4]

[1] "Arthur Rimbaud," *Œuvres complètes*, p. 512.

[2] Etiemble, *Le Mythe de Rimbaud*, Vol. I: *Genèse du mythe* (Paris: Gallimard, 1954); Vol. II: *Structure du mythe* (1952); Vol. IV: *L'Année du centenaire* (1961).

[3] Robert Faurisson, *A-t-on lu Rimbaud* (Paris: Pauvert, 1962).

[4] Yves Bonnefoy, *Rimbaud par lui-même* (Paris: Le Seuil, 1961); W. H. Frohock, *Rimbaud's Poetic Practice: Image and Theme in the Major Poems* (Cambridge, Mass.: Harvard University Press, 1963); John Porter Houston, *The Design of Rimbaud's Poetry* (New Haven: Yale University Press, 1963).

It is my hope that the following pages can be considered a modest contribution along the same lines, in particular to the study of Rimbaud's rhetoric, which for the most part has been neglected.[5]

I wish to center my remarks on one of the most striking *Illuminations* which was published for the first time with four other prose poems in the 1895 edition of the collected poetry. To gauge the contemporary reaction of one avid admirer of his work, we may turn to Paul Valéry, who wrote to André Gide on 6 December 1895 in these terms: "Ces inédits sont miraculeux (soyons exacts!). Ce sont d'étonnantes Illuminations, des meilleures. Je voudrais passer deux heures avec toi et avec elles."[6] Now, with regard to "Génie," we do not have the original manuscript or any drafts, as we possess for much of Rimbaud's poetry, nor have we any means of establishing the date of composition, even if we may incline, as Suzanne Bernard and others have done, to the years 1872-1873.[7] (I shall, moreover, suggest that its technique appears to have more than a little in common with "Voyelles," which was composed in 1871 and could well stand at the root of later developments.)

But if indefiniteness surrounds its genesis, there has been little reluctance on the part of critics to hail it and analyze its meaning. The interpretations have been extraordinarily diverse; for a summary of the positions adopted, one can

[5] See in particular: Francis Scarfe, "A Stylistic Interpretation of Rimbaud" (*Archivum Linguisticum*, Vol. 3, Fascicule 2 [1951], pp. 166-192)—on the "de-aestheticizing process," the "aestheticizing" of the unpoetic, pejorative vocabulary, the use of the imperative; and Suzanne Bernard, *Le Poème en prose de Baudelaire jusqu'à nos jours* (Paris: Nizet, 1959), especially the chapter "Rimbaud et la création d'une nouvelle langue poétique." Yet, alongside many precise comments, at least one of Madame Bernard's observations must surprise us (p. 183): "Très justement, Rivière notait qu'on pourrait dire des *Illuminations*, sans trop exagérer, qu'elles sont écrites en style de journal: et nous avons là en effet, pour une part, le 'carnet de notes' d'un voyageur."

[6] *Correspondance André Gide-Paul Valéry* (Paris: Gallimard, 1955), p. 253.

[7] Suzanne Bernard, *Œuvres d'Arthur Rimbaud* (Paris: Garnier, 1960), pp. 536-538 (henceforth designated as *Œuvres*).

do no better than refer to Madame Bernard's notes to her critical edition, which by and large are just as valid today as they were in 1960. She distinguishes two main groups of exegetes: those who identify the Genie, or Genius, with Rimbaud himself (these include Wallace Fowlie, Rolland de Renéville, Mario Matucci, and, one might add, René Char),[8] and those who take him to be either Christ (Ernest Delahaye) or the symbol of new Love, as predicted, before Rimbaud, by Michelet, Quinet, Vermersch, and others (Antoine Adam, André Dhôtel, Madame Bernard).[9] Yet the first theory fails, in my opinion, to come to grips with the details of tone and language, or with the fact that the discourse is about "Génie," not a pronouncement in the first person; and—putting aside for the moment any internal observations—it can hardly be made to square with the impersonal nature of the greater part of the *Illuminations*. As for the second approach, although one would not deny the importance of the visionary philosophers of French Romanticism, who doubtless impregnated and informed Rimbaud to a high degree, it is surely an over-

[8] René Char writes: "Dans le poème 'Génie,' il s'est décrit comme dans nul autre poème. C'est en nous donnant congé, en effet, qu'il conclut. Comme Nietzsche, comme Lautréamont, après avoir tout exigé de nous, il nous demande de le 'renvoyer.' Dernière et essentielle exigence. Lui qui ne s'est satisfait de rien, comment pourrions-nous nous satisfaire de lui? Sa marche ne connaît qu'un terme: la mort, qui n'est une grande affaire que de ce côté-ci" ("Introduction aux *Œuvres* d'Arthur Rimbaud," reprinted in *René Char*, ed. Pierre Guerre [Paris: Seghers, 1961], p. 191).

[9] For Yves Bonnefoy, who calls it "l'extraordinaire 'Génie,' un des plus beaux poèmes de notre langue" (*op.cit.*, p. 147), it is a kind of summit of Rimbaud's work and his highest aspiration: "un acte de bouleversante intuition, l'instant de vision où une pensée s'accomplit [. . .]. Il a évoqué [. . .] ce que je puis nommer notre possible de gloire" (pp. 147-148). Of the many other commentaries on the poem we should surely pay attention to the last pages of Jean-Pierre Richard's essay "Rimbaud ou la poésie du devenir" (*Poésie et profondeur* [Paris: Le Seuil, 1955], pp. 187-250), in which he says: "le poème de Rimbaud qui nous donne l'idée la plus exacte peut-être du *bonheur* poétique rimbaldien, c'est aussi et précisément le poème où Rimbaud solitaire rêve au miracle d'un 'Génie' qui réunirait êtres et objets séparés, et qui rétablirait entre eux un courant tout humain, une nappe horizontale de solidarité" (p. 249).

simplification to say that the poem conveys an extrinsic doctrine.[10] On the contrary, I wish to suggest that the subject is an idea, but "une idée qui vient des mots," as Mallarmé would observe: for here, I believe, the language of poetry itself has the first and last say.

FREEDOM of style Rimbaud needed in order to break the more imperiously with traditional forms and matter and to allow him, in the instance we have in hand, to propose a new godhead or tutelary spirit having the attributes of supreme love that resolves all contradictions, yet is as magically seductive as an Oriental sprite. In "Les Sœurs de charité," written in 1871, he already associates the word "génie" with beauty, love, sensuous mystery:

> Le jeune homme dont l'œil est brillant, la peau brune,
> Le beau corps de vingt ans qui devrait aller nu,
> Et qu'eût, le front cerclé de cuivre, sous la lune
> Adoré dans la Perse, un Génie inconnu.[11]

The subject as he developed it required, then, a language that was not tied to the dictates of conventional prosody and its implied eloquence, to the confines of prose narrative or logic. In this he succeeded admirably and gave us a piece that contains, as we shall find, a fervor and necessity of its own.

> Il est l'affection et le présent puisqu'il a fait la maison
> ouverte à l'hiver écumeux et à la rumeur de l'été, lui
> qui a purifié les boissons et les aliments, lui qui est le
> charme des lieux fuyants et le délice surhumain des
> stations. Il est l'affection et l'avenir, la force et l'amour

---

[10] Cf. J. P. Houston, *op.cit.*, p. 200: "Rimbaud's critics have sometimes done him the disservice of treating his thought as if it were unique, thereby making him seem more eccentric than anything else. An unfortunate result of this is that his poems have been assumed to be susceptible of any interpretation whatsoever. Only when we become conscious of the character and direction of romantic myth-making can we begin to discern the nature of Rimbaud's imagination and the themology of his work."

[11] "Les Sœurs de charité," *Œuvres*, p. 108.

74

que nous, debout dans les rages et les ennuis, nous voyons passer dans le ciel de tempête et les drapeaux d'extase.

Il est l'amour, mesure parfaite et réinventée, raison merveilleuse et imprévue, et l'éternité: machine aimée des qualités fatales. Nous avons tous eu l'épouvante de sa concession et de la nôtre: ô jouissance de notre santé, élan de nos facultés, affection égoïste et passion pour lui, lui qui nous aime pour sa vie infinie . . .

Et nous nous le rappelons et il voyage. . . Et si l'Adoration s'en va, sonne, sa promesse sonne: "Arrière ces superstitions, ces anciens corps, ces ménages et ces âges. C'est cette époque-ci qui a sombré!"

Il ne s'en ira pas, il ne redescendra pas d'un ciel, il n'accomplira pas la rédemption des colères de femmes et des gaîtés des hommes et de tout ce péché: car c'est fait, lui étant, et étant aimé.

O ses souffles, ses têtes, ses courses; la terrible célérité de la perfection des formes et de l'action.

O fécondité de l'esprit et immensité de l'univers!

Son corps! Le dégagement rêvé, le brisement de la grâce croisée de violence nouvelle!

Sa vue, sa vue! tous les agenouillages anciens et les peines *relevées* à sa suite.

Son jour! l'abolition de toutes souffrances sonores et mouvantes dans la musique plus intense.

Son pas! les migrations plus énormes que les anciennes invasions!

O lui et nous! l'orgueil plus bienveillant que les charités perdues!

O monde! et le chant clair des malheurs nouveaux!

Il nous a connus tous et nous a tous aimés. Sachons, cette nuit d'hiver, de cap en cap, du pôle tumultueux au château, de la foule à la plage, de regards en regards, forces et sentiments las, le héler et le voir, et le renvoyer, et sous les marées et au haut des déserts de neige, suivre ses vues, ses souffles, son corps, son jour.[12]

---

[12] *Œuvres*, pp. 308-309.

The basic technique by which structure was imposed on formlessness was, it seems to me, the adoption of a genre to set the rhetorical pattern. Rimbaud chose the sermon, which of course has no rigid form but is arranged according to familiar articulations: in "Génie" the voice of faith begins by declaring its conviction, naming the qualities of its divinity; then it presents the sure promise of redemption; thirdly we hear, in company with a changed diction, a hymn of adoration; finally, the poet-preacher presents the spiritual message he draws for himself and for us. It is evident that the four parts are typical of a literary kind that combines praise and didacticism and is able, as Rimbaud shows in this piece, to range widely in tone and manner. Upon this canvas, and the Christian connotations it provided, he could give a dazzling demonstration of a visionary language which he constructed part by part, at the furthest remove, I take it, from a trance.

In this manner the internal structure of the two opening paragraphs is a gradation of three statements, expressed in parallel terms and arranged in ascending order, which define the miraculous *being* of the god ("Il est l'affection et le présent," "Il est l'affection et l'avenir," "Il est l'amour [. . .] et l'éternité"), followed by a fourth sentence which indicates his relationship to all men. We have thus, in spite of the discontinuity of the development on a logical level, a rhythmic progression that culminates in a sequence of exclamations. The unknown and essentially unreal god, who is from the start a consummated past, a transformed present, and a future that must be followed to be won—both near us and beyond—is evoked in an overture that persuades us by its nervous force and dynamism.

An examination of the vocabulary of these lines is instructive. Tenderness is the keynote: "affection" (found three times), "amour" (twice), "aimer" (twice); while other words reinforce this emotive aura ("charme," "jouissance de notre santé," "élan de nos facultés") and introduce religious associations ("délice surhumain," "extase," "passion pour lui"). Alongside we observe the poetic consciousness exulting in its taste for novelty and order, or rather novelty within order, as translated in the sense and rhythm: "mesure parfaite et réinventée, raison merveilleuse et imprévue"; while even "éternité" is reduced to our grasp by the apposition used to qualify it ("machine aimée des qualités fatales"), which I take to be neither ironic nor derogatory—the tone excludes this—but a metaphor that describes, in a purposely concrete way that answers the demands of reason, the channel and the very vehicle by which fate expresses itself. Finally, we note the properly religious note of awe ("épouvante," "ciel de tempête"), which will be taken up later in the poem.

The first words of "Génie" offer, then, a mythical figure of grace, seductiveness, marvel, terror, and the corresponding meaning the poet finds in it for the body and the mind. Nevertheless, we need to pursue our study further if we are to appreciate the way the vocabulary is disposed in order to give the text a peculiar, wholly original, energy. In this regard we may look first of all at a few words from the opening sentence:

> . . . puisqu'il a fait la maison ouverte à l'hiver
> écumeux et à la rumeur de l'été. . . .

The phrase conjures up for us the familiarity of a home not closed upon itself but, like this poetry itself, open to apparent contradictions and diametrically opposed images. We might perhaps have expected "saison" rather than "maison," but Rimbaud's is a Verlainian *méprise*, a creative dissonance. The word may also recall, for the reader acquainted with the *Illuminations* as a whole, other images of warmth and childhood wonder: "L'essaim des feuilles d'or entoure la maison du général" ("Enfance"); "Quand le monde sera réduit [. . .] en une maison musicale pour notre claire sympathie" ("Phrases"); "ils furent rois toute une matinée où les tentures carminées se relevèrent sur les maisons" ("Royauté"). Winter and summer can both be welcomed here in their difference: on the one hand, the froth of spray, or snow, perhaps the wild wastes of cold; on the other, throbbing heat and the manifold agitation of nature or men. We may observe, incidentally, that the bond between the contrasting terms receives added pertinence by the assonance of "écumeux" and "rumeur."

> . . . lui qui a purifié les boissons et les aliments. . . .

These words surprise less, and reassure, giving us, within a clear resolution of complementary terms, an allusion to the Eucharist; and just as Rimbaud's sermon seeks to abolish and replace traditional ones, so his new Christ surpasses the other by consecrating all food and all drink. Such is Rimbaud's thirst for purification, which would renew the world and transcend the notions of good and evil: "On nous a promis," he writes in "Matinée d'ivresse,"—"on nous a promis d'enterrer dans l'ombre l'arbre du bien et du mal, de déporter les honnêtetés tyranniques, afin que nous amenions notre très pur amour."

> . . . lui qui est le charme des lieux fuyants et le
> délice surhumain des stations. . . .

Rimbaud presents the balance of two rhythmic groups and the parallel between "charme" and "délice surhumain"; he also evokes the direct contrast between "lieux fuyants" and "stations," which paradoxically brings together evanescence and permanency, tenuousness and stability. By this technique he creates, for the least tangible of themes, a plastic depth of remarkable beauty, and indeed, as I shall endeavor to show, the veritable sense of his poem.

We find the same means used in the second sentence, in which "force et amour" links the tender and strong in a marriage Rimbaud constantly sought ("O palmes! diamant! —Amour, force!—plus haut que toutes joies et gloires!—de toutes façons, partout,—démon, dieu,—Jeunesse de cet être-ci: moi!" ["Angoisse"]), but which too often cruelly escaped him ("l'horrible quantité de force et de science que le sort a toujours éloignée de moi" ["Ouvriers"]). In like manner, the phrase "nous, debout dans les rages et les ennuis" presents the poles of frenzy and boredom in a contrast as brusque as winter and summer, or storm and ecstasy in the following line: "dans le ciel de tempête et les drapeaux d'extase." Rimbaud conveys a visionary presence as glimpsed in the sky, a fugitive dream, like a child's: "le petit valet suivant l'allée dont le front touche le ciel" ("Enfance"), "la douceur fleurie des étoiles et du ciel et du reste" ("Mystique"); but grammatical coordination, placing side by side the most opposed facets, overleaps contradictions without negating them and unites the tempests of disarray and the banners of a spiritual jubilation that makes us think of the conquistadors of poetry—"eux chassés dans l'extase harmonique" ("Mouvement").

I have mentioned the balance of rhythm and verbal structure in the appositions of the third sentence: "mesure parfaite et réinventée, raison merveilleuse et imprévue." The emphasis in each corresponding (we might almost say, congruent) phrase is on newness that is within the bounds of reason but is reason's pleasure and surprise, like the imagined forms of "Jeunesse": "Des êtres parfaits, imprévus, s'offriront à tes expériences." Thus Rimbaud prepares us for the next word and a startling apposition ("l'éternité: machine aimée des qualités fatales"), which raises the tone once again and, by the delimited image of timelessness, underlines the poet's insistence on intellectual control.

Following the triple enumeration that carries us forward, so to speak, by its own impetus, the last sentence provides a remarkable example of verbal composition.

> Nous avons tous eu l'épouvante de sa concession
> et de la nôtre. . . .

Rimbaud begins with the expression of fear, the recognition of a high reciprocity: we yield to the god, and he to us, in mutual surrender and acceptance, like an act of love. Now the cry of joy can come in its fullness:

> . . . ô jouissance de notre santé, élan de nos facultés. . . .

The body rejoices in its well-being, a vigorous self-posses-
sion that reminds us of the amorous consummation of the
Prince and his Genie: "Le Prince et le Génie s'anéantirent
probablement dans la santé essentielle" ("Conte"). The
second short phrase points up the sharp incisiveness of
the acute and energetic rhythm of the preceding one, con-
veying the parallel inactivation of mind and soul. We
think of a similar exultation in "Solde": "Elan insensé et
infini aux splendeurs invisibles, aux délices insensibles."

> . . . affection égoïste et passion pour lui, lui qui
> nous aime pour sa vie infinie. . . .

The principle operative here is again one of balanced
contrast: the word "affection," which no longer describes
the god but the complementary love of men—both poet
and listeners—expresses our wholly personal pleasure (as
in the adagio of "Jeunesse": "Ah! l'égoïsme infini de l'adoles-
cence, l'optimisme studieux: que le monde était plein de
fleurs cet été! . . ."); but it is linked in a paradoxical way
to sacrificial devotion to the god ("passion"), in imitation
of his sacrifice for us ("concession"). After these two
phrases, which sum up a complex tension of forces with
admirable concision, the last line offers a kind of incanta-
tion, made deeply resonant by the repetition of the vowel
"i" as by the strength and simplicity of the eight words
used. It also provides a manifest ambiguity: for if the god
has previously been associated with eternity, hence an in-
finite love—"pour sa vie infinie"—these words may also
be taken to express a self-interest and self-centeredness
(like the "affection égoïste" of men): as one might say, not
"Je t'aime pour la vie" but "pour *ma* vie." In this sense,
it is clear, the dual interpretation is in total accord with the
rhetoric of paradox which we discovered in the previous
lines.

The second section is shorter than the first, although com-
posed similarly of two paragraphs.

Et nous nous le rappelons et il voyage . . . Et si
l'Adoration s'en va, sonne, sa promesse sonne: "Arrière
ces superstitions, ces anciens corps, ces ménages et ces
âges. C'est cette époque-ci qui a sombré!"

Il ne s'en ira pas, il ne redescendra pas d'un ciel,
il n'accomplira pas la rédemption des colères de femmes
et des gaîtés des hommes et de tout ce péché: car c'est
fait, lui étant, et étant aimé.

Rimbaud now eschews the technique of enumeration and
definition for the statement of a promise and the "gospel"
of present redemption, accomplishing a transition that in-
volves considerable discontinuity by way of a simple co-
ordinative conjunction. The tone, if no less firm and deci-
sive, is gentler, as alliteration (for instance: "C'est cette
époque-ci qui a sombré"), repetition ("sonne, sa promesse
sonne"), internal rhyme ("voyage," "ménages," "âges"; and
"sombré," "péché," "aimé" at points of particular empha-
sis) lend a singing quality to the lines.

The poet suggests by religious terms the supernatural
power of the object of his vision ("Adoration"), the trans-
formation the god brings ("rédemption"), the idols he re-
places ("superstitions"), the promised salvation. "Adora-
tion," written with a capital letter, indicates an uniqueness
even more precious than that of "Being Beauteous" ("Des
sifflements de mort et des cercles de musique font monter,
s'élargir et trembler comme un spectre ce corps adoré"),
for in "Génie" we have a plain allusion to the worship of
Christ. Indeed, all the details of this section are imbued
with a religious fervor that bespeaks some miraculous ful-
fillment of desire: "cette promesse surhumaine faite à notre
corps et à notre âme créés: cette promesse, cette démence!"
("Matinée d'ivresse").

The Christian vocabulary gives emotional force and color-
ing to the lines. But another aspect of the language we
must observe is the emphasis on motion ("s'en va," "Arrière,"
"sombré," "redescendra"). When we examine these uses

81

in detail we find that they are central to the structure, which hinges on their paradoxical development. Thus, if the first part of the section revolves about the notion of the god's departure, the second insists symmetrically on the notion that the god will not return, will not descend once more from the sky in millennial splendor—since he is already present. No doubt a tension of this kind is at the heart of Christianity, evoking both the Messianic Christ and Christ who is the Holy Ghost, but Rimbaud makes of it the principle which dramatically abolishes from these lines prose continuity for verbal freedom and an intrinsic balance of forces.

Et nous nous le rappelons et il voyage. . . .

The first sentence already contains the pattern of movement in one direction complemented by movement in another, a beckoning that is answered by a departure rather than a return. The god maintains his distance, affirms his separateness, although there is no rude rebuttal of our desires. The word "voyage" is frequently found in Rimbaud to denote his enthusiasm for spiritual adventure— the "voyages métaphysiques" of "Dévotion," or the enterprise undertaken in the name of all men by the lone sailors of "Mouvement"—"voyageurs entourés des trombes du val et du strom."

Et si l'Adoration s'en va, sonne, sa promesse sonne. . . .

The form of the sentence, the alliteration, the peculiar elliptic introduction of "sonne," which is subsequently repeated and justified by the subject "promesse," have for us, we might say, before anything else a precise auditory charm; but this charm is inseparable from the semantic strength of the two terms "Adoration" and "promesse," pregnant with Christian overtones, that balance each other, just as the god's departure is balanced by his consoling presence. "Sonner," we might observe, is used in two other *Illuminations* in a similarly effective way, to convey a music of the imagination: "Pendant que les fonds publics

82

s'écoulent en fêtes de fraternité, il sonne une cloche de feu rose dans les nuages" ("Phrases"); and again: "Sur les plates-formes au milieu des gouffres les Rolands sonnent leurs bravoures" ("Villes": "Ce sont des villes").

> "Arrière, ces superstitions, ces anciens corps, ces ménages et ces âges. C'est cette époque-ci qui a sombré!"

The language has the obliquity and portentousness of an oracle. Castigating with zeal that which the god rejects, it helps to define his nature. But the enumeration has a disorder that teases and is meant to tease: we are obliged to provide a link between these discontinuous notions, the more so because of the rhyme "ménages"-"âges," which brings together two apparently unmarriageable terms. "Superstitions" figures all a "true" religion eliminates. As for "anciens corps," its relative concreteness surprises us after "superstitions"; it denotes the need for new forms of beauty and vigor, which finds frequent expression in Rimbaud: "Oh! nos os sont revêtus d'un nouveau corps amoureux," he exclaims in "Being Beauteous"; and in "Matinée d'ivresse": "Hourra pour l'œuvre inouïe et pour le corps merveilleux pour la première fois!" "Ménages" might be said to echo Jesus' call to be ready to give up family ties to follow him and, more specifically, Rimbaud's own "Drôle de ménage!" by which he described his relationship with the Mad Virgin of *Une Saison en enfer*; or, pointedly, in "Conte": "Il prévoyait d'étonnantes révolutions de l'amour." In "âges" we can see the refusal, constant throughout his work, of time unredeemed by love, such as we find expressed in his touching "Chanson de la plus haute tour," which avoids pathos by its lively pentameter:

> Oisive jeunesse
> A tout asservie,
> Par délicatesse
> J'ai perdu ma vie.
> Ah! Que le temps vienne
> Où les cœurs s'éprennent.[13]

---

[13] *Œuvres*, p. 158.

The god's last sentence contains a change of vision, for the transformation hoped for is already present. Rimbaud's cry "La vraie vie est ailleurs" is here and now fulfilled, since old lives and times have been engulfed in a new flood ("sombré"), the one he called for in "Après le déluge": "Sourds, étang,—Ecume, roule sur le pont et par-dessus les bois; draps noirs et orgues—éclairs et tonnerre,—montez et relevez les Déluges." The verb "sombrer" evokes this image of a total purification by water, Rimbaud having led us to the center of his rhetoric of vision, and announcing that what seems to exist does not, that our reality is illusion. We also see, however, that these last two sentences are not gratuitous but are woven into a single pattern of paradox. On the one hand the urgent call is to brush aside prevailing errors; on the other, we have a statement couched as an exclamation: the clearing away has no longer to be realized in the present or future, but already is; and time that was to be renewed has sunk like a stricken ship. The fundamental link between the two propositions is thus not so much logical, I take it, as structural.

Il ne s'en ira pas, il ne redescendra pas d'un ciel,
il n'accomplira pas la rédemption des colères de femmes
et des gaîtés des hommes et de tout ce péché. . . .

Rimbaud's technique consists of a series of negations that surprise us by their apparent rejection of what has been said about the god's departure, and by the failure of charity that seems at first to be implied. The entire development is constructed around Christian imagery of the Second Coming, but the statements serve to illustrate the wholly different attitude of this savior. Of the details in the third part, which gives a full rhythmic expansiveness after the two shorter meters, we may ask the reason for "colères" and "gaîtés"; but we recognize that these terms find their justification within the framework of the poem itself, in the contrast they represent between two sexes and two emotions. In their diversity they compose the "old" world tainted by the idea of sin—"L'arbre du bien et du

mal" referred to in "Matinée d'ivresse"—which will be abol-
ished; while the turn of phrase "tout ce péché" suggests
the lightness and detachment with which it is conceived
in relation to the new salvation.

 . . . car c'est fait, lui étant, et étant aimé.

The last line answers the series of negatives, and the un-
rest engendered, with the assurance of a present solace,
thereby reversing the current of seeming unconcern. The
expression has a remarkable impact which directly depends
on simplicity of words, striking repetition, above all con-
centrated construction. One has only to attempt to trans-
late the sentence to measure the economy of Rimbaud's
means. (A few other examples of absolute phrases of this
kind come to mind, as being a syntactical form that ap-
pealed to Rimbaud because of its concision: thus in "Bot-
tom," "La réalité étant trop épineuse pour mon grand
caractère.") The sentence offers then a harmonious ac-
cord, a tension resolved, the complementarity between the
god who loves here and now and those who love him.

 O ses souffles, ses têtes, ses courses; la terrible célérité
 de la perfection des formes et de l'action.
 O fécondité de l'esprit et immensité de l'univers!
 Son corps! le dégagement rêvé, le brisement de la
 grâce croisée de violence nouvelle!
 Sa vue, sa vue! tous les agenouillages anciens et les
 peines *relevées* à sa suite.
 Son jour! l'abolition de toutes souffrances sonores et
 mouvantes dans la musique plus intense.
 Son pas! les migrations plus énormes que les anciennes
 invasions.
 O lui et nous! l'orgueil plus bienveillant que les
 charités perdues.
 O monde! et le chant clair des malheurs nouveaux!

The poem now moves into its third phase, as it presents
a song of praise and wonderment at the grandeur of the
god. It is properly Biblical in flavor, falling into the fervent

tone and the verses of the psalmist, imitating by its ampli-
tude the resonant fullness it evokes—"la musique plus in-
tense." In this it is close to "A une Raison," certainly one
of the most exalted pieces of visionary lyricism in the
Illuminations:

> Un coup de ton doigt sur le tambour décharge tous
> les sons et commence la nouvelle harmonie.
> Un pas de toi c'est la levée des nouveaux hommes et
> leur en marche.
> Ta tête se détourne: le nouvel amour! Ta tête se
> retourne:—le nouvel amour!
> "Change nos lots, crible les fléaux, à commencer par
> le temps," te chantent ces enfants. "Elève n'importe où
> la substance de nos fortunes et de nos vœux," on t'en prie.
> Arrivée de toujours, qui t'en iras partout.

Yet there are differences: in "Génie" the language is
patently depersonalized ("perfection," "célérité," "fécon-
dité," "immensité," "dégagement"), while "A une Raison"
is addressed to a feminine figure who is envisaged with a
certain particularity. Moreover, "Génie" refers not only to
the beauty of the present transformed but also to the past
("tous les agenouillages anciens," "les anciennes invasions"),
which leads Rimbaud to introduce specific mention of the
elements of conflict that make grace doubly precious ("ter-
rible," "violence," "malheurs").

We must also note the art with which, as in the previous
sections, multiplicity is contained within a framework, rapid
movement within form. These eight exclamations—or "ac-
clamations," as Claudel would put it—that offer aspects of
the god's glory are arranged with a view to a structural bal-
ance of four central verses surrounded by two preliminary
and two concluding ones. This is evident if only from the
change in the syntactical pattern, verses one and two be-
ing invocations that take up the mode already adopted at
the end of the first section, while the central ones are the
enumeration of the divine attributes, as each image is

echoed in a grandiose phrase. Yet in its detail the composition, as we shall find, is even more subtly conceived.

O ses souffles, ses têtes, ses courses; la terrible
célérité des formes et de l'action.

The enumeration can only surprise the reader by its apparent gratuitousness. The details indicated in the first line seem to have no cohesion; and the nouns in the second half, especially the Latinate "célérité," are equally disconcerting by their abstraction. Rimbaud is obviously wielding terms that in the first place fail to satisfy our expectations of order. However, it becomes clear that the verse turns on the tension between forms and action, realized states ("perfection") and dynamic effort ("terrible célérité"); and it is the alliance of these contradictory states that continues to give the verse vitality even after we have grasped the antithesis on which it is based.

"Souffles" serves to open the evocation of the miraculous being in his variety. It is used, we may observe, in a similar way in "Nocturne vulgaire," to introduce and conclude a fantastic vision: "Un souffle ouvre des brèches opéradiques dans les cloisons," "Un souffle disperse les limites du foyer"; but in "Génie" the plural, likewise applied to "têtes" and "courses," suggests the manifold nature and action of the god. As for "têtes," we are reminded of its parallel use in "A une Raison," where Rimbaud describes the magic wrought by a glance of his goddess Reason ("Ta tête se détourne: le nouvel amour! Ta tête se retourne: le nouvel amour!"), as well as of the emphasis on lucidity and strength of will with which it is associated elsewhere (thus: "quelques noces où ma forte tête m'empêcha de monter au diapason de mes camarades," he writes in "Vies"). "Courses" brings to mind other images of supernatural freshness that Rimbaud associates with childhood: those in "Enfance" ("Il y a une petite voiture abandonnée dans le taillis, ou qui descend le sentier en courant, enrubannée") and, in particular, the wonderful race in "Aube" between mistress Dawn and the pursuing child ("A la grand'ville elle fuyait parmi les clochers et les dômes, et courant comme un mendiant sur les quais de marbre, je la chassais").

We have referred to the word "célérité," suggestive of a sudden, ever-changing marvel. I find only one use of it elsewhere, in "Mouvement," where Rimbaud speaks of "La célérité de la rampe" that carries forward the adventurers who will win a new world of vision. There are, however, striking images of speed: "les talus de gauche," he writes in "Ornières," "tiennent dans leur ombre violette les mille rapides ornières de la route humide"—like figures in a dream; and a dream atmosphere will be explicitly attached to swiftness in "Veillées": "Rêve intense et rapide de groupes sentimentaux avec des êtres de tous les caractères parmi toutes les apparences." To qualify this notion by the epithet "terrible," as Rimbaud does in "Génie," translates the effect of awe, a divine terror: "O terrible frisson des amours novices" ("H"); or: "Rire des enfants, discrétion des esclaves, austérité des vierges, horreur des figures et des objets d'ici, sacrés soyez-vous par le souvenir de cette veille" ("Matinée d'ivresse").

Against swiftness Rimbaud places wholeness, the accomplished shape, the perfected handiwork. He had already described the consummate form of love in the first section as a "mesure parfaite." To this use of "perfection" the next word "formes" corresponds in the same way as "action" will correspond to "célérité." It is a recurrent point of reference in the *Illuminations*, the word in its nominal and verbal modes evoking an ideal image: "Tels qu'un dieu aux énormes yeux bleus et aux formes de neige, la mer et le ciel attirent aux terrasses de marbre la foule des jeunes et fortes roses" ("Fleurs"); "O Douceurs, ô monde, ô musique! Et là, les formes, les sueurs, les chevelures et les yeux, flottant" ("Barbare"); "La bande en haut du tableau est formée de la rumeur tournante et bondissante des coques des mers" ("Mystique"). On the contrary, "action" is undetermined and indeterminate, and in fact precisely represents in one piece, by way of an unexpected verb, a state of transcendence: "Là, la moralité des êtres actuels se décorpore en sa passion ou en son action" ("H").

O fécondité de l'esprit et immensité de l'univers!

The second invocation contains the balance of two phrases which correspond structurally to the harmonious contrast between the fertile mind and a universe alive with meaning. In the confrontation of microcosm and macrocosm the poet finds an exciting and inexhaustible accord, like the reflection of "fécondité" in "immensité." Throughout the *Illuminations* there are numerous echoes of the same notion of fertility: "Les richesses jaillissant à chaque démarche" ("Solde"); "Je vous indiquerais les richesses inouïes" ("Vies"); again, in "Jeunesse": "La terre avait des versants fertiles en princes et en artistes." Likewise, we find a characteristic emphasis on hugeness: "les ornières immenses du reflux" ("Marine"); "Les Corps, les voix, l'immense opulence inquestionable" ("Solde"); "j'ai senti un peu son immense corps" ("Aube"). With regard to "esprit," the word occurs on several other occasions in the *Illuminations*, his symphony of the mind, once being significantly given an enclosed space and form: "Les calculs de côté, l'inévitable descente du ciel, et la visite des souvenirs et la séance des rythmes occupent la demeure, la tête et le monde de l'esprit" ("Jeunesse"). On the other hand, Rimbaud uses "univers" in only one other prose poem, "Jeunesse," where it expresses the world at its most essential and ideal: "Mais à présent, ce labeur comblé, toi, tes calculs, toi, tes impatiences, ne sont plus que votre danse et votre voix, non fixées et point forcées, quoique d'un double événement d'invention et de succès une raison, en l'humanité fraternelle et discrète par l'univers sans images. . . ."

Son corps! Le dégagement rêvé, le brisement de la grâce croisée de violence nouvelle!

The first of four verses in honor of the attributes of the god refers to his body—a new body as distinct from the old one ("ces anciens corps") of the second section. Yet whereas we might have expected visual imagery to follow, the description is wholly abstract: the two nouns stand together as clearly as "fécondité" and "immensité" in the previous verse, and convey a paradoxical idea rather than a precise image. "Le dégagement rêvé" denotes a purging of dross, an unfettering (thus, in "Being Beauteous": "Les couleurs propres de la vie se foncent, dansent, et se dégagent autour de la Vision, sur le chantier"; and in "Solde": "l'occasion, unique, de dégager nos sens"). In the second phrase the corresponding term "brisement" signifies the breaking—of waves, for instance—or the fine unfurling of grace, at the other extreme from the non-violent separation implied in "dégagement." In a similar way Rimbaud establishes the contrast between "grâce" and "violence," the first term conveying selfless bounty, divine goodness, beauty, which accompany in the *Illuminations* the sum of all energies and seductiveness ("Gracieux fils de Pan," Rimbaud writes in "Antique"); but this grace is surprisingly and harmoniously wedded—the word "croisée" is a favorite one ("Des accords mineurs se croisent et filent" in "Les Ponts"; "Du détroit d'indigo aux mers d'Ossian, sur le sable rose et orange qu'a lavé le ciel vineux, viennent de monter et de se croiser des boulevards de cristal" in "Métropolitain")—with violence, which is unlike and yet its complement. The polarity has, then, a particular structural justification in "Génie" although, needless to say, "violence" recurs frequently throughout Rimbaud's work as a token of its rebellious intent: "O le plus violent Paradis de la grimace enragée!" ("Parade"); it is his will to make things new, and the vaulting ambition he proclaims with a verbal tension similar to that of "Génie" in "Matinée d'ivresse": "L'élégance, la science, la violence!"

Sa vue, sa vue! tous les agenouillages anciens et les peines *relevées* à sa suite.

If the evocation of the god's body corresponded to the category of *forms*, in the terms of the opening verse of this section, the second belongs to that of *action*. "Vue" describes the act of seeing, here the god's magical glance. It takes up a previous image ("que [. . .] nous voyons passer dans le ciel de tempête et les drapeaux d'extase") and one that follows ("Sachons . . . le voir") by pointing to the active response of the object of our contemplation. Yet Rimbaud does not describe the glance itself but its effect —raising the lowly and humble and those that labor and are heavy burdened ("peines" designates penalties inflicted, suffering borne, toil pursued)—and imitates Christian promises. The salvation he speaks of, however, is already accomplished. "Agenouillages" is a masterly coinage which is wonderfully economical. Its suffix conveys an emotional commitment that is absent from "agenouillement" and calls to mind not only "ménages" and "âges" in "Génie," but also Rimbaud's predilection for this ending in other pieces (for example: "veuvages," "naufrages," "ravages," "saccage," "sauvage," "orages"). The term that answers it and provides the structural balance is "relevées," synonymous with uprightness, nobility—like "rédemption" in the previous section, or "reconstituées" in "Solde" ("Les Voix reconstituées"), or "revêtus" in "Being Beauteous" ("Oh! nos os sont revêtus d'un nouveau corps amoureux"), or the use of the verb "relever" itself in "Royauté" ("En effet, ils furent rois toute une matinée où les tentures carminées se relevèrent sur les maisons"). Thus the words depict an attitude righted, an imbalance adjusted.

> Son jour! l'abolition de toutes souffrances sonores
> et mouvantes dans la musique plus intense.

The god's splendor, which is the contrary of "cette époque-ci" in the second section, causes pain to disappear. Rimbaud does not attempt to express, after Dante, eternal light, but translates it in terms of emotion and sensation, above all sound. In fact, verbal energy is based on the contrast between two kinds of music: one formed of the burden of experience like some huge *Pathetic Symphony* ("toutes souffrances sonores et mouvantes"), the other a fullness free of private passion. Music is of course a central image in Rimbaud, particularly in the *Illuminations*, in which it serves to suggest, in a way not unlike Apollinaire, the ideal he creates as well as the ideal he seeks to capture, the two of which must, so he dreams, ultimately coincide. He writes of his art in "Vagabonds": "Je créais, par delà la campagne traversée par des bandes de musique rare, les fantômes du futur luxe nocturne"; and in "Vies": "Je suis un inventeur bien autrement méritant que tous ceux qui m'ont précédé; un musicien même, qui ai trouvé quelque chose comme la clef de l'amour." Similarly, thinking of his desirable goal, he writes in "Barbare": "O Douceurs, ô monde, ô musique!" and again, with fantastic imagery: "La musique, virement des gouffres et choc des glaçons aux astres"; in "Villes": "Des châteaux bâtis en os sort la musique inconnue"; and in "Phrases": "une maison musicale pour notre claire sympathie." Such a harmony, complete, ample, complex, would transcend the chorus of personal feeling.

> Son pas! les migrations plus énormes que les anciennes invasions!

In the last verse that affirms in exultant terms the attributes of the god, the poet alludes to another aspect of his action; and in so doing he echoes a verse from "A une Raison" that we have already seen: "Un pas de toi c'est la levée des nouveaux hommes et leur en marche." In "Génie," however, the syntax is exclamatory, the image more comprehensive; and the two nouns "migrations" and "invasions" provide suggestive foils for each other: the latter offering the idea of conquest and military power (we remember that Rimbaud was writing shortly after the Franco-Prussian war), the former that of peaceful movement toward a new land. Rimbaud suggests in both cases diversity of action (by the plural number) and breadth of scale. The epithet "énormes," we note, underlines this, as it frequently does when the poet is presenting his images of the ideal: "O les énormes avenues du pays saint" ("Vies"); "L'énorme passade du courant" ("Mouvement"); "ce monde où je subis tous les succès civils, respecté de l'enfance étrange et des affections énormes" ("Guerre").

> O lui et nous! l'orgueil plus bienveillant que les
> charités perdues!

The section concludes on two verses that return to a tone of invocation, and now express the interrelationship between the god and ourselves. Once again the technique consists of contrasting the old and new, past and present, and of placing two similar terms side by side. Here "bienveillant" is almost synonymous with "charités," but eschews the connotations of Christian convention. Yet Rimbaud paradoxically links altruism with "orgueil" so as to conjure up an idea of pride which comes from knowing the god and being known by him, and from inducing love for others. We see then that the phrase is built on a simple antithesis that is pointed up by the parallel of two charities, and by the direct opposition between "orgueil" and "charités."

> O monde! et le chant clair des malheurs nouveaux!

Almost a regular alexandrine, this verse is notable for the beauty of its rhythm, supported by the alliteration of "monde" and "malheurs," and for the admirable way we move from back vowels to front, then to back again, as the phrase begins and ends on the same closed "o." To conclude his hymn Rimbaud turns, not to the god and the self, but the world, the new creation which is the product of his imagination, like the one he discovered as a child: "Dans un grenier où je fus enfermé à douze ans j'ai connu le monde, j'ai illustré la comédie humaine" ("Vies"), or that of "Ouvriers" ("O l'autre monde, l'habitation bénie par le ciel et les ombrages"), or "Barbare" ("Les brasiers, pleuvant aux rafales de givre,—Douceurs!—les jeux à la pluie du vent de diamants jetée par le cœur terrestre éternellement carbonisé pour nous.—O monde!"). Such is the vision in which the poet delights, the illumination he composes.

Yet the last words state a persistent tension at the heart of the poem, for it is not happiness that now sings in a clear voice, but unhappiness. We have already seen the importance of the image of music as a means of suggesting the ideal; to the same end "chanter" and its derivatives recur frequently, whether to describe a bird's song that pierces our sensibility: "Au bois il y a un oiseau, son chant vous arrête et vous fait rougir" ("Enfance"), or the couple who depart for a country of desire and sing as they go: "Aux accidents atmosphériques les plus surprenants, / Un couple de jeunesse, s'isole sur l'arche, / Est-ce ancienne sauvagerie qu'on pardonne? / Et chante et se poste" ("Mouvement"), or a transformed city: "Et une heure je suis descendu dans le mouvement d'un boulevard de Bagdad où des compagnies ont chanté la joie du travail nouveau" ("Villes"). "Clair" is associated with unclouded charm and happy renewal, as in the image of the orange-lipped girl of "Enfance"—"dans le clair déluge qui sourd des prés"—and of the dwelling place made of music in "Phrases." Thus, in using the terms "chant" and "clair," Rimbaud establishes a direct contrast with "malheurs," playing one against the other and reminding us that, if the new harmony is triumphant, its greatness does not lie in facility but in the conflict it transcends.

> Il nous a connus tous et nous a tous aimés. Sachons,
> cette nuit d'hiver, de cap en cap, du pôle tumultueux
> au château, de la foule à la plage, de regards en regards,
> forces et sentiments las, le héler et le voir, et le renvoyer,
> et sous les marées et au haut des déserts de neige, suivre
> ses vues, ses souffles, son corps, son jour.

The last lines take up once again certain words of the third section ("vues," "souffles," "corps," "jour") to provide a recapitulation. Yet the tone and intent have changed: instead of a psalm of praise the poet draws his lesson from what has been said, concluding with an injunction. He uses two sentences of an entirely different length and structure: the first is brief and simple in its vocabulary, the second composed of a long series of short phrases and a wide-ranging vocabulary which, by what it expresses as by the grandeur of its rhythm, articulates the dream of a total response.

The general form of the section consists of a pattern of proposition and counter-proposition. The god has known and loved us: let us know and love him. The same characteristic features, it will be recalled, we found in the last sentence of the first section ("ô jouissance de notre santé") and in the second verse of section three ("O fécondité de l'esprit et immensité de l'univers!"). Yet in both cases the reciprocity was the subject of excited exclamation, whereas it has now become the diptych of an argument. We shall also discover that, in addition to this balance, the second sentence offers other elements of contrast and complementarity as well. It is indeed a complex, extraordinarily controlled piece of writing.

Il nous a connus tous et nous a tous aimés.

The sentence has the decisiveness and symmetry of a classical alexandrine; and the repetition of "nous" and "tous" and of the same syntactical form, the simplicity of vocabulary, are also factors that combine to give great power. The past tense cannot surprise us (although it has been questioned by some critics), since the analogy is with Christ, whose incarnation, this act of love, was the way he came to "know" men. In parallel manner Rimbaud suggests that the god has come to know us, has demonstrated once and for all his love for us, just as he has accomplished once and for all (again the perfect tense is used) the miracle of constructing a home that embraces both winter and summer and purifying food and drink (section one). We might note that in "Vies," "connaître" has a force similar to the one we find here in suggesting spiritual and imaginative penetration: "j'ai connu le monde."

Sachons, cette nuit d'hiver. . . .

The imperative is that of the preacher addressing the faithful, showing the way. It echoes "connus" in the first sentence as a natural complement and consequence. As for the phrase "cette nuit d'hiver," it is sufficiently justified by the contrast with the last words, "son jour" preparing as it does the god's effulgence. Yet we should not forget other occasions in the *Illuminations* on which Rimbaud associates night and winter, so that the image becomes a characteristic one. Thus in "Après le déluge": "Et le Splendide-Hôtel fut bâti dans le chaos des glaces et de nuit du pôle"; in "Vies": "à quelque fête de nuit dans une cité du Nord, j'ai rencontré toutes les femmes des anciens peintres"; and in "Dévotion": "Ce soir, à Circeto des hautes glaces, grasse comme le poisson, et enluminée comme les dix mois de la nuit rouge,—(son cœur ambre et spunk),—pour ma seule prière muette comme ces régions de nuit et précédant des bravoures plus violentes que ce chaos polaire."

> ... de cap en cap, du pôle tumultueux au château, de la foule à la plage, de regards en regards, forces et sentiments las. ...

The five discontinuous phrases hold up the resolution of the sense as we await the complement of "sachons"; but at the same time they provide wonderful resonance for the sentence. The emphasis on breadth is found in the repetition of "cap"—vast in its very indetermination—and "regards," which includes all that is absorbed with each new glance, the visible and the yet unseen. In the other phrases Rimbaud uses contrast instead of repetition, the first case being the most disconcerting because of the particularity of the language. What is this pole, this castle? The sense, I suggest, lies in the linguistic pattern, in the difference between the image of violently disturbed remoteness and that of a Nervalian structure of the living past, its calm, its graciousness: pathetic when abandoned ("Le château est à vendre; les persiennes sont détachées" ["Enfance"]) but magical ("Des châteaux bâtis en os sort la musique inconnue" ["Villes"]), as reassuring for the imagination as "maison" in section one. As for the phrase "de la foule à la plage," it contains the antithesis of a multitude—men, women, flowers (in "Jeunesse": "Dans tes environs affluera rêveusement la curiosité d'anciennes foules et de luxes oisifs"; in "Fleurs": "la mer et le ciel attirent aux terrasses de marbre la foule des jeunes et fortes roses") and a virgin strand at the beginning of time (in "Phrases": "Quand le monde sera réduit [. . .] en une plage pour deux enfants fidèles"; in "Enfance": "Cette idole [. . .] court sur des plages nommées, par des vagues sans vaisseaux, de noms féroce-ment grecs, slaves, celtiques"). The last phrase of the series, even more patently antithetical, suggests in an elliptical construction the union of energy and fatigue, especially linked with the erotic in Rimbaud: "force," we recall, was used in the first section in relation to love; while "senti-ments las" is love's languorousness (we think of the enig-matic "H": "Sa solitude est la mécanique érotique, sa las-situde, la dynamique amoureuse"). Rimbaud expresses, then, a total diversity of strength and weakness, activity and inertia, which is to be submitted to a single end.

. . . le héler et le voir, et le renvoyer. . . .

In these words the technique of contrast is once again apparent. We find an echo of the opening of the second section ("Et nous nous le rappelons et il voyage. . ."); how-ever, the second half of the phrase emphasizes our need to affirm the god's separateness from us. For he must be hailed, and recognized as the source of meaning and mir-acle, but also distanced; we must see his glory but ac-knowledge it as external and separate, and transcending our particular needs. In fact he must be like the language of the poem, that is, humanly meaningful and yet strange, near and yet unsoundable. The paradox of sending him further on ahead is the means we have of preserving the nature of love, so that it remains both "affection égoïste" and "passion pour lui."

. . . et sous les marées et au haut des déserts de neige. . . .

97

Yet again, the phrase obeys the rhetorical principle of antithesis, bringing together height and depth, sea and desert and snow, the movement of tides and the stillness of landscapes. A whole world is suggested in its variety, redeemed by the presence of the god.

> . . . suivre ses vues, ses souffles, son corps, son jour.

In conformity with the best models of classical eloquence, the conclusion turns for its matter to what has gone before, and repeats four of the god's attributes that were praised in the third section. Rimbaud does not, however, utter them mechanically, in the same order, but arranges his terms of "action" and "forme" with a rare art of sound (alliteration, assonance, rhythm) and sense, so that the climax is reached with the last word, part of whose brilliance comes, as we observed, from the image of night by which it is preceded.

In "Génie" we find, then, an apocalyptic myth presented with idealism and sensuousness, lucidity and precision, and the unique resources of variety of an author who is the complete master of his language. Poetry is at its least anecdotal and least figurative as Rimbaud requires of his reader the readiness to respond to his scheme of words in its constantly changing variations; to a sequence of four diverse tones; to a pattern that uses symmetry and dissymmetry to evoke the idea of a hard-won harmony and inclusiveness. No better example could be given, I think, of his visionary poetics, for "Génie" offers a wholly spiritual vision that is not the fruit of description but of a rhetoric of vision built up image by image, phrase by carefully controlled phrase. Is not, moreover, this tension between consciousness and transcendence already inherent in the title *Illuminations*? The word designates epiphanies, but also, as Verlaine noted, "colored plates," "painted plates"—illustrations that have been prepared by the artist and printed for our delectation.

At the beginning of our reading I endeavored to suggest the relevance of the framework of the sermon and the effectiveness with which it is handled. It is no doubt worth underlining at this point that similar techniques are far from rare in Rimbaud's work. One might recall the frequency of pastiches and parodies in his regular verse—perhaps as a normal sequel to the borrowed nature of his style in Latin; and that even for a masterpiece such as "Le Bateau ivre" the reader cannot afford to ignore the literary tradition to which it corresponds and the Parnassian poems it echoes.[14] In the prose poems the practice is less evident, although of very real significance in my eyes, since I find that frames of reference are being constantly adapted, as in "Génie," to new ends. Some of these are plainly non-literary, like the palaver of a street-caller in "Solde" ("A vendre ce que les Juifs n'ont pas vendu, ce que noblesse et crime n'ont pas goûté"); or the harangue of "Démocratie" ("Conscrits du bon vouloir, nous aurons la philosophie féroce; ignorants pour la science, roués pour le confort; la crevaison pour le monde qui va. C'est la vraie marche. En avant, route!"); or the children's round in "A une Raison" ("—Change nos lots, crible les fléaux, à commencer par le temps, te chantent ces enfants"); or the riddle of "H" ("trouvez Hortense"); or the description of the setting of a comic opera in "Scènes" ("L'opéra-comique se divise sur notre scène à l'arête de l'intersection de dix cloisons dressées de la galerie aux feux"); or the rendering of a public spectacle, a "Parade" at a fair ("Dans des costumes improvisés avec le goût du mauvais rêve ils jouent des

[14] On this subject, it is worth recalling what Maurice Blanchot wrote twenty-five years ago in an essay on *Les Fleurs du mal* (*Faux pas* [Paris: Gallimard, 1943], p. 194): "Ces trois poètes"—he is discussing Baudelaire, Rimbaud, Lautréamont—"ne sont pas seulement attirés par le désir de scandaliser en se faisant gloire d'une défaillance morale et esthétique. Ils sentent que la poésie peut cesser d'être originale, que son efficacité, sa pureté, sa force d'origine ne sont pas nécessairement brisées dans l'étau des réminiscences et sous le poids du déjà dit et qu'un poète réussit parfois à s'exprimer lui-même et d'une manière qui lui est propre en s'exprimant comme un autre. Ce paradoxe a toutes sortes de sens. Mais on a le droit d'y voir aussi un acte de foi dans le langage et dans la rhétorique qui, souvent, de ce qui a vieilli, tirent un charme nouveau fait pour durer éternellement."

complaintes, des tragédies de malandrins et de demi-dieux spirituels comme l'histoire ou les religions ne l'ont jamais été"). All these, I believe—and one might add to the list— point up the novelty of Rimbaud's poetry as projected against a familiar scheme of expression and enabling him to establish with it a subtle counterpoint of verbal tension. Yet the same remark would apply to several other pieces where the echo is patently literary. We can thus see that "Conte" adopts the style and tone of the *Thousand and One Nights* ("Un Prince était vexé de ne s'être employé jamais qu'à la perfection de générosités vulgaires"). In the same way "Aube," which tells with mythological grandeur in the first person singular of a child's dream of capturing the dawn goddess ("J'ai embrassé l'aube d'été"), draws much of its impact from its modulation of the narrative ballad; the first of the "Veillées" I take to be his song without words in the mode of Verlaine ("L'air et le monde point cherchés. La vie. / —Etait-ce donc ceci? / —Et le rêve fraîchit"); while "Barbare," with its constant repetitions, composes a primitive charm, its last words inviting us to chant it again *da capo*. It touches a religious note, as does "Dévotion" in even more specific manner by its ex-voto, and the Biblical verses of "Après le déluge" where the poet's voice imitates the prophet's.

One could develop at length such observations, and I believe it would be useful to do so; but I hope to have indicated here, and above all by what we found in "Génie," that Rimbaud, a master rhetorician, consciously exploits this stylistic device. Nothing, it seems to me, could be further from the unpromoted outpourings of the sensibility. I cannot, therefore, subscribe to this statement by one of his latest critics: "Where Mallarmé's work seems superintended and controlled, Rimbaud's strikes us, in contrast, as approaching spontaneous and uncensored utterance. With Mallarmé we equate the intellect, but with Rimbaud the subconscious."[15] On the contrary, I find a poet who is acutely aware of traditional languages ("prodigieux linguiste," as Verlaine called him) and of the need to begin again in a

15 W. H. Frohock, *op.cit.*, p. 9.

prose that draws its strength from recognizable patterns; and, by establishing a paradoxical relationship to his own manner, he sensitizes anew and surprises his readers. It is, I feel, a vital part of his extraordinary skill and artistic suppleness with respect to what had gone before. "Lions," said Valéry, "are but made of the goats they consume."

Yet just as I find a concerted use of this technique, so the mastery of linguistic detail, and the linguistic analysis it presupposes, may be traced throughout his work until it reaches its peak in the *Illuminations*. Indeed, we may say that no other French poet before him, with the exception of Baudelaire, his direct ancestor in this as in many things, and Mallarmé, gives evidence of having submitted the language of poetry to such meticulous scrutiny. To designate his procedure elsewhere would of course require a study at least as attentive as our reading of "Génie"; but I should like to suggest briefly a few traits of rhetorical method as it applies in four pieces from the *Illuminations*.

We might thus take for a start the opening section of "Enfance" ("Cette idole, yeux noirs et crin jaune"), in which one discovers the symbol of ideal feminine beauty that offers the marriage of diverse races and multiple legends, of sky, plants, and sea ("nudité qu'ombrent, traversent et habillent les arcs-en-ciel, la flore, la mer"), smallness and greatness, activity and languorousness, tyrannical beauty and pathetic sweetness, whose variety is caught up in a dance of linguistic contrasts and balances. Each sentence stems from the ambition to totalize apparent contradictions in a harmony, which is at the other extreme from the boredom of conventional courtesy and courtship: "Quel ennui, l'heure du 'cher corps' et 'cher cœur.'" Such irony attests the artist's control, like his previous aside when describing the girl in the flood of freshness: "les fleurs de rêve tintent, éclatent, éclairent"—reminding us that his poem is directed and that, if dream has a part in his creation, it assuredly does not dominate it.

"Being Beauteous" is another fine example of Rimbaud's command of a nonreferential language that contains an intrinsic tension. As in "Génie" and "Enfance" he evokes an ideal figure: not Genius, not Woman, but Beauty. We are introduced into an atmosphere divorced from things mundane ("le monde, loin derrière nous"), to a magical purification of nature (beyond "les couleurs propres de la vie"). The rhetorical pattern turns on the tension between grandeur and death, for Beauty is both majestic and touched by suffering and mortality ("sifflements de mort," "blessures," "frissons," "sifflements mortels"). Death is in fact, the poem declares, the very condition of Beauty's existence. It is also inherent in our act of contemplation and worship, transforming us into lovers, fascinating us with its ashen face, finally exacting supreme sacrifice ("Le canon sur lequel je dois m'abattre à travers la mêlée des arbres et de l'air léger!"). The linguistic ambiguity is developed with admirable force, and concludes strikingly on the image of love and war caught in inextricable union by way of the single word "canon."

Another poem that has attracted a great deal of attention is "Matinée d'ivresse." The interpretations have been quite diverse, although most frequently of a biographical kind. It seems clear, however, that it presents one of the most intensely excited expressions in the *Illuminations*, the theme of which is contained in the paradoxical phrases of the opening: "Fanfare atroce où je ne trébuche point! Chevalet féerique!" We are told that the ideal of love, elegance, science—this promised world, this madness ("cette promesse, cette démence")—which will witness the long-sought abolition of good and evil and of the tyranny of conventions ("les honnêtetés tyranniques") must come out of torture, poison, murder. Rimbaud's language is a cry of pain and of exultation, shouted with a Dionysiac enthusiasm which does not exclude a glance to the past and the future (three times we have the intoned construction "cela commença," "cela finit," or "finira") and the lucidity of violence implied in the words "Nous t'affirmons, méthode!" From the structural point of view this morning fanfare thus offers a splendid intermingling of contrasts that demonstrate once again Rimbaud's artistic integrity, his organic conception of the whole.

The last "illumination" I wish briefly to examine is written in an entirely different style. "Mouvement," composed in free verse, has a tremendous forward drive which takes us with it precipitately to the end of the third section before the final lines at last propose an image that is, as it were, immobile ("un couple de jeunesse [. . .] se poste"). It is a hymn in honor of the heroic adventure of those by whom humanity survives, for their ship is an ark not so much of conservation as of discovery. In the midst of swirling destruction they are confident, steadfast, and can sing. As carefully planned as "Génie," the poem is likewise made up of four parts: first the boat's rapid passing is described; next the voyagers, their cargo of knowledge; then an affirmation couched in general terms, to the effect that such a departure, and a similar voyage, always occur when they are most needed for mankind's salvation. Within this framework, the peculiar tension and energy of Rimbaud's admirable poem come from the variations in rhythm and sound, the freshness of imagery, the sudden changes of focus as in the opening lines ("Le mouvement de lacet sur la berge des chutes du fleuve, / Le gouffre à l'étambot, / La célérité de la rampe, / L'énorme passade du courant"). But it is also attributable in very considerable measure to the concerted antithesis of technical terms (emphasized by *-ique* endings: "chimique," "hydraulique," "harmonique," "atmosphérique") and natural images, and to a whole series of direct linguistic contrasts: "repos" and "vertige," "lumière diluvienne" and "terribles soirs d'études," "extase harmonique" and "héroïsme de la découverte," "accidents atmosphériques" and "arche," "jeunesse" and "ancienne sauvagerie"; similarly, we note the complex of contrasting details in a single line: "Les appareils, le sang, les fleurs, le feu, les bijoux." Such is Rimbaud's song of calculation and exultation, science and vision, the elements of which are united by a controlled language. Moreover, the introduction of "On voit" and the question "Est-ce ancienne sauvagerie" remind us that the speaker continues to survey his own mood and style with careful eye.

Now, it is evident that a strict analysis would be necessary to show the validity of these remarks and, above all, the art with which the modulations are introduced and the pattern kept open to surprising developments. I have suggested that Rimbaud's real master in this is Baudelaire, whose great poems are built around paradoxes that are worked out with all the resources of majestic or acerbic harmonies. But in his revolt against classical prosody Rimbaud could carry this technique to its limits, rejecting the coherence of a line of argument or evocation in order to play out the variations of a given linguistic structure. His object was not paradox under the sign of psychological tension, but of a nonreferential and all-embracing ideal. At the same time he undermined traditional discourse from within. No one, it appears, has characterized the implications of this approach more acutely than Valéry, when he spoke of "ce point extrême, paroxystique de l'irritation volontaire de la fonction de la parole."[16] It was to produce in another vein pieces like "Entends comme brame. . . ," in which the Verlainian tone and mood remain, but eliminate what we normally expect of poetic language:

> Loin des claires meules
> des caps, des beaux toits
> ces chers Anciens veulent
> ce philtre sournois . . .
>
> Or ni fériale
> ni astrale! n'est
> la brume qu'exhale
> ce nocturne effet.
>
> Néanmoins ils restent,
> —Sicile, Allemagne,
> dans ce brouillard triste
> et blêmi, justement![17]

[16] Letter to Jean-Marie Carré, 23 February 1943, *Lettres à quelques-uns* (Paris: Gallimard, 1952), p. 240.
[17] "Entends comme brame . . . ," *Œuvres*, p. 173.

This indeed appears to represent an end, the achievement of "l'incohérence harmonique," as it has been called,[18] or "une espèce d'hypnose ouverte."[19] But in the *Illuminations,* it seems to me, the intention is wholly different, as the lucid poet carries composition to a very high degree of refinement.

Our realization of the conscious force of this art in "Génie," and in the *Illuminations* as a whole, may also help us to see other poems in a different light with respect to the curve of his evolution. It would again require close argument to carry out a project of this kind, but I wish to choose as a single significant point the sonnet "Voyelles." One has naturally some reluctance to take up a poem that has been so often and so extensively dissected—with what passion a glance at Etiemble's book is enough to show. The battle is still very much alive: witness the reactions to Faurisson's article, which was mentioned earlier. After a period when the theory of "colored hearing" was more or less ponderously expounded, other modes have seen their day, the erotic no less justifiably, one supposes, than many others. Among English and American critics this exuberance of interpretations has of late resulted in an attitude of rather understandable deflation: "I think that on artistic grounds it hardly deserves its fame," observes J. P. Houston; and W. H. Frohock: "when one simply reads the poem without appealing to preconceptions, the chance that Rim-

[18] *Lettres à quelques-uns,* p. 240. Cf. "Vraiment ce bougre-là a deviné et créé la littérature qui reste toujours *au-dessus* du lecteur" (*Correspondance Gide-Valéry,* letter of 9 October 1906, p. 411); again: "Voyance de Rimbaud. Il essaie de se placer dans un état qui lui permette de former des combinaisons verbales de *pure résonance* (*états-instables*)" (*Cahiers* [Paris: Centre National de la Recherche Scientifique, 1957-1961], XVI, 703); again: " 'Génie' de Rimbaud réside en ce que *seul,* il a trouvé çà et là quelques combinaisons de mots de puissance comparable à celle de certaines sensations étrangement *agaçantes*—et certaines autres qui semblent balbutiées par un *impénétrable*—un homme qui parle à un autre qu'on ne voit pas, et non à vous qui êtes là—tel un dormeur et son balbutiement" (*Cahiers,* XV, 457).

[19] Paul Claudel, "Arthur Rimbaud," *Œuvres en prose,* ed. Jacques Petit and Charles Galpérine (Paris: Gallimard, Pléiade, 1965), p. 517.

baud's imagination was playing a gratuitous game seems considerable."[20]

We cannot attempt to resume the present state of the argument, which would take up considerable space. This has, moreover, been laboriously done at various times by Emilie Noulet, Etiemble, and Suzanne Bernard;[21] while Rolland de Renéville, in the 1963 edition of the Pléiade collected works, noted still further exegetical attempts before affirming: "De ces diverses interprétations, et des polémiques qu'elles ont parfois entraînées, nous retiendrons que le problème qu'elles s'attachent à résoudre demeure entier."[22] It does however appear to me that an approach by way of the texture of language and the imaginative structure has been left aside for more seductive theses, and that it may well be appropriate to suggest a reading which explores first and foremost the system of verbal forces, like the one we sought to follow in "Génie." From this viewpoint "Voyelles" is not the expression of a scientific poetics, nor a subjective vision as such; rather is it the triumph of an artist who wills his technique of contrast and complementarity with panache, yet refined power.

A noir, E blanc, I rouge, U vert, O bleu: voyelles,
Je dirai quelque jour vos naissances latentes:

[20] J. P. Houston, *op.cit.*, p. 64; W. H. Frohock, *op.cit.*, p. 133.
[21] Emilie Noulet, *Le Premier Visage de Rimbaud* (Brussels: Palais des Académies, 1953); Etiemble, *Le Mythe de Rimbaud*, Vol. II: *Structure du mythe* (1954) and *Le Sonnet des Voyelles* (Paris: Gallimard, 1968), in which the author concludes his review of the various interpretations of the poem with these words of dismissal: "Il est temps, grand temps qu'on en finisse avec *Voyelles*, poème incohérent, vaguement construit, bourré d'allusions littéraires, de latinismes, d'images livresques, et qui, si je dois à toute force lui trouver un sens, c'est tout bêtement celui-ci: après avoir sacrifié en deux vers idiots à la mode des voyelles colorées, Rimbaud s'oublie heureusement et se borne à grouper, entre l'image de la mort physique et celle du jugement dernier, des objets noirs, blancs, rouges, verts ou bleus, tous on ne peut plus banals, sans aucun rapport avec les voyelles qu'ils 'illustrent', mais qui faisaient partie de son univers personnel: la nature, la vie, l'amour, la science, de ce que tout homme oppose pour vivre aux obsessions macabres" (p. 233).
[22] *Œuvres complètes*, ed. Roland de Renéville and Jules Mouquet (Paris: Gallimard, Pléiade, 1963), p. 727.

A, noir corset velu des mouches éclatantes
Qui bombinent autour des puanteurs cruelles,

Golfes d'ombre; E, candeurs des vapeurs et des tentes,
Lances des glaciers fiers, rois blancs, frissons d'ombelles;
I, pourpres, sang craché, rire des lèvres belles
Dans la colère ou les ivresses pénitentes;

U, cycles, vibrements divins des mers virides,
Paix des pâtis semés d'animaux, paix des rides
Que l'alchimie imprime aux grands fronts studieux;

O, suprême Clairon plein des strideurs étranges,
Silences traversés des Mondes et des Anges:
—O l'Oméga, rayon violet de Ses Yeux![23]

It would seem that "Voyelles" was the last of the many sonnets Rimbaud composed, if we except, reasonably no doubt, the prose poem that is entitled "Sonnet" in the *Illuminations*. The structure based on five rhymes is not classical (abba-baab-ccd-eed), nor is the great preponderance of feminine endings (twelve out of fourteen), by which our expectation of the final balance of masculine rhymes is dramatically heightened; yet one cannot deny that the formal cohesion is impressive. There is, however, as much difference between—let us say—"Ma Bohême" and "Voyelles" as between Mallarmé's "Angoisse" and "Le vierge, le vivace et le bel aujourd'hui." Here the sonnet is no longer the instrument of personal expression and of the well-turned phrase, but an idea within a poem designedly impersonal.

Certainly one may well recall, as we approach the poem, the famous comment of Verlaine, who was among the first to read and admire: "Cet un peu fumiste, mais si extraordinairement miraculeux de détail, *Sonnet des Voyelles* qui a fait faire à M. René Ghil de si cocasses théories"; and again: "L'intense beauté de ce chef-d'œuvre le dispense, à mes humbles yeux, d'une exactitude théorique dont je pense que l'extrêmement spirituel Rimbaud se fichait

---

[23] *Œuvres*, p. 110.

pas mal."[24] Verlaine dismisses the claims of those who would find in it a manifesto and theoretical illustration—therein does not lie its worth. He also admits the possible presence of some mystification ("un peu fumiste"): Rimbaud speaks in an oracular tone, announcing that he possesses a secret which one day he will name; he proposes a series of equivalents between the central elements of our language, the colors they are supposed to evoke, and the images that accompany them: five vowels, and their visual consonance. This is indeed arbitrary. On the other hand it is justified, I think, if we suppose on the part of the speaker the elevated tone and attitude of a visionary who speaks with precision of an ideal and not of reality. "Je fixais des vertiges," he writes in "Alchimie du verbe." Nevertheless, Verlaine insists at the same time on the artistry of "Voyelles," the poetic charge written uniquely into its images and their arrangement ("si extraordinairement miraculeux de détail"). His observation appears to me wholly valid and points to the incantatory effect of the poem as well as the intensity of the parts, which spring from a will, similar to that contained in "Génie," to create as if despite the world and its appearances.

The vowels provide Rimbaud with a sequence that is complete in itself and at the soul of expression. We have before us five moments that establish a scale symbolic of universality, just as the colors introduce a prism of contrast (black and white) and complementarity (red and green) which closes on the cardinal blue of the ideal, and violet at the end of the spectrum. But the images that accompany each moment are not dictated by a single movement of emotion

[24] *OC*, VIII, 263; V, 361. Verlaine also refers (IV, 17) to "l'œuvre de sa toute jeune adolescence,—gourme sublime, miraculeuse puberté." On the relationship between Verlaine and Rimbaud, see C. A. Hackett, "Verlaine's Influence on Rimbaud," in *Studies in Modern French Literature, Presented to P. Mansell Jones* (Manchester: Manchester University Press, 1961), pp. 163-180; Octave Nadal, *Paul Verlaine* (Paris: Mercure de France, 1961), pp. 35-42; Antoine Fongaro, "Les Echos verlainiens chez Rimbaud et le problème des *Illuminations*" (*Revue des Sciences humaines*, No. 106 [April-June 1962], pp. 263-272).

or vision but, as I should like to submit, by a paradoxical alliance of terms. As in "Génie," so here: Rimbaud achieves remarkable impact by his use of brief phrases that have no connection other than that of their position, either of contradiction or balance. Thus A is identified both with brightness ("éclatantes") and shadow ("ombre"), with the smallness of flies and the greatness of gulfs; E: both deserts ("candeurs des vapeurs et des tentes") and glaciers ("lances des glaciers fiers"), proud nakedness of men ("rois blancs") and timid shadow of flowers ("frissons d'ombelles"—the Latin *umbella* designating a parasol); I: the blood of suffering ("sang craché") and laughter ("rire des lèvres belles"), anger ("colère") and equally passionate repentance ("ivresses pénitentes"); U: the diversity—not without visual analogy—of sea, prairies, and the furrowed brow of the scholar, and the direct contrast between cyclical movement and vibration on the one hand ("cycles," "vibrements") and immobility on the other ("paix," "paix"). Finally, the poem introduces a daring antithesis as O evokes both a stirring clarion call, a searing fanfare ("suprême Clairon," "strideurs"), and silence ("silences"), before concluding its group of words suggestive of a beatific vision on a further silence—the divine radiance of a glance.

It seems to me, then, that "Voyelles" shows us once more the rhetorical procedure and technical mastery of "Génie" and other poems we have mentioned. In the disposition of his imagery Rimbaud attains verbal dynamism, plasticity, resonance, bending a traditional form to his own goals of beauty, violence, totalization by way of his art of language. However, his poem is not merely a gratuitous demonstration but, in the same sense as "Génie," has shape and coherence. It progresses from the linking of repulsion and cruelty with mystery and attraction, to brilliant images, to anger and penitence, then to the ocean swell, and the stillness of pastoral calm and of magic transformation ("alchimie") at the end of long desire; and at last, to the supreme union of strange music and silence that echoes with cosmic motion and exultation. The hidden origin of the sonnet (its "naissances latentes" of the second line, the "traduction" of *Une Saison en enfer*) would from this angle seem not impossible to supply: is it not the idea of love—"mesure parfaite et réinventée, raison merveilleuse et imprévue"—of which the poem, this complex self-sustaining structure, offers us an emblem?

THE APPROACH attempted in these pages with respect to "Voyelles" and "Génie," and all too briefly in the case of other poems, is based on the belief that Rimbaud's use of language offers a remarkable example of conscious control of words and forms, which needs to be followed into its nooks and crannies to be known. We come to understand that his themes are comparatively few for a great poet, echoing those of the religious visionaries of the nineteenth century and, more profoundly still, his own orthodox upbringing and adolescent idealism; yet Verlaine was surely right by and large to say of the *Illuminations*: "D'idée générale il n'y en a pas, ou du moins nous n'en trouvons pas." For Rimbaud the sense might be resumed vaguely as love, science, violence—that was enough. We can even go so far as to observe that, had some of the *Illuminations* been mislaid, what we would be lacking would be not so much a vital part of his message as stylistically unique statements that are each the unravelling of a particular linguistic adventure.

It is true, of course, that certain traits characterize his rhetoric as a whole, such as his revolt against rational and lyrical discourse in search of discontinuity, ellipsis, dramatic intensity. "La morale et la langue sont réduites à leur plus simple expression, enfin!"[25] There is also the taste, which begins with his Latin verse and continues throughout his career, for using his prosodic and linguistic gifts in pastiche and parody. It was this that provided his work with the pricks to kick against, and that obviously gave so much vigor to his art, as we found in the poems examined. Nevertheless, as I have suggested, we miss the essence of

[25] *Œuvres*, p. 274.

Rimbaud when we generalize. René Char has made a re-
mark in which one might wholeheartedly concur: "A l'in-
térieur d'un poème de Rimbaud chaque strophe, chaque
verset, chaque phrase vit d'une vie poétique autonome."[26]

Thus I would venture to conclude that he pursued in the
early 1870's a severe scrutiny of style which bears com-
parison with Mallarmé's preoccupations of almost the same
date; that he was led to "exhaust" the contents of words,
their role as signifiers, so that, as it were, the sign alone
appeared to remain (what Claudel called from another
point of view in his seminal essay on Rimbaud "une décan-
tation spirituelle des éléments de ce monde");[27] and that,
having rejected the referential use of language, he pro-
ceeded to handle words in such a way as to compose care-
fully articulated patterns, primarily independent of any
particular subject, and possessing a specific gravity of their
own. "Trouver une langue," he wrote in his letter to De-
meney; and again: "Toujours pleins du *Nombre* et de
l'*Harmonie*, ces poèmes seront faits pour rester."[28] We find
that he achieved exceptional mastery of the plastic character
of language, willing its effects however far they were from
the normal rhetoric of nineteenth-century French literature,
eliminating the persona with as much ruthlessness as Mal-
larmé. In the *Derniers vers*, the *Fêtes de la patience*, and
the *Illuminations* it is not self-expression that has primacy
but rather its contrary: a verbal construction that only at
second remove, as in a glass, reflects the poet's ideal and
allows us to glimpse his face. It was, I take it, his manner of
discovering and demonstrating a truth he was later to
abandon: that the "genius" of his desire did not preexist
language and form, nor was it identifiable with them, but
lay magnificently—"flamme et cristal, fleuves et fleurs et
grande voix de bronze d'or" as Verlaine said[29]—in the in-
terplay of their paradoxes.

[26] *René Char*, p. 191.
[27] Paul Claudel, *Œuvres en prose*, p. 247.
[28] *Œuvres*, pp. 347-348.
[29] *OC*, V, 356.

Chapter IV

"Magic" and "Movement" in Claudel and Valéry

O_F Claudel and Valéry it may well be said that no two writers offer a more striking contrast; so much so that André Gide, their mutual correspondent depicted them as exemplary of the French dialogue: "Toujours, en regard d'un Pascal, un Montaigne," he affirmed, "et de nos jours, en face d'un Claudel, un Valéry. Parfois c'est une des voix qui l'emporte en force et en magnificence. Mais malheur aux temps où l'autre serait réduite au silence!"[1] Now, it is true that the very mention of their names suggests a series of implicit polarities, but we should not forget that each was acutely aware of the other's existence and tended to some extent to modify his own position accordingly. One could in fact predicate, without applying excessive subtlety, that in a sense there are Claudelian "influences" on Valéry, and vice versa. My object, then, is to show a relationship that has not received more than cursory acknowledgment and to adduce in the process some rare material which may serve our investigation.

On the level of personal interchange relatively little needs to be said, although the contacts were in fact more numerous than is commonly thought. With their provincial backgrounds—one was from the North, the other from the South

---

[1] André Gide, *Journal* (1939-1949), (Paris: Gallimard, Pléiade, 1954), 13 February 1943, p. 191; and in English, in *The Cornhill Magazine*, No. 969 (Winter 1946), under the title "Le Dialogue français." Cf. Georges Cattaui, *Orphisme et prophétie chez les poètes français* (Paris: Plon, 1965), p. 172: "Le dialogue Claudel-Valéry ne s'impose pas moins à nous que les grandes controverses d'Abélard et de saint Bernard, de Descartes et de Pascal, de Bossuet et de Fénelon, en un pays dont l'équilibre naît de l'alternance et de la dialectique." For Valéry also such differences were a vital aspect of French intellectual life: "Le contraste et même les contradictions sont presque essentiels à la France" ("Images de la France," *Œuvres*, II, 1008).

—the two young poets, who were almost exact contemporaries, met first of all on a few occasions at Mallarmé's *mardis*, each of them drawing his own conclusions and conceiving under the same charm works of remarkable originality. The creator of *Monsieur Teste* was impressed above all by the exquisitely organized intellect that was revealed in Mallarmé's use of language; while Claudel, as he showed in *Connaissance de l'Est*, absorbed in his own way the concept of the poem as "l'explication orphique de la Terre": every object *means* something, and offers a sign which it is the poet's duty actively to discover.[2] Thus it was that both of them collaborated in the homage presented to Mallarmé by his younger admirers in 1897, for which they wrote tributary sonnets. Valéry's is no doubt more controlled in its imagery, just as it is more patently a pastiche.[3] But by then Claudel was in China. It was not until November 1903 that the first item of the thin packet of their correspondence was written, when Valéry took the initiative by requesting Claudel to send him a copy of an essay later to be in-

[2] "Mallarmé est le premier qui se soit placé devant l'extérieur, non pas comme devant un spectacle, ou comme un thème à devoirs français, mais comme devant un texte, avec cette question: *Qu'est-ce que ça veut dire?*" (P. Claudel, *Œuvres en prose*, p. 511).

[3] It would be possible to show how germane the images of Valéry's "Valvins" are to the *Divagations* and the poems of Mallarmé, especially "L'Après-midi d'un faune." One might even say that this desire is manifest in the opening words of the first line: "Si tu veux dénouer la forêt qui t'aère . . . ," which echo a statement Mallarmé made on one occasion and which Claudel reports: "Il croyait à la valeur suprême et incantatoire du langage et le mouvement de sa pensée épousait naturellement les formes syntactiques. Je lui ai entendu parler d'un poème qui se serait appelé simplement *Si tu*, et qu'il est en effet très possible de concevoir" ("Notes sur Mallarmé," *Œuvres en prose*, p. 514). Yet despite intentional echoes of this kind, Mallarmé considered that the sonnet was truly characteristic of the young poet: "Ah! heureux et vagabond et comme je vous imiterais, cela va venir et, en attendant, la voile invite, dans vos vers, qui en sont le frisson, avec plus de blancheur que je ne lui en connus. Tout de vous ce morceau Valéry, ému et riche abstraitement" (Letter of 29 March 1897). On the other hand, in recording his reading of Henri Mondor's *Vie de Mallarmé*, Claudel calls his own tribute to Mallarmé "un sonnet ridicule" ("Huitième cahier," 1937-1942, p. 98 [as yet unpublished]).

corporated in his *Art poétique*. In the November 1903 number of the *Mercure de France* Claudel had inserted the following item: "*Connaissance du Temps* est le titre d'un opuscule de cinquante pages environ que M. Paul Claudel va prochainement faire imprimer à Foutchéou. Les personnes que ce livre intéresserait sont priés d'adresser leurs demandes à l'auteur, à Foutchéou (Chine)."[4] Valéry's reply was couched in the following terms:

> Paris, le 2 novembre 1903.
>
> Monsieur,
>
> Je me mets au nombre des personnes que la *Connaissance du Temps* intéresserait.
>
> Je vous remercie maintenant. Pourquoi ne pas vous rappeler enfin quelques rencontres autrefois, chez Mallarmé? Croyez, Monsieur, que je ne les ai pas oubliées.[5]

This short formal note was not to be followed by a long series of letters, for we must describe their exchanges as desultory, if not without moments of real warmth. The courteousness of some of Valéry's letters in particular is at times disarming: on 23 September 1923, for example, shortly after the earthquake that destroyed the French Embassy in Tokyo, he wrote from Paris:

> Mon cher Claudel,
>
> Laissez-moi vous dire la joie avec laquelle j'ai lu le télégramme qui disait enfin que "le personnel de l'Ambassade était sauf."
>
> Je vous serre les mains, et tout mon cœur remercie ce qui vous a préservé, vous et les vôtres, dans cet affreux mouvement de la Terre.[6]

Here the abstract thinker, the nonbeliever addressing the Catholic, finds terms which warmly, urbanely, make due

[4] Letter quoted in the "Revue du mois," *Mercure de France*, No. 167 (November 1903), p. 576.

[5] I am happy to express my deep gratitude to Monsieur Pierre Claudel, who graciously allowed me to consult the precious documents that concern this subject in the poet's apartment, in the Boulevard Lannes, and to Madame Paul Valéry.

[6] Letter of 9 September 1923.

allowance for another's feelings. In the same way, when in March 1935 Claudel failed to be elected to the Académie Française, which preferred Claude Farrère, Valéry wrote: "L'affaire d'hier m'a tellement écœuré que je n'ai pas eu le courage de vous écrire à l'issue de cette dégradante séance [. . .]. Quant à moi, je suis honteux d'avoir vu cela. Vous à l'Académie, il y eût eu quelque chose de changé dans cette étrange vieille."[7] He referred to the same matter once again in May of that year: "Je vous jure qu'après la colère initiale, je ris et rigole de bon cœur de voir la confusion des Amalécites."[8] Nine years later, it was Claudel's turn to refuse to allow himself to be elected because, with Maurras still a member, his scorn was scathing ("Il m'était impossible d'accepter d'être le collègue de cette immonde canaille" [30 October 1944]). In this instance, Valéry's reply to his friend may be considered a model of balanced counsel which might rather be expected from one who himself was a retired ambassador:

> J'ignorais qu'il vous eût dénoncé. C'est inconcevable! Il y a de la folie dans son cas, ce qui confirmerait d'ailleurs les prétentions à la logique de ses thèses et diatribes.
> Toutefois je me permets de vous mettre en garde contre l'impression que vous pourriez donner de vous acharner contre lui. Vous sentez toute la partie que l'on en pourrait tirer contre vous—et même contre la foi qui est la vôtre. Grand poète et croyant, il faut laisser tomber, mon ami, tout ce qui n'augmente ni votre gloire ni votre espoir.[9]

We might mention finally the letters exchanged during the war. These reveal a Valéry profoundly tired in body and mind, who, in turning to Claudel, offered him a token of affection. Vichy was in control when he wrote in deeply touching terms to Claudel, who was at Brangues in the Isère: "Car enfin, *je désespère des gens*. Vous me comprenez,

---

[7] Letter of 29 March 1935.   [8] Letter of 13 May 1935.
[9] Letter of 4 November 1944.

je sens que vous sentez ce que je sens, ce m'est une consolation dans toute cette amertume généralisée de penser à cette simple et profonde similitude. Combien j'ai regretté de n'avoir pu vous voir à Lyon! Que de choses se seraient dites —toutes seules!" and again, one month later: "Croyez que je pense à vous comme l'homme pensait à l'homme pendant le déluge!"[10] A deep and simple likeness one with the other: in the midst of his depression he reached out to a man with whom he shared, despite so many dissimilar points of view, unswerving values. Claudel replied with a generousness that does not disappoint us. We find him writing that year in these terms: "Ne vous laissez pas abattre, mon cher Ami! Les beaux jours ne sont peut-être pas bien loin, et vous avez une œuvre contre laquelle toute la méchanceté des hommes ne peut rien. C'est du marbre. Je vous salue et je vous embrasse";[11] and shortly afterwards: "Serrons les dents. Je vous le dis avec la plus *entière certitude*. Dieu est grand et nous sortirons de cette épreuve plus tôt peut-être que vous ne pensez. Courage et vive la France!"[12] It was during the same period that Valéry, touched by the way Claudel singled out his new version of *Profusion du soir* ("Je ne connaissais pas le fragment de poème sur le soleil couchant que je trouve dans l'*Album de vers anciens*. Il est admirable"),[13] wrote to say he would dedicate it to him if the volume was ever republished. And indeed, the poem bears Claudel's name in the 1945 edition.[14]

Yet undoubtedly the finest item of their correspondence dates from 1921, when Valéry made a penetrating appraisal

[10] Letters of 10 September and 16 October 1942.
[11] Letter of 18 September 1942.
[12] Letter of 20 October 1942.
[13] Letter of 25 September 1942. Claudel begins his letter thus: "Que j'ai été heureux de recevoir ce beau livre et de posséder sous un format commode l'ensemble de votre œuvre poétique. Il ne quitte plus ma table de travail, et c'est une jouissance toujours renouvelée de le rouvrir. C'est un cadeau magnifique que vous faites à notre pauvre France humiliée." In Valéry's twenty-sixth *Cahier* (p. 366) we read a note dated 10 September 1942: "Carte de Claudel qui me fait plaisir (Profusion du soir.)"
[14] In the Pléiade edition the name of the dedicatee has regrettably been omitted.

of their attitudes in response to a rather facile contrast drawn by a critic. In his letter he acknowledged the ease with which such an apparent antagonism could be postulated: "il est vrai que nous ne sommes pas aisément conciliables pour un observateur pris au hasard. Il est vrai que je suis fondé sur un doute, et que vous l'êtes sur une foi. Il est vrai que votre grande œuvre est, en quelque sorte, active ou acte; et que la mienne, ces quelques pages, est purement spéculative." But, he went on, this divergence does not offer grounds for hostility, but rather for understanding and appreciation. "Et moi je ne vois entre nous que des motifs d'estime, et des certitudes de confiance. J'ai pour vous une considération singulière, que ne trouble pas ce que je fais. Vous sentez qu'il n'est pas possible que je ne vous place pas en un rang où je ne vois aujourd'hui personne d'autre."[15] We must underscore the honesty of Valéry's attitude toward a poet who might have been expected to stir in him a prick of jealousy, or grudging approval. Instead, at a time when Claudel had still not achieved full public acclaim, Valéry was warm in his recognition and unreserved in his praise. At the end of his letter he summed up the affinity he felt for Claudel in a scientific metaphor of the kind often encountered in his notebooks: "l'abîme entre nous est océan, distance géodésique, longitude,—non substantiel."

In Valéry's other writings as well, quite apart from his correspondence, a number of implicit and explicit allusions illustrate his interest in Claudel's art if not his metaphysics, which he never went so far as to discuss. His many references to *vers libre* may, for example, be viewed as a kind of counterpoint to Claudel's condemnation of classical prosody. For him it constituted useless freedom, undirected movement: "Avec le système des 'vers libres' ou des facilités illimitées, le poème se fait toujours. Ce n'est pas une entreprise qui puisse avorter, un être qui n'arrive pas à la vie, une construction qui puisse se fermer."[16] (But he

[15] Letter of 25 September 1921, *Lettres à quelques-uns*, p. 136.
[16] *Cahiers*, V, 652.

knew that in Claudel there is another form of discipline, a pattern of symbol and sound around a given motif which replaces more evident control.) In the same way, he criticized Claudel's prose because it lacked the strict framework of an analytical sequence of definitions: "Littérature de substitutions. Ainsi la prose de Cl. qui peut se démonter par substitutions. Littérature de gens qui ne savent que dire—et forts de leur besoin d'écrire etc. Il faudrait que le système des choses substituées soit ordonné."[17] (But this remark only serves to underline a characteristic of Claudel's style which had been consciously elaborated by him after the fashion of a musical composer; and, whether it be poetry or prose, Claudel's procedure is the same—oblique, and yet constantly turning on a single theme.) In the same way the *Calepin d'un poète*, originally published in 1928, reproduces a passage from a notebook of 1911 in which Valéry replaces the initial "C," designating no doubt Claudel (*Cahiers*, IV, 704), with an "X": "C. voudrait faire croire qu'une métaphore est une communication du ciel. —Une métaphore est *ce qui arrive* quand on *regarde de telle façon*—comme un éternuement est ce qui arrive quand on regarde un soleil.—De quelle façon? Vous le sentez. Un jour, on saura peut-être le *dire* très précisément.—Fais ceci et cela,—et voici toutes les métaphores du monde. . . ." (Here is, of course, the fundamental distinction between a Christian symbolism and a stylistics, faith and linguistic analysis, a particular *scheme* of metaphors and the uncommitted sensibility. Nevertheless, Claudel would be the first to admit that his point of view was fixed from the start.)

Such annotations would tend at first to suggest that Valéry was resolutely opposed to Claudel's art, but we

[17] *Cahiers*, IV, 128. We find a brief note concerning Valéry's reactions at the première of *Le Soulier de satin* in November 1943 at the Comédie Française. He concludes: "J'ai éprouvé ce que les situations, les mimiques et les tons de voix peuvent faire éprouver. Mais cela est valeur indéterminée. Et il y a toujours beaucoup de ridicules dans ces effets dès que l'on se reprend, repris par tel détail qui rompt le jet d'eau sur lequel dansait l'œuf creux" (*Cahiers*, XXVII, 752).

must remember that he mentioned him specifically as one of the few select authors he consulted when he came to writing *La Jeune Parque*; at the same time, in the notebook that offers a running commentary on his poetic ideas concerning the Parque's long monologue of self-consciousness, we find a brief but perspicacious remark: "Cl. prend pour repère l'état sauvage, l'état mort, de manière à exprimer toute chose à partir de l'inertie, et comme à tâtons et ce truc fait sentir au lecteur l'effort pour que la chose soit. Il exprime ce que les auteurs en général prennent comme donné."[18] The reader will recognize these words as true of a poet who brings a world into being, conveys the "naissance" of things and the poet's "co-naissance," and imbues his work with the dynamic will to find a direction, a sense that can be indicated only by approximations. The passage dates from 1917; but nearly twenty years later, in January 1935, Valéry was led to examine Claudel's work in similar terms after hearing the poet-ambassador read his *Jeanne d'Arc* in Brussels: "Je constate *once more* une différence totale de manière de 'voir' entre nous[. . .]. Ce qu'il voit accessoire, 'infiniment petit', je le trouve essentiel, et réciproquement. Le parti pris est hardi, neuf, peut faire grand effet. Il cherche une très forte naïveté qui permet le symbolisme, et dessine une composition."[19] The definition we find in the last sentence might be interpreted by some readers as missing the whole point of Claudel's art, for they would want to emphasize matter rather than method. On the other hand, one might consider it to be a marvelously appropriate observation that applies to an individual aesthetic approach as well as to its message. Claudel, we might say, moves between a periphery and a center; or, more precisely perhaps, it is a case of a periphery in search of its center. He gives us the sensation of an isolated detail tending toward its principle, coming to know itself in relation to other things in proportion as every de-

[18] *Cahiers*, VI, 752.
[19] "Notes personnelles: Ephémérides," quoted by Agathe Rouart-Valéry, *Œuvres*, I, 61.

sire, like those of the adventurers in *Ballade,* is absorbed into the ocean of all desire.[20] Such an art presupposes both naïveté and intellectual rigorousness, a language that is superficially unpretentious, even self-deflating, even humorous, and an overriding spiritual attitude that makes us conceive of objects and events as symbols, and the poem as the discovery of the sacred nature of the universe. Valéry was far from unaware that in Claudel everything is in movement with respect to a point named God, whereas in his own thought the central reference is none but the self. The infinite greatness of the former was opposed to the infinite smallness of the self, an all-embracing "Otherness" to self-contained consciousness. We can appreciate how keenly he grasped this distinction and, with admirable concision, formulated it in his private journal.

One final comment on Claudel deserves our attention, since in making it Valéry pointed up a comparison with his own poetic ambitions. On 27 October 1944, a short time after the Liberation, he was invited by de Gaulle to attend a poetry reading under the title "Poets of the Resistance" at the Comédie Française (and found some irony in his being included—he the poet of *La Jeune Parque* and "Le Cimetière marin"—among their number!). During the performance Jean-Louis Barrault's reading of one of Claudel's poems gave him grounds for meditation: "Je pense en écoutant à la diversité des effets. A la grande question Diction-chant, et Diction-déclamation—c'est-à-dire 'Magie' et 'Mouvement,' *deux modes de propagation. C'est de la physique de la sensibilité* que j'esquisse."[21] Here one finds him drawing the same fundamental contrast, now envisaged in the light of the effect a particular work has on its reader: Claudel's poetry depends on a progressive development, a dramatic structure, a compelling voice, while his own seeks to cancel out movement by the symmetry and

[20] See my article, "Claudel's Art of 'Provocation,'" *Essays in French Literature,* No. 1 (November 1964), pp. 30-58.

[21] *Cahiers,* XXIX, 201.

complementarity of its parts, its goal being enchantment and not incitation.

These remarks, then, are valuable, if restricted in scope. Claudel may have called on his readers to look beyond appearances to the center, beyond the poem to its meaning ("O grammairien dans mes vers! Ne cherche point le chemin, cherche le centre!"),[22] yet we know very well that it is only by seeking out the means and discovering the path that the reader can truly find the center. Valéry's observations indicate, I believe, a loyal and perceptive response to an art that by its essence was distant from his own.

The change of tone when we approach Claudel on Valéry is considerable. He was never inclined to minimize the differences, or to seek to please, and we do not have to look long to find him bringing into the open, in typically blunt fashion, the main differences as he felt them. His first letter, provoked by a reading of the 1919 edition of the Leonardo essays, took Valéry to task for his criticism of the dogma of the resurrection of the body. In his "Note et digression" Valéry had written: "L'Eglise,—pour autant que l'Eglise est thomiste,—ne donne pas à l'âme séparée une existence bien enviable. Rien de plus pauvre que cette âme qui a perdu son corps."[23] Although Claudel's answer attempted a defense of St. Thomas, and supplied references to the Gospel parable of the Rich Man (Luke 14) and to St. Paul, he allowed that the dogma had not been fully formulated ("Les textes de St. Thomas sont insuffisants[. . .]. D'ailleurs sa théorie purement intellectualiste est à mon avis ce qu'il y a de plus faible dans son œuvre . . ."). Yet what interests us much more than this inevitably inconclusive discussion is a postscript that raises the whole question of inspiration as distinct from conscious effort, to which Claudel alluded in various manners on later occasions. "Comme vous êtes dur pour les 'genies'! Et croyez-vous qu'une belle flambée de sarments et de genêts secs ne soit

---

[22] "Cinq Grandes Odes," *Œuvre poétique* (Paris: Gallimard, Pléiade, 1957), p. 227.
[23] "Note et digression," *Œuvres*, I, 1214.

pas suffisante en elle-même, quand elle ne servirait pas
à faire du café ou à faire marcher une saloperie de ma-
chine quelconque."[24] The indictment of Valéry's position is
phrased with admirable force. This was Claudel's basic
belief, that had no common measure with an attitude that
placed man's dignity in an act of lucid construction. (As
Valéry put it: "j'aimerais infiniment mieux écrire en toute
conscience et dans une entière lucidité quelque chose de
faible, que d'enfanter à la faveur d'une transe et hors de
moi-même un chef-d'œuvre d'entre les plus beaux").[25] Both
poets were outspoken in their stand; and yet I think that
their practice is in no sense antagonistic, for, if Claudel
never neglects the technical details of creation and is
acutely aware of the ruses of art, as one might expect of a
former pupil of Mallarmé, Valéry does not fail to give due
weight to chance and the unforeseeable developments of
"genius." Might not in fact Emilie Teste well answer to
the name of Anima?

[24] Letter of 13 November 1919. Claudel returned on a number of
occasions to this same point with reference to Valéry: "Quand Paul
Valéry nous dit que 'l'enthousiasme n'est pas un état d'esprit
d'écrivain' il entend que les mouvements violents de la passion ne
viennent pas troubler cet état suspendu de sensibilité délicate qui lui
est indispensable. Mais il y a un enthousiasme froid où notre ami
n'oserait refuser à la critique quelque chose du tré-pied de la pythie.
Plus encore que l'intelligence, pour ce patient de la Muse, les oreilles
pleines du murmure préalable, il s'agit de convenance" ("L'Enthou-
siasme," *Œuvres en prose*, pp. 1394-1395); again: "Cette inspiration
sur laquelle mon ami Paul Valéry a écrit tant de choses que son art
magnifique d'ailleurs n'est pas sans contredire . . ." ("L'Art et la
foi," *Œuvres en prose*, p. 65); elsewhere: "Paul Valéry s'est acharné
toute sa vie, jusqu'à lasser ses lecteurs—et cependant son œuvre est
là qui suffisait à lui donner le démenti le plus net—à nier l'inspiration.
Plus une idée est fausse et plus il est naturel qu'on essaye de remédier
à la fausseté par l'insistance. Et cependant, depuis les temps les plus
reculés, s'il y a un fait bien reconnu et établi, c'est celui de l'inspira-
tion poétique" ("La Poésie est un art," *Œuvres complètes*, XVIII,
18); "En littérature, la prédominance de la cause efficiente a inspiré
la théorie de l'art pour l'art. Ce n'est pas ce que l'écrivain a à dire
qui est important, c'est la manière dont il le dit. Toute l'œuvre théo-
rique de Paul Valéry est consacrée à promouvoir cette insanité, que
l'œuvre de ce beau poète est là heureusement pour contredire."
("L'Esprit de prophétie," *Œuvres complètes*, XXI, 402).
[25] "Lettre sur Mallarmé," *Œuvres*, I, 640.

Another letter, written shortly after, acknowledged the receipt of a copy of the *Album de vers anciens* in its original version (not of *Charmes,* as incorrectly stated in the Bibliothèque Nationale catalogue of 1956). It affords a precise confrontation of views on the problem of versification, since Claudel calls attention to the fact that the title of Valéry's collection refers not only to "old" poems conceived twenty to thirty years before, and "old" legends rehandled (Helen, Venus, Narcissus, Semiramis), but also to the "old" prosody, *l'ancien vers,* which had been respected by Valéry.

Copenhague le 19 janvier 1920[26]

Cher Ami,

C'est une joie pour moi de posséder maintenant ces beaux vers dont la plupart m'étaient inconnus. Les deux poèmes de la fin sont vraiment superbes, ruisselants de lumière. Vous êtes vraiment le seul qui me feriez hésiter dans la condamnation qu'autrement je serais de plus en plus disposé à faire de l'ancien vers. Je suis frappé de l'immobilité qu'il peut donner à un concept, à une idée, à une forme, comme à une chose désormais établie pour toujours et qui vraiment et réellement est devenue un objet. Le très beau vers est presque toujours solitaire:

Toi qui sur le néant en sais plus que les morts
Qui se soucie de la ligne parallèle?

De même chez vous:

Déjà contre la nuit lutte l'âpre trompette
Une lèvre vivante attaque l'air glacé

La rime est nécessaire, on serait désappointé si elle n'arrivait pas, mais néanmoins elle apporte une déconvenue.

De même:

Ose l'abîme!

Après cela il n'y a plus que le blanc qui est possible.

---

[26] The date should be 1921, not 1920, since the *Album de vers anciens* appeared in the course of 1920. The volume does not, however, bear the exact date of publication.

Je vous dis cela à cause de notre conversation de l'autre
jour. Je sais très bien qu'à côté du vers "libre" qu'on
devrait plutôt appeler le vers lyrique ou dramatique, il
y a un autre vers qui est possible, dans lequel le nombre
est l'élément essentiel et préalable, une espèce de lan-
gage ambrosiaque, de clef avec une facilité divine pour
l'expression de tout. C'est à peu près ce que donne
l'hexamètre virgilien, mais je doute que notre alexandrin,
malgré les réussites rares et merveilleuses de Mallarmé
et de vous, en soit spécifiquement capable.

Je vous serre la main et suis heureux de vous dire ma
vive et sincère admiration.

P. Claudel.

The two poems Claudel singles out, "Anne" ("Anne qui
se mélange au drap pâle et délaisse") and "Sémiramis"
("Dès l'aube, chers rayons, mon front songe à vous
ceindre!"), translate the primal energies of day and of
the awakening sensibility: they are indeed, as Claudel re-
marks, aflood with light. Both are composed, moreover, in
the same way, of twelve-syllable quatrains with alternate
rhymes. Our first reaction may well be to say, especially
with regard to "Sémiramis," that this form has the great
forward surge that befits a dramatic monologue; but do we
not see on reflection that Claudel is right to speak of "im-
mobility," that Valéry's poem develops as a kind of sensu-
ous transmutation of its own substance? It is not an anec-
dote or a legend, but a chant, a "psalm" (the name Va-
léry gave it in one of his manuscripts),[27] a language closed
on itself like a sphere. This was the law of necessity the

---

[27] Cf. my book *Lecture de Valéry: une étude de "Charmes"* (Paris:
Presses Universitaires de France, 1963), p. 11. In his *Mémoires impro-
visés* (Paris: Gallimard, 1954), Claudel discusses Valéry's observance
of prosodic discipline and concludes in these terms: "La contrainte
par elle-même ne me semble pas un élément de beauté. Vous voyez
un acrobate, par exemple, qui fait des tours, des contorsions effroyables
pour arriver à passer entre les barreaux de sa chaise. Evidemment, la
contrainte est un élément gymnastique pour lui. Est-ce que c'est un
élément de plaisir pour ceux qui le regardent? Je trouve cela fort
douteux" (p. 47).

poet sought to create, and which could not admit the "Oui, mais . . ." of Claudel: an undivided garment it had to be, its sound and sense indissolvable. Claudel, on the other hand, did not fail to make use of discontinuity for the dramatic possibilities it offers, and he shows that Valéry's poetic work, like that of any great poet writing in a regular prosodic form, could well be rewritten, the best lines isolated, the so-called padding stripped away. Many a reader would no doubt agree; but it should not be forgotten that it was *only* the continuum, the achievement of a balanced fullness, that mattered in the eyes of Valéry—the "discours-chant," as he put it, with its intrinsic necessity of sound and sense, its pattern more than its message, and not the "discours-déclamation."

Concerning the last part of this letter, I am not sure one would find Valéry of the opinion, as Claudel implies, that all things can be expressed in the measured language of the gods. We recognize that Claudel is referring to the Mallarméan conception of poetry when he speaks of a key for expressing everything and recalls the famous affirmation that "rien ne demeurera sans être proféré." Yet this was a mystical approach which certainly had no parallel in the author of the *Cahiers*. Nor could Claudel know, at the time of writing these lines, just how dazzling would be the prosodic diversity of the twenty-one poems of *Charmes*, the formidable mastery of the decasyllable in "Le Cimetière marin," the octosyllable in "La Pythie" and the "Ebauche d'un serpent," the heptasyllable in "Aurore" and "Palme," and several other meters as well. Not concerned to make the alexandrine, as Mallarmé had done, the fundamental instrument of his art, he brilliantly demonstrated that it was but one among several.

The cordiality of this letter, together with the considered criticism it provides, was echoed on a number of other occasions: Claudel did not stint his applause, at the same time as he let it be known that his position was dissimilar. Here, for example, was the comment he sent from Brangues in October 1942 on receiving Valéry's preface to Father

Cyprien's translation of St. John of the Cross: "Mon cher Valéry—Je ne sais si je vous ai remercié du précieux volume du Père Cyprien qui m'est bien parvenu. Moins sensible que vous au prestige de la difficulté vaincue, je dois avouer que je préfère le texte biblique à la double paraphrase un peu trop alambiquée de S. Jean de la Croix, et un peu trop distinguée du Père Cyprien. Mais que votre préface est intelligente et quel beau français. Je vous serre la main affectueusement."[28] No postcard could put more briefly or politely a view that was so averse to Valéry's claim (Father Cyprien, he had written, is "l'un des plus parfaits poètes de France [. . .] jusqu'ici à peu près inconnu").[29] A like note is struck by the final item of their correspondence, dating from June 1944, when, in thanking Valéry for a copy of *Variété V* which had just appeared, Claudel again praised the form and manner of the book but emphasized his radical criticism of the thought.

Brangues le 24 juin 1944.

Mon cher Ami,

C'est bien dégoûtant de ma part de ne pas vous avoir encore remercié de l'envoi de vos deux livres. N'y voyez pas négligence de ma part. Mais plutôt le désir et la difficulté pour moi de vous exprimer toute ma pensée à leur sujet. Le plaisir, comme l'admiration, est certain et il est intense. J'ai toujours admiré vos vers, mais devant votre prose le moment pour moi n'était pas venu. Il est venu cette fois! Je ne puis pas dire que je suis d'accord avec vous, tant s'en faut! Mais il me faudrait beaucoup de temps et de réflexion pour mettre mes idées sur pied. En gros je dirais que vous me paraissez une magnifique intelligence *désaffectée*, je veux dire qui ne se rattache pas à un principe, pour moi Dieu. De là cette impression de désolation qui imprègne votre lumineuse atmosphère. Quel théologien étonnant vous auriez pu faire!

Je vous serre affectueusement la main.

Paul Claudel.

[28] Letter of 23 October 1942.
[29] "Cantiques spirituels," *Œuvres*, I, 445.

J'ai écrit à Gallimard de m'envoyer les 4 autres vols de *Variété*.[30]

In Claudel's familiar style, admiration and censure commingle. He pulls no punches, and most certainly says what he means: on the one hand pointing to the luminousness of Valéry's essays, on the other emphasizing what is for him the solitude and misery of man without God. The expression "intelligence désaffectée" strikes us especially because it is not only an unusual metaphor ("désaffectée" normally qualifies buildings which have been put to another purpose, such as a deconsecrated church) but implies the concept of intelligence at its finest as being of necessity based on God. May we not add that it also suggests a personal detail about Valéry, whose approach presupposes, Claudel seems to say, the Principle he has rejected, the Christianity he replaced by an insatiable thirst for analysis? From this point of view the light of his mind, this thought concerned with itself, becomes plainly Luciferian, its strength desolate and savoring of death:

> Beau serpent, bercé dans le bleu!
> Je siffle, avec délicatesse,
> Offrant à la gloire de Dieu
> Le triomphe de ma tristesse. . . .[31]

We note that Claudel could not refrain from humorously remarking in conclusion that Valéry would have made an extraordinary theologian; and this is surely true of a thinker who, however untheological his preoccupations, handled ideas with such sensuous precision.

I take it then that the tone of Claudel's letters over the quarter-century for which we have them has been clearly established: they reveal a most lively interest in Valéry, although deep reticence with regard to his aesthetic and philosophical position. Yet there are in particular three other texts devoted to Valéry's poetry and written along-

---

[30] Letter of 24 June 1944.
[31] Valéry, "Ebauche d'un serpent," *Œuvres*, I, 146.

side this correspondence which, quite as acutely as Valéry's own notes on Claudel, go to the heart of the matter. The first of them, a comment that places Valéry in the tradition of Mallarmé, seems perhaps today to make an excessive identification of the two poets.

> . . . un professeur, Stéphane Mallarmé, qui nous a gardés tous pendant de longues années à son cours du soir, fit une trouvaille. On pouvait fabriquer et "étudier" cet objet prosodique qu'il nous était loisible de saisir entre les doigts, avec ses lignes simplifiées, non moins que la *figure* d'un livre scientifique, non plus seulement comme un bibelot, mais comme un document et un texte et le *mot* même de la Création. Découverte capitale et bien supérieure à l'instrument particulier qui l'avait permise, taillé dans le transparent et le nul à la manière d'une lentille. C'est ainsi qu'aujourd'hui un grand poète, M. Paul Valéry, transcrit les objets contingents et passagers dans le monde éternel et lumineux de l'Idée.[32]

The statement might be said to apply to a few pieces like "Les Grenades" and "Au Platane," in which such a transposition ("du fait à l'idéal," as Mallarmé described it) takes place; but even here it is certainly exaggerated to suggest that the process can be compared to the mystical explanation of the earth which Mallarmé dreamed of and to which all his poetry and prose refers. The Valéryan world has no sacramental role in naming the elements of a spiritual unity; there is no precise *meaning* for objects as Mallarmé conceived it, that is to say, as an exact relationship to a center; in fact, as we know, the world for Valéry has no substance except insofar as it is the locus of the mind's action and self-discovery. Thus "Les Grenades" offers, not a transcription of lush fruit, but the self-reflective procedure of the analytical imagination which discovers the structure of an *I* that was capable of creating a poem, while "Au Platane" constitutes a lesson in humility for the conscious-

[32] "Positions et propositions sur le vers français," *Œuvres en prose*, p. 12.

ness that had overleaped its limits and sought to appropriate the tree. Indeed, however much these and other poems of *Charmes* outwardly resemble the compositions of Mallarmé, their inner sense is clearly different, and their form is not finalistic. "Pour *lui*, l'œuvre; pour moi, le moi" is the manner in which Valéry formulated the essential difference between his poetic master and himself.[33] In this regard it is surely Claudel who is much closer to Mallarmé in conceiving poetry as the act of realizing the world's true meaning; and in 1952, when he returned to this question in his *Mémoires improvisés*, he pointed out the speculative nature of Valéry's approach in contrast to his own confident affirmation: "La différence, c'est qu'il ne prenait pas les êtres et les choses au sérieux. Il se figurait qu'il était devant un spectacle qui n'a pas beaucoup de sens, tandis que moi je suis persuadé qu'il a un sens, comme celui du Sphinx: 'Devine, ou je te dévore.'"[34]

It is certain that Claudel gave much thought in 1925 and 1926 to the writings of Valéry, both during his stay in France from March 1925 to January 1926, when the passage from *Positions et propositions* was written, and on his return to Tokyo. The text of "Le Poète et le shamisen," dated June 1926, sums up his attitude toward Valéry's art at that time.[35] By its very genre, we may note, it is already a kind of response: it adopts the dialogue form in the same way as *Eupalinos ou l'architecte* and *L'Ame et la danse*, which had recently appeared, but instead of Socratic figures and an ideal atmosphere, it proposes a lively exchange between the Poet and the traditional long-necked lute. His samisen is of course far from being a classical or romantic lyre in the European tradition, for it unceremoniously breaks through high-sounding phrases with its vigorous accompaniment ("ses petites remarques sèches") and summons the poet to order; for example: "un peu plus tu allais me pincer et

[33] *Cahiers*, XXIII, 147.

[34] *Mémoires improvisés*, p. 69.

[35] Originally published in *Commerce*, IX (Autumn 1926), of which Valéry was one of the founders, and later included in *L'Oiseau noir dans le soleil levant*.

alors bzing! voilà tout ce paysage industrieusement con-
fectionné qui instantanément, comme ces images bouddhis-
tes dessinées sur le sable avec des barbes de plume, fout le
camp"; and again, to conclude the dialogue with a good
deflating pinch of American salt: "Du moins c'est ce que
disait le Gouverneur de la Caroline du Nord au Gouverneur
de la Caroline du Sud, ou quelque chose d'approchant."
Nevertheless, although the conversation seems to follow
the most capricious meanderings, it unfolds carefully, ac-
cording to a logic of its own—like the leaves of a cabbage,
says Claudel, or a painting that the artist begins from
every side with a view to finding the middle, or the peonies
in the garden of Kawasaki, or a journey across every man-
ner of green knoll, or the musical edifice that is built up
stage by stage with the left hand whilst so many arpeggi
are being showered by the right. Now the real object of
this divertimento being the art of composition, it includes an
illuminating comparison between Greek and Japanese prac-
tice and their aims, as well as a central criticism of Valéry
in relation to Claudel himself. It finally leads to the con-
clusion, not that the world was made to find its expression
in a Beautiful Poem, as Mallarmé dreamt, nor that it is
sufficient for poetry to provide a few perfect applications
of a language: literature for Claudel can never be an end
in itself, but a direction and a path, a color and a music, a
perfume and a breath of redness, in sum, a rose that tells
the heart's pure and secret desire—which for him could
only be God: "Au fond des pétales blancs de la pivoine je
respire l'exhalation de cette rougeur par qui l'âme est pré-
cédée.—La rose n'est que la forme un instant tout haut
de ce que le cœur tout bas appelle ses délices." Such is
his way of suggesting the ideal structure of a poem; and
such is the manner in which this particular dialogue is con-
ceived and formally constituted.

The section specifically treating Valéry follows a discus-
sion on the Tao laws of composition and the Japanese no-
tion of beauty. The poet evokes the Islands of the Inner
Sea as he woke to contemplate them in the light of one

May morning, which allows him to make the transition to his remarks on *La Jeune Parque*, whose original title was *Iles*, and to quote two fragments that refer to the islands the Parque glimpses in the sunrise, and the "islands" of the waking sensibility ("îles de mon sein nu"). But the various verbal islands that go to make up Valéry's poem are not bathed in mist or mystery like those of Japan, but possess the Apollonian clarity of Mediterranean art. Claudel describes them pregnantly in these terms: "les îles de Valéry sont complètes de la base au faîte comme des cyclades, elles sont parfaites comme des porcelaines, elles sont aussi indigènes à la Méditerranée que les rascasses et les oursins et le rouleau de malachite bleue qui passe sous les pêcheurs de thons." One could not wish for a more suggestive comment on the sensuous will to define and delimit, that leads us quite naturally to the hub of Claudel's statement as found in the next exchange:

LE SHAMISEN: Ici il ne serait pas difficile de tirer de moi une espèce de gamme déglinguée qui ressemblerait assez au mot "intellectuel."

LE POÈTE: Quelle bêtise! Valéry est avant tout un voluptueux et tout son art est une attention voluptueuse. C'est l'esprit attentif à la chair et l'enveloppant d'une espèce de conscience épidermique, le plaisir atteint par la définition, tout un beau corps gagné, ainsi que par un frisson, par un réseau de propositions exquises. Rappelez-vous la qualité du modelé chez les peintres Vénitiens, le Corrège par exemple ou Titien.

LE SHAMISEN: De là chez Valéry . . .

LE POÈTE: Je prends esprit dans un sens demi-physique, une intelligence dont les narines seraient l'organe par qui nous prenons l'inspiration même de la vie.

LE SHAMISEN: De là chez Valéry ce thème continuel de Narcisse, l'obsession du serpent, ces lignes qui se recherchent,

    Il

        (quelque chose, le poison, je crois)

Il colore une vierge à soi-même enlacée,
ces vers parallèles qui sont l'un de l'autre images (avec
un frisson qui les brise quelquefois), s'épousent et se
composent, autour de ce centre secret que le doigt de
la Belle Dame du Prado précisément indique. Pendant
qu'un artiste à demi tourné vers elle, mais pas jusqu'à
la voir!—les perceptions latérales!—joue de l'orgue
ou d'un instrument qui me ressemble. L'Île toujours,
quoi![36]

He underlines the marriage of body and mind, a passionate
interrelationship between the senses and the intellect: this
is Valéry's art of seduction, the charm that consists of grasp-
ing, "comprehending" the secrets of the sensibility, in the
same way as the poem charms its reader.

> O Courbes, méandre,
> Secrets du menteur,
> Est-il art plus tendre
> Que cette lenteur?[37]

The subtlety of Claudel's analysis we need not emphasize.
Against those critics of his time who could only see for
the most part in Valéry the poet of ideas, he notes the sen-
suous pleasure of this network of entwined figures which
are traced with the plastic genius of a painter. "La Belle
Dame du Prado" he alludes to is one of Titian's three rep-
resentations of Venus, which he had seen the previous year
when he was on a lecture tour in Spain. To him they rep-
resented a kind of fleshly paradise which he later described
at length in an essay on Spanish painting. Titian, he ob-
serves, is "ce poète, d'une volupté où l'esprit fait entendre
à la chair l'appel de la béatitude."[38] In two canvases the
musician in the company of Venus plays a guitar, in the
third an organ; but Claudel combines the details of all
three paintings by speaking of both an organ and an instru-

[36] *Œuvres en prose*, pp. 824-825.
[37] "L'Insinuant," *Œuvres*, I, 137.
[38] "La Peinture espagnole," *Œuvres en prose*, p. 213.

ment that resembles the samisen. Yet the focal point of the composition is clearly indicated: "Tout monte et tout descend vers le ventre. Tout ce que la nature en un puissant soulèvement gonfle, tout ce qu'elle est prête à déverser sur nous d'ambroisie et de moissons passe en un accord sacré, en une transition bienheureuse, à cette hanche suave, à ce corps au nôtre approprié."[39] No less intense is the voluptuousness of Valéry, since what could be more insidious than the appetite of the mind? Claudel no doubt had just read the article entitled "Le Retour de Hollande," in which Valéry had spoken perceptively of Rembrandt, in particular of the "lateral" effects that the eye sees but the mind is incapable of defining, that attack the sensibility at its most vulnerable spot while its attention is held elsewhere.[40] They are present in some paintings, in the music of Wagner, and also, he remarked, in literature, or rather the literature he himself sought to compose. Hence Claudel introduces his reference to lateral perceptions and suggests that they form part of our delight—the hidden and unnamed charm, the sensuous attention—that we savor in reading *La Jeune Parque*.

The last of Claudel's comments on Valéry's poetry that I have come across is to be found in the private journal ("Huitième cahier") for the year 1942, where we note the following entry: "Paul Valéry m'envoie son recueil de Poèmes que je lis avec le plus grand plaisir. On ne saurait pousser plus loin la finesse et le talent technique. C'est merveilleux! Mais comme c'est peu nourrissant et somme toute, futile! Le sujet est toujours cet effort vain et d'avance découragé à se dégager de soi-même."[41] The remark again

---

[39] *Ibid.*, p. 214.

[40] "J'ai longuement rêvé autrefois à cet art subtil de disposer d'un élément assez arbitraire afin d'agir insidieusement sur le spectateur, tandis que son regard est attiré et fixé par des objets nets et reconnaissables [. . .]. Quand j'admirais jadis, dans certains Rembrandts, des modèles de cette action indirecte [. . .] je ne manquais pas de songer aux effets *latéraux* que peuvent produire les harmonies divisées d'un orchestre" (*Œuvres*, I, 852-853).

[41] Paul Claudel, "Huitième cahier" (1937-1942), p. 104 (as yet unpublished). Claudel visited Valéry in July 1945, a few days before

links admiration and criticism as Claudel singles out the
accent of desperate aspiration characteristic of Valéry's
major poems: the attempt by the poet, or the Parque, or the
protagonist of "Le Cimetière marin," to compose a world
transcending reality and sufficient unto itself: "O récom-
pense après une pensée / Qu'un long regard sur le calme
des dieux!" And yet, as we know, this fixity will be broken,
this composition will not only be completed but *known* to
have been completed, and the pressure of everyday activity
will again prevail: "Envolez-vous, pages tout éblouies!" It
is, then, no doubt a vain and foredoomed enterprise in
Claudel's terms; but on the other hand, we must say that
it constitutes for the reader of Valéry an experience of a
unique kind, translating as it were the systole and diastole
of the sensibility, the energies of thought and the forces of
the body, our dreams and our fate. One could not hope for
a more complete representation of "what a man is capable
of" (we recall his persistent query: "Que peut un homme?")
as the poetic self moves between the extremes of man's
striving and his irrefutable limits. Poetry thus expresses the
essential law of a thinker who can make no divine leap
into freedom but seeks to create a sphere of his own which
will be the diamond-point of consciousness. Vain it may
be, but for the mind that refuses to place its raison d'être
beyond itself nothing perhaps is nobler.

ONE MIGHT, I think, most directly bring to mind the con-
trasting character of the imaginations of Valéry and Clau-
del as indicated in this last quotation, and implied in vari-
ous ways in our previous remarks, by looking at a small
sample of their works. Thus we could compare their two
poems of shipwreck ("Ballade," "Sinistre"), which con-

---

his friend's death. In his ninth notebook ("Neuvième cahier," 1943-
1949, p. 35 [as yet unpublished]) we read the following remark:
"20 juillet. Mort de Paul Valéry. De cette génération d'avant-guerre
il ne reste plus qu'André Gide et moi." Two years later he described
him affectionately as "une de ces figures familières qui, en disparais-
sant, diminuent notre propre objection à les rejoindre" ("Le Maître
du tumulte," *Œuvres en prose*, p. 592).

tain the elements of entirely different religious dramas
placed under the sign of Christianity;[42] in the same way,
"Le Cocotier" of *Connaissance de l'Est* would provide a most
suggestive parallel with "Palme";[43] while the three female
voices in the summer night who discover the meaning of
life by way of *La Cantate à trois voix* offer a wonderful
counterpoint to the many-toned voice of *La Jeune Parque*,
which appeared three years later, in 1917. Yet, for the
brevity and beauty of the works concerned, I should like
to choose the treatment of the traditional theme of the bee,
popular among Greek and Latin poets as well as those of
the Renaissance, which the two modern writers transformed
in an individual manner that reflects what has emerged
from their correspondence and mutual criticism. The po-
etic substance in its diversity offers, as we shall find, com-
plementary facets of a poetic idea.

Amusingly enough, Claudel's lines first appeared in a
small regional beekeepers' journal, the *Gazette apicole de
Montfavet* in the Vaucluse (somewhat like Valéry's "Le Vin
perdu," which was later published in a deluxe volume
devoted to wines). One wonders what the original readers
made of it![44] The date was 1925, which would seem to sug-

[42] I have attempted to analyze the spiritual drama expressed in
Valéry's "Sinistre" (see "The 'Shipwreck' of Paul Valéry," *Essays in
French Literature*, No. 3 [November 1966], pp. 38-64).

[43] For a brief comparison between the two poems, see *Lecture de
Valéry*, pp. 244-245.

[44] Among the other thirty-one collaborators in this special Christmas
issue (No. 253, December 1925) devoted to the theme of the bee
were Georges Lecomte, Raymond Poincaré, the Comtesse de Noailles,
Rachilde, Henry Bordeaux, and Alphonse Séché. The variants with
respect to the final version are: title: *Abeilles et pensées*; line 6:
"L'âme *aux roses* comparable"; line 10: "Heureux qui, des *Dieux*
parente." Under its original title the poem was reproduced in *Les
Nouvelles littéraires* of 13 February 1926, p. 2, with the following
comment: "La *Gazette apicole* vient de publier un précieux numéro
auquel ont collaboré une trentaine d'écrivains. Nous sommes heureux
de publier ici le poème envoyé par Paul Claudel." It later appeared
under the title "Abeilles" in *Le Manuscrit autographe* (March-April
1926), where it contained several variants: line 6: "L'âme, *pollen et
pistil*"; line 7: "*Quand vous la sollicitez*"; line 8: "*Sent son silence en
péril*"; line 10: "Heureux qui, des dieux *parentes*"; line 11: "*Vous voit

gest that the poet had perhaps been influenced to some extent by the recent appearance of the "Abeille" of *Charmes;* moreover, we have had occasion to observe that he was paying particular attention to Valéry's writings at this precise period and that his thoughts found expression in "Le Poète et le shamisen" of 1926. On the other hand, if we look at the volume in which this poem was first collected, we find that it is immediately preceded by a translation from the English of Thomas Lovell Beddoes (1803-1849) called "A une grappe de raisins en train de mûrir à ma fenêtre." The original is the last piece of the *Improvisatore,* which Beddoes published when he was not yet eighteen. Significantly, it is also a song of sensuous warmth and spiritual lightness (although Claudel's version is less concrete than his model) which conjures up the "silencieux essaim d'abeilles jaunes," as well as the future wine: "ô nectar dans nos veines, ô parfum de la pensée,—qui exhale jusqu'à nos joues animées par le plaisir—un souffle impalpable. . . ."[45] The original point of departure for Claudel's "Abeille" may, then, have been Valéry, or Beddoes, or even, perhaps, more classical pieces; but in any case his brief poem, of comparable length and motif to Valéry's, shows a highly personal approach, the poet refusing to adopt a loud voice and oratorical style and proceeding by means of soft touches like those in *Cent Phrases pour éventails.* For the

[overscored by the final reading *sent*] sur sa lèvre hésiter"; *"Visiteuses transparentes."* In the *Bulletin Joseph Lotte,* Second Year, No. 13 (December 1930), the "Pages à lire" present the following note: "Nous sommes heureux de publier aujourd'hui les vers suivants de M. Paul Claudel, ambassadeur de France à Washington, qu'il a bien voulu nous envoyer précédés des lignes suivantes: 'Voici les vers—à peu près inédits—que vous me demandez. Je vous les envoie avec mon compliment affectueux aux rédacteurs et aux abonnés du Bulletin Joseph Lotte, que j'ai contribué à fonder, du temps où il s'appelait "le Bulletin des professeurs catholiques de l'Université." ' " The reading is the same as that of the Gallimard volume of *La Cantate à trois voix* in 1931 and subsequent editions, but the poem here bears the date "1925." In the Benoist-Méchin and Blaizot *Bibliographie des œuvres de Paul Claudel* (Paris: Blaizot, 1931) the poem is erroneously described as a sonnet.

[45] "A une grappe de raisins en train de mûrir à ma fenêtre," *La Cantate à trois voix* (Paris: Gallimard, 1948), p. 175.

meter he preferred the *impair*, "plus vague et plus soluble dans l'air," seven of the lines being heptasyllables; nevertheless there is no numerical uniformity, since we also find two octosyllables and three hexasyllables. The same freedom is observed with regard to rhyme: Claudel pays no heed to the prescriptions of traditional prosody which Valéry welcomed so sincerely, and here primarily obeys the dictates of sound, and not the eye. The result is a small song in the line of the classical epigram that is at once general in import, relaxed in tone, and unpretentious. The Latin inscription at the end, concise and suggestive, reinforces the dominant note; while in one early edition the typographical arrangement of the introductory words "Et une abeille pour finir" in the shape of a bee also indicated the smiling restraint with which Claudel envisaged his composition.

> Abeilles et pensées,
> Vous qui points, or, désirs,
> Faites des fleurs pénétrées
> A la fois miel et cire,
>
> Enrichie et dépouillée,
> L'âme au jasmin comparable
> Sent par vous en elle apporté
> Frémir un grain délectable,
>
> Parole prête à l'idée!
> Heureux qui, des dieux parente,
> Te sent sur sa lèvre hésiter,
> Visiteuse transparente!
>
> APIS
> INITIUM DULCORIS[46]

The poem comprises one sentence only, the resolution of which is delayed by stylistic ploys of apposition ("Vous qui points, or, désirs"), inversion ("L'âme au jasmin comparable," "Sent par vous en elle apporté"), and striking syntactic

[46] *La Cantate à trois voix*, p. 179. The poem is reproduced in the *Œuvre poétique* without the Latin inscription.

preciousness which surprises the reader and introduces him
to the pleasures of discovery ("Heureux qui, des dieux
parente / Te sent sur sa lèvre hésiter"). It becomes clear
to us that statement is less the poet's concern than the ex-
clamation of his delight at a simple and miraculous pres-
ence. Instead of exploring the tense meeting between the
sensibility and the sting, he smiles as he pursues a relation-
ship that moves from the second person plural to the fa-
miliar second person singular in the last two lines.

Who or what is this bee, this "beginning of sweetness"?
From the first we know that we are not in the domain of
Valéry's symbolism, since everything is deciphered and
made clear. Not just once, however: there is not a *single*
equivalent for bee, as we find in traditional allegory; on the
contrary, Claudel offers a solution, reveals his theme with-
out mystery, multiplies definitions instead of concealing
them. Thus he allows the image to be explicitly ambivalent,
so that it opens an ample gamut of meanings; for if sug-
gestiveness can be achieved by shadow, it is also eminently
attainable, as the poet shows, by an apparent clarity. In
the first quatrain, from the initial words, the openness of
the scheme of references is established: these bees are not
simply symbols of thoughts, but exist in a parallel way, in
intimate accord with them, exchanging values and as-
sociations but not absorbed by each other. Both, in like man-
ner, are moments in a development, instants of time
("points") which in their smallness are related to the mean-
ing of the whole passage, providing a limit and a form for
the composition of the sense. Precious, perfect, they con-
stitute a substance whose worth is universal, whose purity
is intrinsic ("or"); but far from being inert and compla-
cently centered on their own beauty, as "or" might lead
us to suspect, they are hungry for nourishment, impatient
to obtain satisfaction ("désirs"). Their fertile presences, in
like fashion, make honey and wax from their intercourse
with flowers, golden sweetness, translucid softness—food
and a vital framework for their future diligence. The
poet's thoughts, like the bees, marry the useful and the

pleasurable ("utile dulci") which Horace and the Renaissance theorists had sought.

The second quatrain focuses attention more directly on the object of the bees' visit as the poem becomes more specifically allegorical, if no less impregnated with the richness of nature. The soul is redolent, white, innocent like the jasmine; it has the same exquisite attraction as the flower. At the prompting of the bees it abandons some of its own treasure in an act it conceives not as loss but purification ("dépouillée"), not as impoverishment but paradoxical enrichment ("enrichie"). Its gain is a quivering fertilization, a tender seed that violates and enlivens; as the bee procures sweetness from the flower, so the flower from the bee, and the soul from its newly found thought.

In the last quatrain the poem reaches its most abstract point, since the bee has become a transparent visitor and the flower a joyful self. We have, as it were, gone back from the first stanza, in which honey and wax were acclaimed, and the second stanza, which described the flower of the soul after its union. Here the time of meeting is evoked in universal terms as an event that is constantly destined to bestow a blessing. "Parole prête à l'idée!": language and thought are not granted in some obscurely inspired utterance, for we realize that they participate by way of the poet in a common enterprise, a vital cooperation. Now the poet can proclaim his beatitude, not because he feels himself to be the equal of the gods (Claudel does not write "Heureux qui, des dieux *parent*," as one might expect in Valéry), but because he recognizes that his bee is an angel, light, fragile, unlaboring—divine inspiration, that kisses his lips and bends all things to an essential pattern and a single orientation.

What in Valéry would be stylistic negligence is part of Claudel's scheme. Irregularity of meter, imperfect rhymes, the repetition of the important word "sent," the lack of strong alliteration and assonance take away certainly from the intensity and sensuous unity such as we find in Valéry; instead they bespeak Claudel's vision, whereby words are not enclosed in a prosodic and semantic necessity but bathe in apparent freedom, perform willingly, so to speak, like the soul and the bee, in a plan that allows room for preciousness. Of a secret control we are aware as the composition is carefully ordered to lead us from the edge to the center, back from the fruits that crown the bee's visit to the pleasures of union itself. No poem could be less truly subject to the whims of chance, less independent of a particular philosophy and its corresponding poetics.

As for the other "Abeille," we find in it a wholly different approach. Valéry, we know, sought to escape from chance by the observance of certain arbitrary conventions, to "deduce the incantation" (*deducere carmen*)[47] in which the reader would discover a representation of his consciousness at its freest and most complete. Poetry as he conceived it offers us the experience of a heightened sensibility and knowledge in which man does not cease to be a man, subject to our common desires and fears, but also finds the delight of wholeness that is legendarily vouchsafed to the gods alone. Thus his "Abeille" is the sonnet of impassioned consciousness, or murmuring desire as seen through the eyes of an amorous woman who unnaturally, savagely, awaits the sting to consummate union in a moment of pain. She is conscious of her own virgin beauty, but her body no longer wishes to be self-sufficient. The exclamations, the imperatives are multiplied throughout as her ardent appeal continues and insists, and the words are charged with erotic overtones. There is, however, a note of elegant and refined song in the echoing sixth and fourteenth lines; while the images of light and awakening in the last tercet will finally bring the assurance of joyful resolution.

> Quelle, et si fine, et si mortelle,
> Que soit ta pointe, blonde abeille,
> Je n'ai, sur ma tendre corbeille,
> Jeté qu'un songe de dentelle.

[47] Valéry placed this epigraph on the title page of *Charmes* in the collected edition of his work which appeared in 1933 and in the 1941 edition.

Pique du sein la gourde belle,
Sur qui l'Amour meurt ou sommeille,
Qu'un peu de moi-même vermeille
Vienne à la chair ronde et rebelle!

J'ai grand besoin d'un prompt tourment:
Un mal vif et bien terminé
Vaut mieux qu'un supplice dormant!

Soit donc mon sens illuminé
Par cette infime alerte d'or
Sans qui l'Amour meurt ou s'endort![48]

Rarely do we find in an octosyllabic sonnet the nervous tension of "L'Abeille," which is quite absent from Claudel's poem. The first word introduces us to an atmosphere of excitement: by its sound, by its syntax, it is already, as it were, the sting of the bee. The rhythm is broken up into short movements, proceeding after the first surprising utterance to two other exclamations in the first line ("Quelle, et si fine, et si mortelle"). Emotion is ready to accept whatever consequence desire may entail, be it suffering or death itself. The speaker is not naïve, since she knows from past experience—or simply by the desperate nature of her own thirst—that the bee bears a sting. But appearance is enough ("blonde abeille") and the four feminine rhymes—their insistence, the surrender to murmuring fascination they imply—tell us that the self is past prudence, held by what it sees and hears. A flood of tenderness, the cherished flesh with its fruits ("tendre corbeille") is waiting like the waiting mind, armed with only the scantiest of resistances, a lacework impatient to be pierced.

The tone is heightened as the first words of the second stanza urgently call for action. The self caresses its own body, the fair gourd of its breast where love lies dying or asleep. This sleep, this death is the dull oppression of desire which must be overcome, which the bee alone can resolve. The woman consents to suffer; her blood will be

[48] *Œuvres*, I, 118.

spilt in sacrifice to love. Although beautiful, the flesh is not content with its state ("rebelle"); proud of its charm, it is yet anxious to discover an unsavored happiness.

After the sequence of feminine rhymes comes the brief rapidity of the tercets. In a simple, direct confession the self declares its need for the torment of the sting. Suffering and its outcome are made valid and resolved by each other in the eyes of the speaker, as the conscious use of contrast demonstrates: "mal," "bien," "vif," "terminé." This tense balance the self prefers to the paradoxical union of torture and sleep ("supplice dormant") that evokes unconsummated desire.

The tensions of the first tercet yield to certain satisfaction, the imperative followed by "donc" indicating that the final term of the proposition is about to be put. Now the self is turned wholly toward the illumination of its sensibility when the smallest of pricks ("infime alerte") will bring a golden dawn of light and vitality. The last line echoes line 6:

> Sur qui l'Amour meurt ou sommeille . . .
> Sans qui l'Amour meurt ou s'endort!

The parallelism points up the contrast: while in the first case oppression weighs heavily on the woman, in the second there is detachment, and liberation from the sleep and death that have preceded the sting. Nevertheless, although the words suggest this detachment, the very repetition shows us that there is a return to the past: the self has not escaped into the future but has plunged again into its own fascination. The forward-moving sequence has rejoined its past; the woman discovers triumphant illumination and at the same time contentedly surrenders to forces that resemble those of sleep and death. With its final linked rhymes the sonnet ends, so to speak, on a sigh of pleasure.

The law of "L'Abeille" is voluptuous, as the self willingly offers its treasure to the bee. The speaker is a woman, and the tone of her song feminine, caught between self-love and desire. For her the act of love does not bring escape but affords a new savoring of her own sweetness, and she accepts all the consequences of the sting—its alliance of pain and delight, sleep and wakefulness, death and life. The bosom which allows the prick goes against the immediate law of its own nature, yet it knows that out of these tensions and hurt will come new enchantment as well as the fresh discovery of the sensibility.

As intrinsically as in Claudel, the form has a precise function in our poetic experience. We have seen that there is a strong line of development which gives a sense of progression, but that this progression is more apparent than real. The first quatrain establishes a balance between the twin seductions of the bee and the self ("blonde abeille," "tendre corbeille"), between fear and invitation; in the next lines the self-love of the speaker is displayed, the roundness of her flesh ("gourde," "ronde"), the surging desire in her breast and in her blood; the first tercet introduces sudden haste ("prompt," "vif") as suffering is evoked, both present pain ("supplice dormant") and the pain that is yet to come ("tourment," "mal"); while the conclusion brings finality ("donc"), both light and pleasure ("sens illuminé," "alerte d'or"), and the tender caress of the self. In this fashion the individual sections propose the same terms of relationship, which are modulated in diverse manners. The theme, like the structure, is in fact a variation around a central point of attraction. The speaker murmurs, dances, moves slowly, then rapier-sharp, and at last is silent: exactly imitating the bee in its game of love and death, she traces out the image of the mind fascinated by its own processes.

It is clear that Valéry's poem can stand alone as the highly controlled expression of a moment of the intellectual sensibility. Yet in a more general sense we may also say that it presupposes an author who was the analyst of the *Cahiers*, and his daily exercise or constitutional on the theme of mental functions which he undertook at the age of twenty-one. He aimed to offer a clear and precise representation of thought, to reduce its vagueness to form, so that his central concern was not with the subject of any particular meditation—"l'écume des choses"[49]—but with its vital moments, which he conceived with intensity and passion: "J'aime la pensée véritable comme d'autres aiment le nu, qu'ils dessineraient toute leur vie."[50] Thus the hazards of consciousness could be noted and, as it were, willed; thus the analyst could stand at the proud center of his universe, uncommitted to any single event; thus the poet could find in a symbolism of his own making the magic formula for intellectual clarity. He once declared: "Je ne suis poète que par raccroc," and such of course is the case: the *Cahiers* were his prime preoccupation; but is it not also true that this apparently fortuitous enterprise is the crystal by which desire was transmuted into illumination, thought into a law, analysis into composition? A poem like "L'Abeille" revolves around a self that is the principle of an ordered structure which escapes the ruins of time, however briefly, however illusorily. The glory of the "intelligence désaffectée" is to make of its tragic separateness a fugitive triumph. But the other "Abeille" of grace and fructification echoes a fundamental experience of rebirth, the inspiration of one Christmas Day when time for Claudel gained new meaning and which *Connaissance du temps*, and later *Art poétique*, were to expound. His poetry is the restatement of this insight, the rediscovery of a unique relationship by way of naïvely Christian symbols. No position could in a way be more utterly divergent from Valéry's. Yet to work out this divergence was the task to which both of them devoted their lives, the one exultantly, the other in anguish but with equal dedication.

The debate could not of course be resolved, nor is this what one seeks. It is moving, however, to savor the courtesy and mutual respect of a confrontation in which the whole of their attitudes was implied and—in the last resort, each in his own way—their confidence in poetry, less for any intrinsic truth it might contain than as the means of con-

[49] "Les événements sont l'écume des choses. Mais *c'est la mer qui m'intéresse*" ("Propos me concernant," *Œuvres*, II, 1508).
[50] *Cahiers*, IV, 881.

signing their most cherished aspirations. Our last word will be that of the nonbeliever, which by its ambiguity is, I think, amply suggestive of the poetic impulse in both Claudel and Valéry: "Tout vrai poème n'est précisément qu'une espèce de *consécration*—liturgique!—de certains mots";[51] and again: "La plus belle poésie," he observes in a notebook contemporaneous with *Charmes*, "a la voix d'une femme idéale, Mademoiselle Ame."[52]

[51] *Cahiers*, XXV, 589.
[52] *Cahiers*, V, 170.

Chapter V

Claudel's Art of Composition

IN THE twenty years between 1897 and 1917 three poems of night, surely among the finest that have been written, crown the achievement of French Symbolism. If we were to look closely we would find in them, I believe, a basic continuity, however divergent their tones and temper, for *Un Coup de dés*, *La Cantate à trois voix*, and *La Jeune Parque* depict man in the presence of fatality, abstracted from trivial details, meditating on the ends of life. In each is a vital commitment and a searching appraisal under the solitary light of the stars; in each, to the various tensions it contains, is an individual resolution—the glory of the Mallarméan artist, spiritual joy in Claudel, Valéry's clear-eyed acceptance of action—wherein aesthetics and philosophy combine.

It is my aim to describe in the following pages the genesis of the longest of these works. In many respects, intrinsically and chronologically, *La Cantate à trois voix* is Claudel's central expression, that bears within it, as it were, the others. For myself, I know of nothing he wrote that is more moving, about which I should wish to say, as he once said of *Phèdre*: "C'est un de ces moments où un écrivain, le pauvre imbécile! il apprend ce que c'est que d'être un homme de génie!"[1]

I have called *La Cantate à trois voix* central. After *Partage de midi* and *L'Otage*, after the *Cinq Grandes Odes* also, but before *Corona benignitatis anni Dei* and of course

---

[1] "Conversation sur Jean Racine," *Œuvres en prose* (1965), p. 463. Cf. Jacques Madaule: "jamais son chant ne s'était élevé aussi pur, 'comme un grand jet d'eau claire'" (*Le Drame de Paul Claudel* [Paris: Desclée de Brouwer, 1947], p. 306); and Julius Wilhelm ("Paul Claudels Cantate à trois voix," *Studia Romanica* [1955], p. 431): "Obwohl die 'Cantate à trois voix' zu den wunderbarsten lyrischen Dichtungen des neueren Frankreichs zählt, ist sie nur wenig bekannt."

Le Soulier de satin, it forms part of the rich new orientation of his career that began with the separation from Ysé, his marriage and return to China, and reached maturity when he came back to Europe, having been appointed French consul in Prague from December 1909. He later described his inner transformation in quite precise terms. "A partir de 1910," he told Jean Amrouche, "la géologie de mon talent, si vous voulez, pour employer un mot très prétentieux, est changée: il ne s'agit plus d'une pente plus ou moins accidentée à gravir, il s'agit d'un terrain plan, permettant les points de vue, permettant l'exercice d'un talent de composition, si je peux dire. La composition domine l'inspiration."[2] If all was not forgotten of his previous grief, he could at last see it as a kind of parable in an embracing view of the world. On the one hand it would constitute the hidden substance and energy of his plays, their bitter drama; on the other, his sense of liberation— "le côté apaisé, le côté joyeux, le côté même à certain point de vue triomphal"[3]—was channeled into purely lyrical works like *La Cantate à trois voix*. He felt after his crucial experience that he fully possessed, in thought and flesh, the meaning of sacrifice. Now was the ripeness, the golden hour:

> Et puis l'heure de l'or, la longue heure de la maturité est venue. Le paysage âcre et heurté où nulle note ne veut rien céder aux autres de son intensité native et de son cri propre, ne s'est pas seulement simplifié, il s'est ouvert, il s'est élargi, et l'espace y fait accueil à la durée. Le poète a pris possession de son domaine: à la rencontre des deux diamètres, il exploite les quatre horizons. Car c'est à lui, héritier du premier Adam, que l'Eternel a

---

[2] *Mémoires improvisés*, p. 231. Cf. *ibid.*, p. 162: "quelque chose de nouveau qui se dégage et que je dois probablement à mon étude et de la Bible et de saint Thomas, c'est-à-dire la résolution d'arriver à la substance, d'arriver au fait, au substantif, pas seulement de borner ma poésie à un rôle décoratif, mais à un rôle substantiel, réel, de tâcher de voir les choses telles qu'elles sont dans leurs rapports philosophiques les unes avec les autres."

[3] *Ibid.*, p. 267.

livré le Paradis terrestre, ce Paradis dont il aperçoit avec surprise qu'il n'était jamais sorti, pour en faire à ses frères et à ses enfants communication [. . .]. L'heure est venue de la fraction du pain. . . .[4]

It was in such propitious circumstances that *La Cantate* was written and published in Claudel's forty-sixth year, just as *Un Coup de dés* and *La Jeune Parque*, by a hazard one might think appropriate, appeared in the forty-sixth year of both Mallarmé and Valéry.

A glance at any of the current editions of the poem shows that Claudel clearly indicated the date and place of composition: "Château d'Hostel en Valromay, juin 1911." We know, indeed, that he and his wife arrived in the village of Hostel in the Southern Juras, at the home of his father-in-law Antoine Sainte-Marie Perrin, on 10 June 1911; that he stayed for the best part of a month, despite a brief visit to Paris and Villeneuve; and that he left again on July 12 for Prague. Yet it is evident that the poem was not actually written during this period, but in Prague ("où est le centre de l'Europe, où est le nœud de ses eaux") and later in Frankfurt, toward the end of 1911 and in the following year. Claudel's dating is thus rather a poetic or sentimental attribution than a historical one. The time of writing can be placed with some accuracy by way of a letter he sent to

[4] "Introduction à Francis Jammes," *Œuvres en prose*, p. 567. The example of bucolic calm offered by Jammes' work was not lost on Claudel, and he praised in particular the *Géorgiques chrétiennes* of 1912. Nearly thirty years after the composition of *La Cantate à trois voix* he recalled this poem, and his attitude when writing it, in terms that echoed his comment on Jammes: "au travers de l'illimité, à la mesure de son pas et de ses bras étendus, / Il y trace et délimite son domaine. Quelque chose lui appartient désormais, et où il n'y a plus qu'à répandre la semence de la moisson future" ("Le Jet de pierre," *Œuvres complètes*, XIV, 195). With regard to this transformation of the man and the poet one thinks also of Saint-John Perse's remarks, which have recourse to another metaphor: "Pour ceux qui l'ont connu dans sa première maturité, mâchant encore le mors de l'insatisfaction humaine, et seul, l'apparition de ce visiteur nocturne, marqué du signe de l'élection, fut une des plus belles intrusions de notre histoire littéraire" ("Silence pour Claudel," *Nouvelle revue française* [September 1955], p. 387).

Madame Perrin in March 1912. He writes: "Je travaille avec patience depuis six mois à une espèce de cantate avec la modeste espérance d'arriver enfin à savoir ce que je veux dire: mais je crois que j'arriverai à la fin sans y être parvenu."[5] To his mother-in-law he speaks with the unpretentiousness of a man engaged in the act of composition, discovering his thought by approximations and the interplay of correspondences rather than asserting it. By June 10 of that year, exactly twelve months to the day after his arrival in Hostel, he could see the whole shape and substance of the poem before him and wrote to Gide from Frankfurt in the euphoria of his artistic powers: "Je suis engagé depuis près d'un an dans un long poème composé, sur le mode du bréviaire, de dialogues et de cantiques et consacré à la nuit du Solstice d'été (trois voix de femmes). Cela a pris beaucoup plus de développement que je ne pensais, et je commence à peine à comprendre ce que j'ai voulu dire. Je suis maintenant dans la partie délectable du travail, où l'on est maître de son sujet et où les idées arrivent en abondance."[6] *La Cantate* was finally completed on 10 July 1912.[7] Eighteen months after its publication, in a lecture at the Université des Annales, he gave further details: it was composed, he said on that occasion, "en 1911, en souvenir de l'été merveilleux que nous eûmes cette année-là";[8] while a detailed, if terse, commentary on the various stages of its genesis is contained in an unpublished letter to Jacques Doucet written shortly after the First World War, in which the origin is taken back beyond Hostel to a visual memory of a scene in China:

[5] Letter of 15 March 1913 to Elisabeth Sainte-Marie Perrin (previously unpublished). I wish to express my deep gratitude to Monsieur Pierre Claudel for his kindness in allowing me to consult the private papers and manuscripts of the poet that are quoted in these pages.

[6] *Correspondance Paul Claudel-André Gide* (Paris: Gallimard, 1949), p. 199.

[7] Cf. letter of 10 July 1912 to Gabriel Frizeau, *Correspondance Claudel-Jammes-Frizeau* (Paris: Gallimard, 1952), p. 250.

[8] The lecture, entitled "L'Epopée de 1914-15: poème de la nature, de la foi, de la patrie," was published in the *Journal de l'Université des Annales*, No. 13, Vol. II, 1914-1915.

La première idée de ce poème date de Chinwangtao (Chine) 1909. Elle m'a été suggérée par la vue de trois jeunes femmes dont une à la chevelure rousse, montant ensemble à travers un bois de pins. L'idée prit corps à Hostel pendant le magnifique été de 1911. Je travaillai au poème à Prague, puis à Francfort. On retrouve par endroit dans la seconde partie du poème des traces du paysage allemand. Le "Cantique des chars errants" a été inspiré par une promenade à Wiesbaden.[9]

Twenty-seven years later, in March 1946, he left aside Hostel, Prague, and Frankfurt so as to recall his initial inspiration, both sight and symbol.

Jadis des pages de je ne sais quel roman feuilleté dans un club d'Extrême-Orient, il s'échappa un soulier qui devint, vingt ans après, le *Soulier de satin.* Et qui expliquera pourquoi ces trois têtes de femmes, l'une blonde, l'autre brune, et cette autre rousse, faisant ascension dans un triple entrecroisement à travers une forêt aromatique vers je ne sais plus quel lieu sacré, s'imposèrent à moi avec l'autorité d'un thème ou d'un symbole?[10]

Thus, he tells us, the seed was a gracious image, the harmony of three female forms, an elemental accord. The red hair no doubt evoked Ysé, and suggested the hymn of Poland that Fausta would sing ("Nous seuls savons ce que nous avons souffert"); but private pathos was absorbed into a higher meaning whose poetic consequences *La Cantate* would develop.

Nevertheless, the fact remains that Hostel had a vital importance in the creative process. Today, as in 1911, the château stands splendidly at one end of a long row of lime trees; at the other, a vantage point overlooks numerous valleys. A description of the scene is to be found in a prose text of 1952, in which Claudel recalled the way

[9] Letter to Jacques Doucet, April 1919, previously unpublished.
[10] Introduction to *La Cantate à trois voix* (Paris: Editions d'art Sagile, 1946).

the mountains as seen from Hostel appear to partici-
pate actively in a network of relationships, a scheme of
questions and answers. "Elles se sont interrompues," he
wrote, "face à face avec d'autres élévations timides, qui
ont l'air, de l'autre côté, avant que de les commenter, de
les interroger."[11] His private journal for 1911 contains
more remarks on the landscape (thus: "Paysage d'Hostel.
Comme une immense ville effondrée, de longs pans de
murailles verticales subsistent à toutes les hauteurs [. . .].
Vaste cuve emplie d'un pur éther")[12]—but fewer than
one might have desired. There is also, in a letter to Gabriel
Frizeau, an eloquent comment on his pleasure at finding
himself once again in Hostel: "Me voici en France depuis
quelques jours, jouissant délicieusement de cet admirable
printemps, et du visage de ce pays de la joie auprès duquel
tous les autres ne sont que ténèbres."[13] For a rather unex-
pected source of additional information, however, we can
consult the "Livre d'Hostel," one of those grand old family
albums popular in generations before our own which was
assiduously and wittily kept by Madame Perrin. The entries
for June and July 1911 refer to exceptionally fine weather
as the family went out to pick wild strawberries, or walked
at night to the windmill of Musieux beneath an admira-

---

[11] "Un Coin de la France," *Œuvres en prose*, p. 1346.
[12] "Journal," 1911, p. 58 (previously unpublished). Claudel was
later to evoke Hostel on the occasion of his father-in-law's death in
his major poem "L'Architecte," written in Rio de Janeiro in 1918:

Heureux celui qui ayant pris femme devant Dieu assume entre
le chemin et le sillon
La demeure qui ne fut pas faite pour un jour, mais pour toutes
les générations!
Tel sur sa colline posté, à l'entrée de ce qu'on appelle le
Val-Romain,
Hostel, dont la tour pointue entre les châtaigners ronds et les
grands séquoïas américains
Domine tout ce paysage que fait le Rhône jusqu'aux glaciers
savoyards,
Et que ce piéton qui arrive d'Allemagne, avec peine jadis
atteignait dans le pas lent des bœufs, tard.
                                        (*Œuvre poétique*, p. 607)
[13] Letter of 14 June 1911, *Correspondance Claudel-Jammes-Frizeau*,
p. 215.

ble sky. The tone may be illustrated by this note for 10 June 1911, which was the date of Claudel's arrival:

> Nous attendons Reine et Paul. Si nos calculs sont justes, ils seront là à six heures et demie.—Mais il pleut.—Le rendez-vous traditionnel au gros tilleul ne sera pas possible. Cette pluie rendra la route moins pénible à nos voyageurs. Ils circulent depuis hier.—Ils ont dû quitter Prague dans la matinée de vendredi.
>
> La pluie cesse, nous allons au tilleul![14] Et les voilà! On voit la voiture! Ils sont au grand tournant! A Chaudossin! A Mury!—Vite nous allons les recevoir au nord. On s'embrasse, on se revoit, on se reconnaît. Les enfants sont un peu pâles. Trente heures de voyage—c'est beaucoup pour ces petits corps. Un bon repas, une bonne nuit, et demain tout ira bien. Il y a du bleu dans le ciel, promesse d'un beau lendemain.[15]

Later we shall find in Claudel's own hand a few lines in memory of a picnic, in which "volaille au *jux*" rhymes with "Castor et Poll*ux*," "cette *crux*" with "un coup de pied au *cux*."[16] At the same time there will be a mock lament to mark his departure for a few days in Paris:

> L'oiseau s'envo-o-le!
> Vers d'autres cieux!
> L'oiseau s'envo-o-o-le!
> Pleurez, mes yeux
> Avec trois chemises et un col
> Adieu! adieu!

---

[14] Cf. "L'Architecte," *Œuvre poétique*, p. 609: "il y a toujours au bout de l'allée des tilleuls ce grand arbre pareil à vous qui de ses branches recouvre la vallée."

[15] It is my pleasure to thank Madame Reibel, its present owner, for allowing me to consult the "Livre d'Hostel."

[16] Entry for the 17 June 1911 (in Claudel's handwriting):
Le dix-sept mai Marie et Paul amis comme Castor et Pollux
Par une chaleur étouffante sont allés déjeuner à Caujux,
De deux bouteilles de Scyssel et d'une volaille au jux,
En compagnie d'un chien affamé qui étudie cette *crux*:
Lequel vaut mieux d'un os de poulet ou d'un coup de pied au cux?

> Pleurez, mes yeux!
> Adieu! adieu!

Such passages enable us to picture the relaxed atmosphere of a well-to-do family enjoying the summer together, at the opposite remove from Claudel's own tense solitude during the period immediately prior to his marriage. China had been left far behind, and he was surrounded by wife, children, and friends. One can well see how this change, in his native country, in a landscape of imposing proportions, should have struck a note of joy and gratitude. He was ready: nature could open up before him, "par le milieu comme une partition sublime."[17]

Was any portion of the poem begun at this time? It is almost impossible to say. Yet if we refer to the isolated jottings in the poet's diary during his stay in Hostel, two notes will attract our attention. The first reads simply: "Une naïve petite étoile tendrement qui dit: Ne m'oubliez pas."[18] As we know, these words will be taken up by Laeta in exactly the same form to end the last interlude, just before the "Cantique de l'Ombre." The second, even more laconic, is also a line found in the final version, at the conclusion of the third interlude that introduces the "Cantique de la Vigne": "La Vigne, le Froment, et l'Ombre."[19] But this not only becomes a line of the poem; it also establishes the correspondence around which *La Cantate* will be constructed, for the three protagonists in the dialogue—Laeta the Latin fiancée, Fausta the Polish wife, Beata the Egyptian widow—represent the Vine, the Grain, and Shadow. By their diversity and convergence they produce a fugue of motifs, each being essential to the suavity that is the poem's object. "Tout passe," writes Claudel, "mais en cette heure du moins de maturité suprême, ces trois choses sont à nous: l'ivresse de la grappe mystique, l'or qui couronne la longue patience de la terre, l'ombre enfin et la nuit, qui, tandis qu'elles en couvrent l'occasion contingente, délivrent

---

[17] "Hector Berlioz," *Œuvres complètes*, XVII, 302.
[18] "Journal," 1911, p. 58.   [19] *Ibid.*

notre joie et notre possession de ce qu'elles ont de périssable."[20]

Now the mention of this triadic development makes us turn from the diary to the manuscripts of the poem, in which we find notes that may well have been written at Hostel in the small pavilion where, as family tradition has it, *La Cantate* was composed. I refer in particular to the original draft of the prelude, in which the poet established his argument and spoke once more of Vine, Grain, and Shadow. But the design had not yet been conceived in its richness, and the distance it would occupy with regard to the poet's own voice was still uncertain. In fact, it becomes clear that the first lines were to be an invocation by the poet himself to his muse, or rather to music. He would praise the intermingling of rhythms and ideas—a subtle and subdued murmur of wood instruments—that opens up a space to be inhabited by the mind, and not a foreign rhythm or obstructive presence.

Partage de l'été—(entre les deux étés)
La Vigne, le Froment et l'Ombre.

Invocation. Hymen de la poésie et de la musique. Le poète ne peut plus se passer de la musique. La musique se refuse à l'étreinte et à la possession: elle échappe, elle

[20] Preface to selections from the poem published in the *Revue de Paris* (March-April 1913), p. 119. It is worth recalling that, when Claudel was writing *L'Otage* in 1908, he conceived the idea of an act which would bring together three women who adumbrate Laeta, Fausta, and Beata: "un acte entre trois femmes, la mère, la veuve, la fiancée" (quoted by André Vachon, *Le Temps et l'espace dans l'œuvre de Paul Claudel* [Paris: Le Seuil, 1965], p. 349n.). In his journal for 1910 we also find a note on the Three Graces of antiquity, written in English and perhaps copied from a reference book: "The Charities or Graces—the temple of the Graces symbolized the mutual services of men to each other, on which society depends." *La Cantate* will marry these notions with that of the Trinity, the three theological virtues ("A la ressemblance des trois Eglises, / Un seul peuple dans les trois Vertus, / Dans la Foi, et la Charité, et l'Espérance, hors de tout espoir humain," we read in the "Cantique du Peuple divisé"), held in a mystical triangulation of desire ("Heureux celui qui aime, mais plus heureux celui qui sert et dont on a besoin, et ces deux que le besoin indissoluble / Relie comme une troisième personne!").

fuit. Rendre la poésie capable de délectation. Non pas un son matériel. La musique sans aucun son purement spirituelle. Par l'harmonie. Non pas un piétinement brutal. Elle dépiste la poursuite, elle échappe au poids et à la capture par l'entrecroisement savant de ses rhythmes [sic] (et de ses idées) entrelacées. Le bois où veut se placer un lieu.

O été, ô lumière. Les 2 étés, celui de juin, celui de juillet.   Son de l'instrument de bois.

J'habite un château (les jeunes femmes, comme des enfants, bruit des billes de billard, éclats de rire en haut).

Jadis (l'idole de bois qu'on amène au travers de la plaine sur un char traîné par les bœufs—le coureur avec les deux petites colonnes de poussière à chaque pied—les vignes et la cascade—les fontaines—le vase virginal)

Parmi les voix les 3 vierges tour à tour—Prenant peu à peu tel visage connu. Plus réelles qu'aucune. Le froment dont l'ombre est de fer ardent.—L'ombre visage fin et sarrazin.

Toutes ensemble en une composition spirituelle.

Finir par la nuit *délicieuse et courte.*

Je ne veux pas qu'une chose à la fois.[21]

---

[21] Previously unpublished. We note also two isolated jottings: at the top of the page, the indication "adagio," which is linked to the other references to music and refers undoubtedly first and foremost to the slow pace and the suavity of the poem as a whole; at the end, under the last line, the words "la terreur," which we may take to evoke an emotion that the poem exorcises, in the same sense as it is found in "La Maison fermée":

> Comme jadis quand Colomb et Magellan eurent rejoint les deux parts de la terre,
> Tous les monstres des vieilles cartes s'évanouirent,
> Ainsi le ciel n'a plus pour nous de terreur, sachant que si loin qu'il s'étend
> Votre mesure n'est pas absente. Votre bonté n'est pas absente.

(*Œuvre poétique*, p. 289)

By the very first word, we can observe that the poem is placed under the same sign of sublimated experience as *Partage de midi*, with its dialectical use of the imagery of midday and midnight. As here, so in the play: at the moment of transition a separation occurs that allows eternity to enter, just as Omega breaks the charmed periphery of the circle.

> O l'année qui se partage dans la nuit!
> La fleur qui est déjà le fruit,
> Semence de tout ce qui commence,
> Or de tout ce qui est fini.

The summer solstice, this "Noël d'été," is a moment of vision, the pivot of light and shadow, flesh and spirit; it concentrates the variations of Vine, Grain, and Shadow. The image of the solstice as a symbolic period of crisis can be traced back through Claudel's work to his earliest writings.[22] But little by little it became in *La Cantate* his own Midsummer Night's Dream of 1911, which was ordered according to the solemnity of a ritual. He told Gide, as we have seen, that the poem was composed "sur le mode du bréviaire,"[23] and later described it as "cette espèce d'Office de la Nuit d'été,"[24] his model being the liturgical dialogue, the alternation of canticles, psalms, quotations, and responses in the official prayer book of the Roman Catholic Church. Here, as in the breviary, the hour and day con-

---

[22] Cf. *La Ville I* (*Œuvres complètes*, VII, 9): "Un très grand jardin dans le milieu de Paris. L'époque du solstice d'été"; *La Ville II* (*ibid.*, p. 144): "Voici pour moi l'heure de la pause suprême; laisse-moi jouir de ce suspens solennel où je suis / [. . .] . . . à chaque entrée des Gémeaux . . . / Il engendre une nouvelle moisson de pensées et de désirs"; *L'Echange I* (*Œuvres complètes*, VIII, 57): "Mais maintenant voici, voici le temps de la paix, / Et le ciel est à lui-même pareil, mais toutes choses poussent sur la terre! / Et la mer improductive demeure dans le repos. / C'est le temps qui est au milieu de l'année, c'est le jour où le soleil s'arrête."

[23] In a parallel way, *Corona benignitatis anni Dei* follows the cycle of the liturgical year; while *La Messe là-bas*, composed in Rio de Janeiro between May and December 1917, adopts the order of the prayers of the Mass (Introït, Kyrie Eleison, Credo, Pater Noster).

[24] *Revue de Paris* (March-April 1913), p. 119.

tain a meaning, a *mysterium*: Claudel depicts a vigil such as that by which Christ's coming is prepared; his poem is a night-course of praise like the progression of Vespers (*vespertina solemnitas*), Nocturns (*nocturna solemnitas*), and Lauds in the early morning, a sequence that represents youth, maturity, and old age; and it is associated naturally with the feast of the nativity of St. John the Baptist on the night of June 23, the shortest of the year, when time is as nothing, merely an interval between spring and summer, an absence of events by which eternity is revealed. "Hic est Praecursor dilectus, et lucerna lucens ante Dominum. . . ."[25] In the silence of meditation a promise irradiates the soul. But we must observe that the moment offered to us in the draft presents an action that would seem to take place in daylight ("O été, ô lumière"), reference being made to night in the second to the last sentence only as the theme of a rapid finale. Needless to say, darkness and stars in the final version will be fully suited to a silence pregnant with meaning, and to the poet's communion with the essence of objects, not their outward appearances.

In the second paragraph the observations on music (which Claudel linked with St. John the Baptist, the voice that precedes the Word),[26] would also require a detailed discussion if one were to place them in context. It is obvious, for one thing, that, in spite of Samson's book *Paul Claudel poète-musicien* and a number of articles, the theme

[25] Claudel's journal shows that he read P. Battifol's *Histoire du bréviaire romain* in 1911 and copied out a long passage ("Aspiciens de longe . . .") that Battifol had quoted, as Claudel observes, "avec une juste admiration." He kept constantly on his desk a copy of the breviary (*Breviarum monasticum . . . pro Congregatione gallica ordinis Sancti Benedicti . . . Pars estiva . . .*), which of course contains the prayers for the feast of the nativity of St. John the Baptist. On the origins of this volume, see the *Catalogue* of the Exposition Paul Claudel held at the Bibliothèque Nationale, February 1968, Item No. 183.

[26] Music is "cette modulation qui, par une disposition de la Providence, a emprunté la gamme, la distinction des sept notes à une hymne de saint Jean-Baptiste, à cette voix qui précède le Verbe" ("La Pensée religieuse de Romain Rolland," *Œuvres en prose*, p. 601).

of music in Claudel has yet to receive the attention it deserves.[27] It must be recognized as vital to his whole approach, both aesthetic and religious. As an indication of its importance one might refer to the lines from his inaugural speech at the Académie Française in March 1947, in which he spoke of the generation of 1900. He said on that occasion, "Il s'était levé sur le monde une certaine attention à la musique, une certaine nostalgie de la réponse, une certaine intolérance de la fatalité, qu'elle fût scientifique ou légale, un certain sentiment irrépressible de notre droit interne, un certain appel de notre conscience morale à la confirmation extérieure."[28] In Claudel's eyes, the discovery of music by the generation of 1900 was part of a spiritual awakening that marked the end of an age of declamation. There was a new need to listen and hear, to wait on an answer, to respond to a divine harmony. For him, music was the way of God. *Non impedias musicam*, he said again and again, adopting the words of Ecclesiasticus. "Hinder not music. Pour not out talk where there is a performance of music, and display not thy wisdom out of season."[29] He applied these words in advising his friends: "Vous êtes comme un musicien à l'orchestre placé devant un morceau de musique, dont on tourne les pages devant lui et qu'il doit déchiffrer à mesure, en faisant attention au texte, au chef d'orchestre qui donne le mouvement et aux camarades si nombreux autour de lui."[30] The same attitude was equally applicable in art: "Ma doctrine poétique se résumerait par le mot de la Sagesse antique: *N'empêchez pas la musique*. Laissez-la émaner toute seule.

---

[27] Joseph Samson, *Claudel poète-musicien* (Geneva: Milieu du monde, 1948); André Espiau de la Maëstre, "Claudel et la musique," *Les Lettres romanes*, Vol. 13, No. 2 (May 1959), pp. 145-176; Karl Schaezler, "Claudel und die Musik," *Hochland* (February 1963), pp. 291-293; R. Bauer, "Claudel et Richard Wagner," *Orbis Litterarum*, IX (1956), 197-214.

[28] "Discours de réception à l'Académie Française," *Œuvres en prose*, p. 651.

[29] Ecclesiasticus 32:3-4.

[30] "Lettre à Madame d'A.," *Œuvres complètes*, XV, 256.

Arrangez-vous pour qu'elle émane."[31] Indeed, one could go so far as to say that it constituted for him a kind of creative technique. One makes of oneself, of one's soul, the springboard for composition:

> J'ai appris à me servir, ainsi que d'un instrument, de ma propre intensité et de la modulation de moi-même. Je critique bienheureusement mon âme par le moyen de ces résonances de toutes parts qu'elle a provoquées au dehors. L'oreille tendue de l'exorde à la conclusion à ma propre justesse, il est arrivé que je chante! il est arrivé que par l'explicitation de ma propre raison d'être et le gouvernement selon tous les modes que j'invente de la rapidité et de la véhémence j'ai atteint délicieusement hors de moi, pour m'en séparer et de nouveau le rejoindre et le suivre et l'entraîner, l'accord![32]

In this respect it is possible to ascertain that, just before the composition of *La Cantate*, Claudel had given much thought to the art of music, his preoccupation with it joined to his new poetics. In letters to Gide and Suarès we find him discussing Wagner, enthusing over certain aspects, criticizing others severely. He also considered Beethoven at some length. But why should he have turned in particular to the cantata? We can have no doubt that his stay in Prague and Frankfurt allowed him ample opportunity to enjoy the music of Bach, who came to represent for him the nonreferential path that leads us, as surely as a heartbeat, toward a goal we surmise from the start: "nous voyons, nous sentons, nous devinons où l'on nous conduit, et tout notre être par avance appréhende le programme auditif avec son ressort et ses reprises, ses conditions, ses renforts et ses obstacles."[33] How could he have escaped reading also—although for this we have no proof— Schweitzer's *J.S. Bach le musicien poète*, which was pub-

---

[31] "La Poésie est un art," *Œuvres complètes*, XVIII, 19.
[32] *Œuvres complètes*, XV, 156-157.
[33] "Le Chemin dans l'art," *Œuvres en prose*, p. 269.

lished in 1905?[34] His viewpoint might seem superficially to
be the direct consequence of Schweitzer's analysis: "Mu-
sique et Poésie s'étreignaient étroitement, chaque dessin
musical correspondant à une idée littéraire. Et c'est ainsi
que ce recueil admiré jusqu'alors comme un modèle de
contrepoint pur, m'apparaissait d'une intensité d'émotion
sans pareille."[35] The parallel between the ideas of Schwei-
tzer and Claudel appears to be somewhat more than for-
tuitous, and it could be pursued. Yet whether some of
Claudel's ideas crystallized around this reading or not, the
fact remains that he saw the form of the cantata as lending
itself to the series of dialogues, and recitatives he wished
to write, by which he could break with the personal voice
of the *Cinq Grandes Odes*. His own music would be an in-
terwoven pattern of rhythms and ideas, of images and sinu-
ous phrases, in which the motif is not stated but suggested,
not declared but composed. The opening of *La Cantate*
establishes the mode that will be developed:

LAETA
Cette heure qui est entre le printemps et l'été . . .

FAUSTA
Entre ce soir et demain l'heure seule qui est laissée . . .

BEATA
Sommeil sans aucun sommeil avant que ne renaisse
le soleil . . .

LAETA
Nuit sans aucune nuit . . .

FAUSTA
Pleine d'oiseaux mystérieux sans cesse et du chant
qu'on entend quand il est fini . . .

LAETA
. . . De feuilles et d'un faible cri, et de mots tout bas,
et du bruit . . .

FAUSTA
De l'eau lointaine qui tombe et du vent qui fuit!

[34] Albert Schweitzer, *J.S. Bach le musicien poète*, preface by
Charles M. Widor (Leipzig: Breitkopf und Härtel, 1905).
[35] Preface by C. M. Widor, *Bach*, p. viii.

BEATA

Ciel tout pur   sans nulle souillure,   Azur
que la large lune emplit!

LAETA

Heure sereine!

FAUSTA

Tristesse et peine . . .

LAETA

Larmes vaines! tristesse et peine qui est vaine . . .

FAUSTA

Larmes en vain, peine vaine . . .

BEATA

De ce jour qui est accompli!

LAETA

Le printemps est déjà fini.

BEATA

Demain c'est le grand Eté qui commence!

FAUSTA

Le jour immense!

LAETA

Le fruit de la terre immense!

FAUSTA

Le jour qui dure!

BEATA

Le ciel tout pur et le soleil par excellence![36]

These lines make us realize—and the original draft already
indicates—that the poet who wrote *La Cantate* could no
longer live without music: "Le poète ne peut plus se passer
de la musique." They are not written in the Claudelian
verset, as the various hymns will be, but in a new line found
briefly in *L'Annonce faite à Marie*, which here receives its
full expansion. It introduces the presence of silence into
our reading, making us aware of a buoyant lightness that
sustains the poem. Claudel rejects the eloquence of rea-
soned or emotional argument for simplicity of words and
syntax, at the other extreme from Hugolian or Baudelairian

[36] "La Cantate à trois voix," *Œuvre poétique*, pp. 321-322.

sequences, and gives us, by the form he has chosen, the very representation of a necessary relationship in which each part calls on the whole, and the whole depends on each. This is indeed a concert that implicitly suggests a hidden conductor, since harmony reigns and the members of the chorus pronounce the words that complete the sense already hinted at, that modulate the same sounds ("heure" establishes the key, as it were: it is found seven times in this opening dialogue, and only twice in the rest of *La Cantate*; it is echoed by "bonheur," "demeure," "pleure," "meurt," "leurre," "sœurs," "explique-leur," "cœur," "fleur," "seul"), providing assonance and rhyme, constructing the musical phrase. We should also note the exquisite care that presides over the alternation of roles between the three sisters, which becomes clear with a little analysis. Thus, to look no further than the above passage, the nineteen exchanges give us the following scheme if we use a to designate Laeta, b for Fausta, and c for Beata: abc-ab-abc-ab-abc-acb-abc. A kind of choral score emerges which shows Claudel using the full resources of his three voices. With every dialogue he brings in a new arrangement, constantly varying his orchestration but just as constantly discovering order within fantasy, direction within freedom.

Turning back to the same draft, we find in the third paragraph an echo of the equinoctial moment of the first lines, the meeting of the two seasons; but now a gentle woodwind, which is the very breath of creation, accompanies it. The poet situates himself in personal terms within this harmony, notes the familiar sounds of a houseful of people—adults in the calm of the billiard room, peals of laughter upstairs —and refers in particular to the young women who disport themselves like so many children. One cannot but think of the atmosphere of Hostel;[37] at the same time another pas-

---

[37] A tender evocation of women and children at Hostel is given in "L'Architecte":

> Comme les hirondelles qui font l'une près de l'autre leurs nids sous l'avancement du toit,
> Dix familles ainsi quand revient l'été occupent toute la hauteur du bâtiment,

sage from the unpublished "Journal," written shortly after Claudel's departure from Hostel, comes to mind: "Scène au clair de la lune sur la terrasse du château: la vieille mère, le jeune homme qui revient seulement pour quelques heures, les deux sœurs, l'une mariée avec ses enfants qui dorment. La lampe de la bicyclette qu'on allume." Here the search was still continuing for the sober structure, the hieratic force of the setting as it was finally established.

By the word "Jadis" in the following lines of the plan a new factor is introduced. Claudel conjures up an image of male determination, of consecrated effort. This is man—"le mâle, le maître, le premier, l'animateur"—as he seeks the goal of duty and desire—vineyard and virgin waters. This ardor the married women have known—"jadis"; Laeta remembers a strength like that of the surging Rhone:

Qu'il est beau, le navire noir que le vent et cette
brise même sur mon visage
    Amène tout droit en quelques instants du fond
de la mer,
    Quand il laisse tomber son antenne, et tourne,
et se couche sur le côté!
    Qu'ils sont beaux, les pieds de celui qui à travers
l'immense plage de sable éblouissant,
        Se met en devoir d'atteindre la patrie,
        Les pieds de celui qui annonce la victoire!

Et par le trou de chaque fenêtre on entend une voix de jeune femme ou d'enfant.
    L'une fait des gammes, et l'autre à grand labeur apprend la vérité,
    Sur les verbes tant actifs que passifs, et sur le nombre des personnes de la Trinité.
    Dès que la porte s'ouvre, c'est un essaim qui s'échappe avec des cris perçants
    Et même quand on croit que tout est parti et que mères et nourrices chacune ont emmené leurs contingents,
    Tout à coup c'est une voix qui caresse et qui gronde et l'on voit au premier étage
    La figure du tout petit que l'on vient de laver et qui apparaît derrière la vitre comme un fromage.

(*Œuvre poétique*, pp. 607-608)

Il vole sur ses pieds ailés, chassant la terre d'un
orteil impétueux,
Et les vierges qui le regardent du haut de la colline
voient deux nuages de poussière tour-à-tour s'élever
sous ses sandales!
Et qu'il est beau, le fiancé, quand enfin, à ce
tournant du Rhône,
Il apparaît, le premier parmi la troupe équestre
de ses frères,
Lui entre tous les jeunes gens de son âge le plus grand
et le plus beau, vêtu d'armes qui jettent l'éclair!
Ah, qu'il la prenne déracinée et perdant l'âme
entre ses bras,
Comme une grande urne pleine d'un vin sans prix
que l'on met debout pour la table d'un dieu, oscillant
sur sa pointe aiguë![38]

We see, then, that this early jotting led directly into the
pattern of physical desire and its spiritual meaning as
worked out from one end to the other of *La Cantate*, pro-
viding also the vocabulary for an especially vigorous de-
velopment that is based on legendary images. For Claudel,
the Christian cantata will subsume the shades of the pagan
past: "Hostel, pressoir et autel, lieu de libation et d'aus-
pices, / Dont indice sous mon pied cette pierre qui sort de
la terre, / Montrant le taureau Phrygien et le couteau du
sacrifice."[39] A consequence of this background is that the
present can be envisaged with fresh detail. The women
now raise their voices in song (whereas the final version
bears their dialogue from the start). Yet they are not
described or defined in any external way, but only gradu-
ally recognized for what they are. Lacking individual out-
lines, they become the very personification of joy: Fausta's

[38] *Œuvre poétique*, pp. 331-332.
[39] *Ibid.*, pp. 330-331. In a pagan framework the Christian meaning
is formed; similarly, in these lines from the journal for 1911: "Le sol
de la forêt couvert de feuilles mortes, origine de la mosaïque. La
figure du Christ se dessinant sur l'automne païen, sur l'immense
jonchée de la forêt païenne."

hope and desire, Laeta's patience and persistence, Beata's renunciation. Such are the divisions that we know without being told and that are more real to us than any fact or fiction—"plus réelles qu'aucune."

Claudel thinks of them in terms of the metaphorical structure, in which shadow is not chill but glowing and the counterpart of grain, in the same way as the Egyptian Beata corresponds to her blond and redheaded companions. She is necessary to the fullness of music, just as darkness allows the true face of things to appear. The word "sarrazin" conjures up the Orient of the Crusades, which must participate in the same conversion. As Beata says in the last recitative, the "Cantique de l'Ombre":

> Jadis au bord de ce fleuve d'Egypte, en ce temps
> de nos noces,
> En ces jours d'un temps étrange et plus long que
> les dieux nous ont comptés et mesurés,
> Tu me disais: "O visage dans les ténèbres! double
> et funèbre iris!
> Laisse-moi regarder tes yeux! Laisse-moi lire ces choses
> qui se peignent sur le mur de ton âme et que toi-même
> ne connais pas!
> Est-il vrai que je vais mourir? dis, ne suis-je donc autre
> chose que cette présence précaire et misérable? est-ce
> dans le temps que je t'ai épousée?
> Trois fois le papillon blanc n'aura pas palpité dans
> le rayon de cette lune Sarrazine
> Que déjà je me suis dispersé!
> Ne suis-je pas autre chose que cette main que tu
> veux saisir et ce poids un instant sur ta couche?
> La nuit passe, le jour revient, Beata!"
> Et je répondais: "Qu'importe le jour? Eteins cette
> lumière!
> Eteins promptement cette lumière qui ne me permet
> de voir que ton visage!"[40]

[40] *Œuvre poétique*, p. 364.

This is the moment—"nuit délicieuse et courte"—that betokens the true light of vision. In the published version it will bathe the poem from beginning to end like the imagery of water in *Le Soulier de satin*.[41]

We may refer by way of conclusion to two lines found in the same manuscript which we have yet to discuss: "Toutes ensemble en une composition spirituelle"; and "Je ne veux pas qu'une chose à la fois." They express the dual ambition of the poet, on the one hand to attune the chorus of three voices, on the other to end his poem self-consciously, like an ode, with an affirmation of the need for correspondence and complementarity, since nothing can exist alone. For him the notion of unity was the foundation of knowledge: "Vraiment le bleu connaît la couleur d'orange, vraiment la main son ombre sur le mur, vraiment et réellement l'angle d'un triangle connaît les deux autres au même sens qu'Isaac a connu Rébecca. Toute chose qui est, de toutes parts, désigne cela sans quoi elle n'aurait pu être."[42] Hence the virtue of a long poem is to enable us to feel, as no short piece could, the proportion of details to the mass, the relevance and the very necessity of parts to a whole. How can we fail to be impressed in *La Cantate* by the breadth of the conception, which comprises over eleven hundred lines of text, some nine thousand words? But the poem has also been planned with exquisite care. It is composed of ten hymns spoken in turn by the three voices of spiritual happiness, together with ten corresponding preludes in which questions find answers, tensions a resolution, as between the left and right hands of a pianist. We attend to a temporal development, from darkness to the approach of dawn as in the night-course of the breviary; at the same time we

---

[41] The Jesuit father of the first scene establishes the frame of the dramatic action: "cette puissance immanquable sous moi qui me reprend et me remonte avec elle comme si pour un moment je ne faisais plus qu'un avec le réjouissement de l'abîme, / Cette vague, voici la dernière pour m'emporter" (*Le Soulier de satin*, first version, *Œuvres complètes*, XII, 13).

[42] "Traité de la co-naissance au monde et de soi-même," *Œuvre poétique*, p. 150.

follow allusively the progress of love, which starts with the
meeting of the rose and the Rhone, the enclosed form of
virginity and the turbulent force that descends into the val-
leys—"Lui, le Violent, avec une souveraine délicatesse
épousant la pente la plus insensible[. . .]. Salut, Rhône,
buveur de la terre et aspirateur de cette rose immense
autour de toi et le trait irrésistible qui donne à tout son
sens!"[43] Then in the "Cantique de la Vigne" comes the
flame which is the sequel to desire, the passion that takes
away judgment and reason: "Ah, s'il méprise la grappe, il
ne fallait pas planter la vigne, et qui méprise le calice, il
ne fallait pas planter la joie!"[44] But solitude follows: the
"Cantique du Peuple divisé" is the tender hymn of exile
and longing, the expectation of reunion, like Poland which
stands at a point where Europe is rent into three parts and
awaits the harvest. Love knows the strains of distance,
which teach it to sing the "Cantique de la Chambre
intérieure," recognizing the purification that is wrought
from sacrifice in the secret places of the heart, the end
that is served: "Car ce n'est aucune molle complaisance
qui nous unit et l'étreinte d'une minute seule, / Mais
la force qui attache la pierre à sa base et la nécessité
pure et simple sans aucune douceur."[45] Now it is mid-
night and the procession of clouds passing across the
sky is a new moment of joy that Laeta takes up: instead
of nostalgia and separation she can exult in the vision
of newlyweds who set out across the shimmering Rhine
on barges laden with hay; the clouds, like the barges, are
the image of the grace that surrounds the lovers: "Pas de
fenêtre si close qu'elle suffise à défendre le dormeur contre
le lait extérieur et contre le temple allumé, / Et de miroir
si absorbé qu'il n'en rétorque un rayon!"[46] It is no longer
the time for looking to the past but to the future, as Fausta
thinks of reunion, the ripening wheat, the sky that changes
from red to changeless gold: "Tout ce qui était de la nuit

[43] *Œuvre poétique*, p. 333.
[44] *Ibid.*, p. 338.   [45] *Ibid.*, p. 345.   [46] *Ibid.*, p. 350.

en moi est devenu comme de l'or."[47] Yet physical reunion
is not enough: Fausta sings of the hard heart that must not
be deceived by false appearances and passing pleasures.
Desire must not be stilled, for it is synonymous with the
soul itself: "Et si le désir devait cesser avec Dieu, / Ah, je
l'envierais à l'Enfer!"[48] The future is at hand, but it offers
our death, and the death of what we love. For Beata this
is not saddening but a further subject for gratitude, as she
sings in the "Cantique des Parfums." Death it is that shows
the essence of love: "Il fallait que celui que j'aime mourût,
/ Afin que notre amour ne fût plus soumis à la mort, / Et que
son cœur devînt respirable à la mienne."[49] The poem can
conclude once again with the words of the widow Beata,
as she describes in the "Cantique de l'Ombre" the precari-
ous moment when night and day touch, like life and death.
This death is a beginning, this shipwreck a homecoming:
"Ah! pas plus moëlleusement une vieille nef au piège de
quelque Célèbe n'épousera la borne occulte sous la mer
/ Que toute mon âme d'avance ne se prête à ce choc
ténébreux!"[50] So the movement has led us from the virgin
flower to transcendence of the self in the same way as one
body ends where another begins, or a single voice in the
night is echoed and developed by those that compose the
harmony.

However, playing across this temporal development are
other lines of internal coherence. There is, for instance,
an evident pattern of departure and return, so that the last
hymn points toward the first and thereby completes the
curve. The haven of consummation is that same lake from

---

[47] *Ibid.*, p. 352. Cf. *Le Jet de pierre* (composed in 1938, published
in 1949), which refers to *La Cantate*:
 . . . tout le milieu de ce livre où tu viens de picorer quelques
grains
 Est plein de blé, de cet or sacramentel que l'on voit à travers les
branches
 Jaunir et blanchir et onduler au loin comme la mer sous les
rayons de la lune!
 (*Œuvres complètes*, XIV, 194-195)
[48] *Œuvre poétique*, p. 356.
[49] *Ibid.*, pp. 359-360.   [50] *Ibid.*, p. 364.

which Laeta was first carried forth by the Rhone; and—
"O visage dans les ténèbres!"—the image of the soul which
Beata turns to her lover is the self-same immaterial flower
of the "Cantique de la Rose": "O paradis dans les ténè-
bres!"[51] Similarly, a strong parallelism is established be-
tween the fifth and last hymns, the "Cantique de la Cham-
bre intérieure" and the "Cantique de l'Ombre," which shows
that the inner chamber of tenderness is not a prison, but a
point of time in the ceaseless river that opens out onto the
ocean. "Et je vois de mes yeux ma prison qui coule et qui
s'en va!/ Je suis l'hôte de ce fleuve ininterrompu."[52] Thus
the plot has shape and elegance. Yet I should like to direct
attention briefly to a further plane of meaning, by which
Claudel indicates the total scale of the whole that the parts
form. Within the poem the ten preludes and hymns are like
the ten white paths that surround Hostel ("Dix routes
blanches, phosphorescentes, qui reparaissent et se nouent
et disparaissent et serpentent");[53] in particular they recall
the systole and diastole of the heart as it ceaselessly pur-
sues its basic count and recognizes the goal it has sought
("Comme cette fleur, la même! qu'on reconnaît, chaque fois

---

[51] Claudel echoes, and at the same time gives new resonance to,
the last line of Mallarmé's "Surgi de la croupe et du bond . . .":

> Le pur baiser d'aucun breuvage
> Que l'inexhaustible veuvage
> Agonise mais ne consent,
>
> Naïf baiser des plus funèbres!
> A rien expirer annonçant
> Une rose dans les ténèbres.

Claudel himself remarked on the correspondence between the two
sections when he spoke of Beata's last hymn in his lecture delivered
in 1915 at the Université des Annales and later reproduced in the
Journal de l'Université des Annales, cited in note 8: "et chaque nuit,
en attendant la nuit suprême, en attendant ce choc sourd et ténébreux
qui annonce à notre barque humaine qu'elle a enfin atteint le port—
*ce port de béatitude d'où, jadis, le Rhône impétueux fit sortir sa sœur
Laeta*—chaque nuit, l'ombre qui est commune aux vivants et aux
morts lui rend celui qu'elle aime" (italics mine).

[52] *Œuvre poétique*, p. 363.

[53] *Ibid.*, p. 330.

que le cœur a battu dix fois!").[54] Claudel was far from being averse to numerical symbolism, and its effects are constantly written into his work. As for the figure ten, it has special appropriateness in *La Cantate* in that it denotes the gamut of absence which, once complete, lets us perceive the nature of spiritual plenty.

> Chaque fois qu'en comptant nous arrivons à dix, il intervient un vide, un blanc, un zéro, et nous avons toute la série à recommencer: le zéro est une ligne fermée qui revient, indéfiniment sur elle-même [. . .]. C'est une coupe vide que nous tenons, c'est une bouche qui s'ouvre pour respirer, c'est le commandement unique en qui tout vient s'engloutir.[55]

One thing at a time is not enough: the three graces must proceed to the full count, tell the extent of sacrifice, before the heart can be rewarded. Like the poet, they know our vital need for music: "Je ne veux pas qu'une chose à la fois."

IN HIS lively dialogue "Jules ou l'homme-aux-deux-cravates," which is a companion piece to "Le Poète et le shamisen," Claudel makes an amusing but revelatory statement about the way poetry comes to be written: "Si vous voulez mon avis, je vous dirai que les poèmes se font à peu près comme les canons. On prend un trou et on met quelque chose autour."[56] There can be no question of building a poem step by step as one builds a house, but of determining by approximations, by the indirections of music, the relationship between the poet himself and an idea, an

---

[54] *Ibid.*, p. 360. The image is prepared twenty-four verses ahead in the same "Cantique des Parfums" by a parenthesis: "(Chaque fois que le cœur a battu dix fois)."

[55] "Au milieu des vitraux de l'Apocalypse," *Œuvres complètes*, XXVI, 102. Cf. *ibid.*, p. 101: "X c'est deux unités qui se traversent, c'est deux bâtons inclinés l'un vers l'autre qui se multiplient en se raturant réciproquement. C'est tout à fait comme zéro qui est à la fois le signe de rien et celui de la multiplication, de l'unité qui se désintègre en s'élargissant quand elle atteint un certain terme."

[56] *Œuvres en prose*, p. 848.

absence, an abyss. In *La Cantate* the "hole" is the absent
lover, around which each of the speakers describes her
separateness and yet comes to know the truth of her own
Latin name, which denies gloom, discovering at the very
moment of apparent pathos the reality of happiness—*"le
bonheur dans le moment."*[57] It is clear, then, that the
manuscript around which we have centered our remarks
contains in limited compass much of the future poem. If
Claudel had still to eliminate the statements of intention
that frame these lines, he had foreshadowed his program
of poetic action, the principal metaphors, the dialogue of
three female voices, the concept of a spiritual and artistic
composition. The process of writing had yet to come and
would involve considerable work in a period which was
among his calmest and most fertile.

We possess several drafts that show the quantity of
preparation required as the plan developed by separate jot-
tings that relate to details of space and time and allow the
allegorical meaning to unravel of its own accord. The ma-
terial, some of it on odd pieces of paper such as a bill for
"Belgischkuchen" from a Prague pastrycook, was carefully
preserved by the poet; and although he did not replace his
papers in chronological order, it is possible to distinguish
the early drafts from the later and the likely line of growth.
They fall into three main categories. First, the "arguments"
of the different parts offer a spare wording that leads us
into the complex structure to follow. One constant concern
was to establish the elements of harmony, the comple-
mentary details that would form the basis of the poem, as
Claudel emphasized in these lines from the original draft
of the "Cantique de la Rose": "empêcher de passer par la
présence des complémentaires. Le lac. La rose fermée sur
elle-même. L'odeur qui empêche de mourir. La femme com-
plète"; and again: "les sépales resserrés—comme l'éternité.

[57] Cf. letter of 14 February 1912 to Gabriel Frizeau: "Je travaille
toujours à ma *Cantate* ayant pour sujet *le bonheur dans le moment*.
C'est assez difficile" (*Correspondance Claudel-Jammes-Frizeau*, p.
243).

/ Ainsi ni commencement ni fin dans le cercle parfait de nos délices. / Où manque la rose, là est le fruit. / Dieu enfermé dans le paradis de nos délices."[58] Here, as it were, is the hymn's topography, the images that will succeed one another and yet remain the same—lake, rose, perfume, woman, paradise—thereby giving us the pleasure of discovering echoes that are like the strands of an intellectual and symbolic network. On other occasions it is the argument that preoccupies Claudel, as he seeks to show evolving attitudes against the background of nature and time. An admirable case is to be found on a draft in which the final resolution was pursued, the speaker's words coinciding with daybreak: "Il faut que le jour me montre cela cela et cela encore pour que j'y renonce. L'ironie. Le passage va recommencer. Cela donc et cela et cela aussi va être détaché de moi. Certitude délicieuse que je suis en marche. Si tout cela est écarté de moi, c'est donc que je suis réservé pour quelque chose de supérieur. / Etonnement—Suspens. Eveil. / Elle voit que le monde recommence à se passer d'elle et elle à se passer du monde."[59] Claudel enters into the dialectics of the image of waking: with dawn, when the things that night encompassed are divided from one another just as the self is divided from the world, the poet finds a lesson of detachment, so that temporal movement comes to suggest to him a movement beyond time, the very experience of transcendence. One needs to add that this particular fragment was not adopted without major modifications in the "Cantique de l'Ombre," but it is nevertheless typical of the way Claudel sketched out the patterns of thought, conceiving the various levels of his poem in schematic terms before putting them to verse.

In a second series of manuscripts the original version of the individual sections strikes us by the power and authority of a language that is found without arduous effort or an elaborate progression word by word. One observes hesitations and revisions, insertions and deletions, but as a rule

[58] Previously unpublished.
[59] Previously unpublished.

the manuscripts are surprisingly close to the definitive reading. Nothing, for instance, could be further from Valéry at work, who brought sound and sense tirelessly into question and held no line inviolate.

The third and final set of manuscripts presents the complete version that was sent to Jacques Doucet in 1919 for inclusion in his private library of documents of contemporary literature. It consists of forty-two pages written on both sides of unlined paper, together with a title page which is disposed in the following way:

Cette heure

qui est entre le printemps et l'été . . .

Cantate

à trois voix

The reading is that of the 1913 edition, although several times the corrections show that words attributed to a certain speaker have now been given by the poet to one or other of her sisters. It also contains variants of punctuation and phrasing, but of a relatively minor nature. In an accompanying letter Claudel observed that he had lately recovered these papers after the long war years: "Le MS. était resté à Hambourg dans un bureau qui vient seulement de m'être envoyé (avril 1919)."[60]

Now, in regard to these versions, I should like to delve some small way further into the detailed processes of Claudel's composition by taking a particular section of *La Cantate*. At the center of the poem is the "Cantique de la Chambre intérieure," which provides us with a striking example of his art. It contains the night of shadow before the golden harvest, when Fausta pronounces the words of sacrifice and expectation, absence and presence. Her eyes are closed in the sleep that abolishes distance and allows her to hear the secret reasons of the heart:

LAETA

Dis-nous, Fausta, le sommeil,

[60] I wish to thank the librarian of the Fonds Doucet, Monsieur François Chapon, for his generous assistance.

BEATA
La patience du cœur qui veille.

These lines, and the hymn she utters (which is referred to, in a parenthesis of the original draft, as the "Cantique du sommeil"), may be considered in the light of a verse from the Song of Solomon: "Ego dormio et cor meum vigilat." Claudel's own gloss of the same line as he translates these words into spiritual terms is no doubt pertinent to our reading: "Le sommeil est ce moment où notre cause est seule à l'œuvre sur nous, où nous lui avons laissé toute la place, où une certaine ligature est imposée à notre résistance"; and again: "Quel que soit notre degré d'expergescence, il y a en nous quelqu'un qui ne cesse d'étudier le Créateur et de fournir à sa présence le synchronisme de son battement."[61] Despite her closed eyes and physical isolation Fausta communes with her husband in the very way the soul communes with God.

The final version comprises forty-two verses and is thus of similar length to the nine other hymns (the shortest has twenty-nine, the longest fifty-four). It would seem to have its origin as a separate poem in a manuscript that teases out elements of metaphor and structure.

La Chambre intérieure   *L'Ombre*
La nuit imitée par l'ombre de ce qui est enfermé.
Ce qui est enfermé, ce qui n'ouvre point d'accès.
Les choses accrues, possédées, économisées,
emmagasinées
De même les gens qui dorment: mouvement vers
l'intérieur: on se retire.
Nuit à l'intérieur de la nuit, il faut la nuit en
nous pour comprendre la nuit
Les grandes *résolutions* de la nuit
Le *sommeil* (Cantique du sommeil).
Passive, cédante, abandonnée comme à l'eau,
entièrement pénétrée.

[61] "Le Cantique des Cantiques," *Œuvres complètes*, XXII, 59 and 61. The rare word "expergescence" describes the action of awakening.

174

> Les choses solennelles dans la nuit, comme *mises*
> *là*, disposées, préparées pour la cérémonie.
> Enveloppées comme des vases.
> Des oracles à toi seul donnés.
> Le solstice, un autre versant, quelque chose en nous
> qui tourne.
>
> *Dialogue*

> Tout est réservé, tout est rangé, mis en ordre.
> Le domaine de soi-seul où nul ne pénètre.
> *L'attente*—la pensée.
> La nuit il n'y a plus de séparation entre les
> âmes, elles sont toutes dans leur chambre.
> La nuit efface ce qui n'est pas nous, ce qui
> n'est pas notre amour.
> J'ai un moyen—Il est quelque part.[62]

With reference to the first section of the draft, only a few words will be adopted in the final version ("accès," "bruit," "retirer," "ombre," "ouvrir," and "sommeil," at the end of the preceding dialogue). It may, then, seem to offer a mere accumulation of disconnected notes, but, as we examine it more closely, we already find several traits of the definitive hymn. For one thing, we observe that from the first line a link is made between this fragment and the "Cantique de l'Ombre," which suggests the importance Claudel ascribed to establishing the balance of the various parts. (Similar cases are to be encountered in his other manuscripts.) A second characteristic is Claudel's emphasis on the notion of closedness—storehouse ("les choses accrues, possédées, économisées, emmagasinées"), home ("mouvement vers l'intérieur: on se retire"), sleep ("nuit à l'intérieur de la nuit")—which is defined here with some apparent ingenuousness by way of a negative formulation: "ce qui n'ouvre point d'accès." It is relevant to observe that the tension between "fermer" and "ouvrir" is at the heart of the final

[62] Previously unpublished.

175

version, as when Fausta speaks of "cette chambre qu'à lui-même il ne faut pas ouvrir, / De peur que je ne lui cède!" and exclaims: "Qu'il ne me rende point la défense trop difficile, / S'il ne veut que je lui ouvre cette porte fatale qui ne permet point le retour!" Thirdly, it becomes clear that the basic idea around which the draft turns, and which will likewise dominate the hymn, is that of knowledge obtained ("il faut la nuit en nous pour comprendre la nuit") and harmony achieved ("les grandes *résolutions* de la nuit"), as of one chord *resolved* into another. A hidden correspondence is revealed between the night of sacrifice within and visible grace without, so that renunciation becomes the condition of plenitude. The second half of the fragment pursues this motif with reference to water imagery, which will be taken up not in "La Chambre intérieure" but in "L'Ombre" ("Avant que la nuit de nouveau nous abandonne, pleine de ceux qui nous sont chers, / Et que cessant de remplir nos demeures, elle reflue de nouveau et nous quitte comme une terre dont l'eau s'exprime!").[63] Thus the soul bathes in sleep, while the diverse facets of nature have become instruments for the performance of a solemn ceremony. Just as the soul is "penetrated" by spiritual waters, so objects resemble vases that are bathed both within and without by air ("enveloppées comme des vases"). Inanimate no longer, they bear witness to the presence of the gods, proffering a truth that strikes the soul in a deeply personal way ("des oracles à toi seul donnés"). Thus the passage conveys the growing invasion of night, and concludes on a precise allusion to the summer solstice, which, like midnight, reveals another slope of time that parallels the transformation of the self.

After these lines a note indicates that the dialogue was to be introduced, and it would seem that Claudel may first have thought of his hymn as ending at this point; however, the fragment that follows contains an essential part of the argument which introduces key words such as "réservé" (Fausta will say: "Ah, du moins qu'il m'épargne! qu'il ne

---

[63] *Œuvre poétique*, p. 363.

sollicite point cette part de mon âme la plus réservée"),
"mis en ordre" ("A quoi tous ces fruits de la terre, si je
n'étais ici au milieu qui tiens la huche, et le moulin, et le
pressoir? et qui ordonne tout"), "domaine" ("A quoi tout
ce domaine"), pensée ("Et je ne sais s'il m'aime, ses des-
seins me sont inconnus et l'accès de sa pensée m'est in-
terdit"), and "chambre" ("Cette chambre qu'à lui-même il
ne faut pas ouvrir / De peur que je ne lui cède!"). It becomes
evident that Claudel has developed a fertile concept in
which the soul is able to affirm the ordered containment
of all things. Objects perform their designated roles in a
universe that is one and complete (as Coventry Patmore
had helped Claudel to see, and as he later expressed in
"La Maison fermée");[64] similarly, the self has a closed
domain of its own, its retreat, its sanctuary of inner medi-
tation. Although Fausta is alone and separated from events,
her lover is as present as thought. She has found a way
("un moyen") of being with him, of overcoming space
and time, for she knows that he exists *somewhere*. What
need has she to have him with her, to trace his every move?
Her conviction, like that of the soul with respect to its Divine
Lover, is enough: "Il est quelque part."

The manuscript gives us, then, much that will come to
occupy a place in the hymn, but it required Claudel's con-
trol of dramatic language and meter and his architectonic
skill to bring these jottings to fruition. If we examine the
subsequent drafts we are surprised to find that they show
little variation from the definitive version and that the poet

---

[64] Cf. letter of 28 January 1908 to Jacques Rivière, written at the
time of composing "La Maison fermée": "Cette idée d'un monde fini
et fermé, d'une terre seule habitée par des êtres vivants et intelli-
gents, que j'ai trouvée dans Coventry Patmore et qui m'a été con-
firmée scientifiquement par Wallace, est pour moi une sorte de
lumière [. . .]. Le ciel est une extase mathématique, et l'infini qui
n'est que l'imparfait n'y a aucune place" (*Correspondance Jacques
Rivière-Paul Claudel* [Paris: Plon, 1926], pp. 129-130). The influence
of Patmore on Claudel has been studied by Alexandre Maurocordato,
Anglo-American Influences in Paul Claudel (Geneva: Droz, 1963)
and Marius-François Guyard, *Recherches claudéliennes* (Paris:
Klincksieck, 1963).

appears to have proceeded in one giant leap from plain argument to the splendor of poetic expression.

Were there any intermediate steps which would have shown a hesitant quest for the right words? Probably not, if we can judge from other cases. Yet one major development must have occurred, which, if we find no trace of it in the extant papers, is clearly written into the hymn. I refer to the architecture of the section that the fragments quoted above do not elaborate. For Fausta's recitative, despite its emotional force, is most economically composed. Indeed, it might well appear to be over-simple, were it not that we are so deeply moved. It consists of four parts that unfold the line of discourse in dynamic manner and with admirable effect. Thus in the first lines Fausta affirms that her husband is not absent but near:

> C'est en vain que la distance et le sort nous divisent!
> Je n'ai qu'à rentrer dans mon cœur pour être avec lui
> et qu'à fermer les yeux
> Pour cesser d'être en ce lieu où il n'est pas.
> Cette liberté du moins, je la lui ai retirée, et il ne
> dépend pas de lui de ne pas être avec moi.[65]

"For faith," says St. Paul, "is the substance of things hoped for, the evidence of things not seen." Fausta rejects appearances and fixes her gaze on a reality beyond. By her very words of denial ("C'est en vain") she calls up an absence that is meaningful, a space that contains a response in the same way as Mallarmé's faun causes ordinary objects to vanish into the "sonore, vaine et monotone ligne" of ideal beauty. Claudel's two lovers are separated by distance and fate; but the first part of the poem has shown, and the second will continue to suggest, that it is in the moment of emptiness, this division of spring from summer, night from day, lover from lover, that time is vanquished and distance overcome. Fausta's utterance is especially energetic as she turns away from the world to her own heart, from

---

[65] *Œuvre poétique*, p. 344.

sight to inner vision. She uses simple words of emotion, not straining after seductive metaphor, reducing all things to the universal "he" and "I" of a direct confrontation. Her syntax offers a series of negatives ("où il n'est pas," "ne dépend pas," "ne pas être") and virtual negatives ("en vain," "je n'ai qu'à," "cesser d'être") which indicate her resoluteness; while the predominance of masculine endings, in the protasis as well as in the apodosis, translates acoustically the confidence of her secret knowledge.

> Et je ne sais s'il m'aime, ses desseins me sont inconnus et l'accès de sa pensée m'est interdit.
> Mais je sais qu'il ne peut se passer de moi.
> Il voyage, et je suis ici. Et où qu'il aille, c'est moi qui lui donne à manger et qui lui permet de vivre!
> Et à quoi, si je n'étais ici, lui serviraient ces moissons autour de nous?
> A quoi tous ces fruits de la terre, si je n'étais ici au milieu qui tiens la huche, et le moulin, et le pressoir? et qui ordonne tout.
> A quoi tout ce domaine,
> S'il n'y avait de toutes parts, par où descendent les chars de foin et, l'hiver, les longs sapins branlants attelés de deux paires de bœufs,
> L'*Alba Via* et les chemins qui conduisent vers la maison?
> S'il n'était loin de moi, si je n'étais loin de mon époux ici, administrant ces biens,
> Le besoin qu'il a de moi ne serait pas aussi grand.
> Car ce n'est aucune molle complaisance qui nous unit et l'étreinte d'une minute seule,
> Mais la force qui attache la pierre à sa base et la nécessité pure et simple sans aucune douceur.

The construction "Et je ne sais. . . . / Mais je sais" marks the transition to a new section that develops the visionary nature of Fausta's hymn. (While "je sais" is found only nine times in the rest of *La Cantate*, it occurs six times in this short sequence, thereby giving special emphasis to her song of faith.) The passage does not merely repeat or prolong

the thought of the opening lines, but provides a comple-
mentary movement in which Fausta describes her hus-
band's inability to escape from the bonds of love. She it is
who gives him the food he requires, an inexhaustible nour-
ishment—"ce qui nourrit le corps à l'âme," of which we
already know from the "Cantique de la Vigne" that it is
not "chose désaltérante";[66] who tends the farm and decides
on everything in the appropriate season; who stands at
the center like the house toward which all paths descend.
In the last four lines the images of food, administrative
order, and home are expressed as "le besoin," "la force,"
"la nécessité," with growing strength. The section thus
possesses a structural coherence, placing the concrete be-
side the abstract, extracting principle from image. It also
takes on particular resonance by the use that is made of
allusions that have already occurred in the poem, such as
"*Alba Via*," which echoes a line of the second dialogue ("en
ce lieu! / D'où l'on découvre l'*Alba Via* et le vaste creux /
Où s'embranchent six vallées comme les rais sur le moyeu");
"pressoir" and "pierre," also found in the second dialogue
("Hostel, pressoir et autel, lieu de libation et d'auspices /
Dont indice sous mon pied cette pierre qui sort de la
terre"); "complaisance," in the "Cantique du Cœur dur"
("Et sache que je ne veux pas même de ta présence, / Si
elle doit m'arrêter sur moi-même! / Et de ta complaisance
si elle est une limite / A ma fuite hors de cette personne
détestée!"); "nécessité," already praised in the third dia-
logue by Beata ("Bienheureuse nécessité!").

> Et je sais qu'il est là tout à l'heure.
> Mais que m'importent ce visage fermé, et ce sourire
> ambigu, et ce cœur qui ne se livre pas!
> Et moi, est-ce que je lui livre le mien?
> Nous ne fîmes pas ces conditions, le jour de nos
> épousailles.
> Qu'il garde son secret, et moi je garde le mien.

[66] *Ibid.*, p. 339.

Ah, s'il m'ouvrait son cœur, voudrais-je le laisser
partir encor?
    Et si je lui ouvrais le mien, s'il connaissait cette place
qu'il a avec moi,
        Il ne me quitterait point de nouveau!
        Dieu m'a posée sa gardienne,
        Moi qui suis faite pour l'aider, vais-je être son entrave?
        Moi qui suis faite pour être son port, et son arsenal,
et sa tour,
        Vais-je être sa prison? vais-je trahir la patrie?
        La force qui lui reste, vais-je la lui retirer?
        Ah, du moins qu'il m'épargne! qu'il ne sollicite point
cette part de mon âme la plus réservée,
        Cette chambre qu'à lui-même il ne faut pas ouvrir,
        De peur que je ne lui cède!
        Qu'il ne me rende point la défense trop difficile,
        S'il ne veut que je lui ouvre cette porte fatale qui ne
permet point le retour!
        Qu'il ne me demande point trop à la fois,
        S'il veut que la moisson devienne de l'or!
        Qu'il ne vienne pas à moi comme dans les songes
avec cet étrange sourire!

In a new section which begins once more with the phrase
"je sais," Fausta turns from the present to the future, as she
thinks of the day when her husband will return. At that
time physical distance will have been overcome and she
will have to guard against another danger: the heart, the
inner chamber that allows her to be at one with him she
loves, must not be violated and occupied, allowing her hus-
band to content himself with a body that would be his
prison. She will not therefore reproach him with being
"close" or refusing to surrender himself wholly. No, both
of them must protect their hidden treasure, accepting "ce
visage fermé, et ce sourire ambigu, et ce cœur qui ne se
livre pas." We may observe that the word "sourire" is used
five times in *La Cantate* to refer to Fausta's husband: in "ce
sourire lentement sur ses lèvres, terrible à voir!" ("Cantique
du Peuple divisé"), "cet austère sourire qui nie la défaite

et refuse la compassion," "ce sourire étrange et ce visage composé" ("Cantique du Cœur dur"), and twice in these lines. Even more significant, perhaps, is the epithet "ambigu," which refers to the interval between two attitudes, as between two seasons, that discovers a potential unexpected richness. Fausta is pointing to the moment of temptation which is also that of her greatest renunciation: another duty is higher, that which she and her husband owe their country. As Claudel wrote: "Tous deux appartiennent à la patrie. Elle doit se montrer avare d'une tendresse qui pourrait le détourner de sa tâche héroïque, et lui, de même, lui montrant son amour, ne doit point lui ôter ce courage qu'elle s'est imposée."[67] The word "patrie," found eleven times in *La Cantate*, denotes the fatherland but also heaven, our lives being a long exile and patient fidelity.

> Ah, qui me rendra la patrie, et cette mer de blé
> obscurément, plus paisible que la soie, qui déferlait
> à mes pieds dans la nuit de juillet vague à vague![68]

These twenty-one verses, which form the longest section of the hymn, have then a striking dramatic force as they develop the notion of sacrifice in three stages (lines 1-5, 6-13, 14-21) and conclude as they began, with an allusion to the smile of inwardness, desirable yet readily endangered.

> Ah, je sais que cette nuit nous trompe et le jour
> reviendra encore!
> Et quand je rêve, je sais que c'est un rêve et que je suis
> dans ses bras cette colonne vivante et voilée qu'on
> étreint comme un candélabre de deuil!
> Que je serve, c'est assez. Je sais qu'un jour je m'éveil-
> lerai entre ses bras!
> Maintenant je dors et si j'ouvre les yeux une seconde,
> Je ne vois autour de moi que de l'or et de tous côtés
> la couleur de la moisson!

[67] Note by Claudel on the "Cantique de la Chambre intérieure," quoted by Jacques Petit in the *Œuvre poétique* of Paul Claudel (rev. edn., 1967), p. 1088.
[68] *Œuvre poétique*, p. 341.

With a new affirmation of faith ("Ah! je sais") the last five verses revert to the visionary tone with which the hymn began, expressing Fausta's belief in the final consummation of desire. Beyond immediate sacrifice lies an abundant light; beyond death, an awakening. The images in the first line form a simple contrast, the syntax of which, by the irregular omission of "que" before "le jour," translates the vigor of Fausta's exclamation. As for the two verses that follow, they convey in a most beautiful manner the meeting of life and death, of mourning under the sign of Christian solemnity and resurrection. Aware that she is asleep— just as in certain exceptional states of second sight—and confident that she will awaken to the fullness of day, Fausta gives voice to her dream. But this dream of the future is already apprehended in the same way that daylight is sensed in night, presence in the midst of absence, eternity in the fugitive moment. The last lines resume the dialectic of time present and time future that is written into the four sections and indicate that happiness assuredly accompanies solitude and sacrifice. The future that Fausta is preparing exists; the harvest of corn that will come is even now golden. She can rejoice, despite the pains of separation, in the paradoxical experience of waiting for that which has been found, contributing to a composition which will be "decomposed" in the absolute harmony: "Le temps est le moyen offert à tout ce qui sera d'être afin de n'être plus. Il est l'*Invitation à mourir*, à toute phrase de se décomposer dans l'accord explicatif et total, de consommer la parole d'adoration à l'oreille de *Sigè* l'Abîme."[69] Claudel can end the recitative on two lines which bring together present and future, sleep and vision, inner austerity and external ripeness. The two caesuras are clearly marked, the rhythms balanced ($5 + 10 / 10 + 5 + 7$), while the sounds echo one

[69] "Art poétique," *Œuvre poétique*, p. 145. One commentator on *La Cantate* writes: "La gamme d'images et de symboles se rapporte à une expérience si occulte qu'afin de la comprendre il faut s'assimiler tout le système spirituel du poète; et l'on ne s'interpose pas sans difficulté dans ce dialogue entre des voix familières" (Alexandre Maurocordato, *L'Ode de Paul Claudel* [Geneva: Droz, 1955], p. 17).

another in a resolution that is symbolic of the meaning of the whole poem (we note in particular the complementarity of "dors" and "de l'or," "j'ouvre les yeux" and "couleur," "une seconde" and "la moisson"). At the same time, the contrast between brevity and breadth of vision underlines the dramatic transfiguration.

Thus Claudel's hymn offers the poetic composition of faith, establishing from the start an elevated tone by the rejection of evidence, maintaining by the use of repetitions, parallelisms, exclamations, and questions a constantly dynamic diction. Yet the four movements are adjusted so as to contain a dialectic that leads us from absence which the heart and an inner necessity transcend to presence which must be tempered by patience and restraint, and finally to an ideal tenderness which is the fruit of aspiration, necessity, sacrifice. Against the background of night the words Fausta pronounces strike us by their sumptuous power, which recalls to us the comment made by Stéphane Mallarmé on *Tête d'or*: "J'admire comme cela sourd et la force du jet!"[70] Yet the overall structure stood, as well as the technique by which all things would be treated as symbolic, delicately finding their reflections on different levels, the simplest anticipating the more obscure, in a subtle interplay of the paradoxes of desire. So the hymn grew, just as *La Cantate* developed, in a way Valéry later described, as we saw in the previous chapter, with wonderful precision: "Il cherche une très forte naïveté qui permet le symbolisme et dessine une composition."[71] In the exchange between composition and naïveté, idea and image, an inclusive pattern and exultant expression, Claudel converted the drama of absence into his poem of love fulfilled.

[70] Letter of March 1893 to Paul Claudel, *Cahiers Paul Claudel I* (Paris: Gallimard, 1959), p. 41.
[71] Valéry, *Œuvres*, I, 61.

Chapter VI

Valéry's "Pureté"

I N A BRILLIANT passage of self-appraisal we find Valéry writing shortly after the First World War: "Je pense en rationaliste archi-pur. Je sens en mystique. Je suis un 'intérieur' et cet intérieur a réussi à faire de son intérieur un extérieur."[1] What strikes us above all in his work is the extraordinary strength of will, the constancy fifty years could not slacken that made him pursue the desired encounter of the "mystique" and the "rationaliste" he contained, the "intérieur" and "extérieur" of the self.

His lifelong search, as we have become acutely aware from his recently published *Cahiers*, sprang from the compulsion to possess a rigorous language. Like the scientist, he knew he had first of all to verify his instruments, to delimit his field of inquiry.[2] In so doing many of the central questions of philosophy appeared to him in a new light, while other "eternal" enigmas seemed wholly to disappear. He writes: "Un problème philosophique est un problème que l'on ne sait pas énoncer"; and again: "Celui qui se méfie du langage n'a besoin d'aucun Kant ni philosophe."[3] His ambition was to perfect a code of meanings for himself, a language he could think with, which would enable him to avoid vague words and vague entities. The *Cahiers* begin with a kind of Cartesian *tabula rasa*: "Je n'ai pas pu supporter," he writes, "de ne pas commencer par le commencement";[4] and, significantly enough for a man who as a poet knew the weight of words, the manner is primarily

[1] *Cahiers*, VII, 855.

[2] "En toute question, et avant tout examen sur le fond, je regarde au langage; j'ai coutume de procéder à la mode des chirurgiens qui purifient d'abord leurs mains et préparent leur champ opératoire. C'est ce que j'appelle le *nettoyage de la situation verbale*" ("Poésie et pensée abstraite," *Œuvres*, II, 1316).

[3] *Cahiers*, XIII, 624; *Cahiers*, I, 345.

[4] *Cahiers*, I, 615.

a linguistic exercise. "Penser au moyen de mes propres définitions, ce fut pour moi une espèce de but."[5]

Mathematics offered an ideal of what such a system of expression should be: precise, universal, coherent. He was profoundly influenced by his reading of Poincaré, whose essays became an enduring source of inspiration. But perhaps even more important was the work of the projective geometers: he speaks with enthusiasm of the three-dimensional spherical space of Riemann, finding that the mobility of perspective it formulates has implications that are certainly not restricted to mathematics, and are particularly relevant to his own representation of the mind as a *locus* of formal relationships. Non-Euclidean geometry, then, strongly influenced the formulation of his research at an early stage; but we also see clearly that through his own wide reading, through his conversations with scientists and mathematicians of his day, he penetrated further into the recent evolution of scientific theory and discovered a fertile vocabulary to translate his own observations about mental processes. Relativity, transformations, functions, entropy, group-theory were all terms he adopted, analogies he relished and incorporated into his language—his "Langage-self." His formal education in science may have been rudimentary, and his technical ability wanting, but he had an intuitive, we might say poetic, sense of its methods. No sorcerer's apprentice playing with he knew not what, he was a man in search of a language both subtle and sure, who felt that contemporary mathematics and the physical sciences offered him a key he could use.

Anti-Freudian, anti-Jungian, he aimed to describe rather than to explain, and, even more than to describe, to comprehend the formal relationship in its general terms. At the center of his thought is a strict relativism which he deduces from the inescapable variability of thought: man, he says, "est une machine pour créer le moment suivant."[6] And what of the self? It too is not a single substance but sev-

[5] *Correspondance André Gide-Paul Valéry*, p. 485.
[6] *Cahiers*, XXIX, 108.

eral; and yet there is one central *I* that is separate from the
mutations of consciousness, and the diversity of the self:
an *I* that like the zero of algebraic equations implies a for-
mal relation which remains constant whatever the par-
ticular contents of thought may be; an *I* that *equals* all
the change that is in the mind but in a sense remains its
master, since it does not alter itself. This is the *Moi pur,*
and to lay claim to it, that is, to be intensely conscious of
its existence, gives us, says Valéry, the ironic distance that
alone enables us to be at last masters in our own domain—
"maîtres chez nous."

He sought, then, to be rigorously exact, to apply to the
vagueness that has surrounded the description of mental
processes a scientific measure, the ideal of consistency and
strict orderliness that would produce a system as necessary
as a musical scale. "Mon idéal serait de construire la gamme
et le système d'accords dont la pensée en général serait la
Musique"; again, toward the end of his life: "J'écris ces
notes, un peu comme on fait des gammes—et elles se ré-
pètent sur les mêmes notes depuis cinquante ans. . . . un
peu comme on se promène à telle heure—chaque jour."[7]
Dry, impersonal, matter-of-fact his language most certainly
had to be, so that it sometimes found its most appropriate
expression in mathematical formulas. Nothing could appar-
ently be less poetic ("ma physionomie toute d'arpentage et
de système métrique"; "Ma nature a horreur du vague").[8]
But the reader of the *Cahiers* who follows this long re-
search finally takes away quite another impression. For
rather than coldly analytical, the mind that delves into the
processes of thought is fascinated by its own inquiry. Al-
though Valéry willed himself to be scornful of any one
thought or to ascribe intrinsic importance to any emotion
or concept, he could not but convey to us how wholly com-
mitted he was to his task. Acknowledging the nature of his
concern, he wrote: "J'aime la pensée véritable comme

---

[7] *Lettres à quelques-uns,* p. 108; *Cahiers,* XXIII, 387.
[8] *Correspondance André Gide-Paul Valéry,* p. 196; *Cahiers,* I, 101.

d'autres aiment le nu, qu'ils dessineraient toute leur vie."[9]
He had rejected the sole pursuit of poetry in order to be an
analyst of the intellect, but his exploration, carried on with-
in the limits he prescribed for himself, became a procedure
that suggests the fervent attitude of a lover. Thus we find
that his patient and concentrated effort of attention con-
tains the representation of one man's lifelong aspiration,
his moments of exultation and depression, his moving pre-
dilection for the beginnings of thought and emotion that
accompany the first light of day. Analysis is here not op-
posed to lyricism but in it rather finds its incentive and
nourishment, and a theme of infinite wonderment. "JE SUIS,
n'est-ce pas extraordinaire? se sentir au-dessus de la mort
comme une pierre se soutiendrait dans l'espace? Cela est
incroyable . . ."; "Mon vrai sujet est toi: Amour de ce qui
est enveloppé, impliqué dans l'esprit. Quoi de plus ardent
que de vouloir ce qu'on implique, posséder sans posséder,
être ce qu'on voudrait savoir, et pouvoir ce qu'on ne sau-
rait se représenter."[10] It is not surprising, then, to discover
that poetic composition furnished him with ample themes
of analysis and that some of his most illuminating remarks
concern the acts of the creative mind. Yet it is also true to
say that analysis is continually leading him to lyrical ex-
pression. The ventures of poetry and abstract thought,
these two pursuits of the intellect, are not opposed, but
participate in the same élan. His is a mind that denies the
divorce of science and lyricism, thought and the imagina-
tion. The poem is in fact a vehicle of speculation and re-
flection, and poetry may of course occur as patently in
prose as in a conventional prosodic form. We therefore
cannot but be struck, when we examine the use of meta-
phor in the *Cahiers*, by the way an image will often emerge
from a page of analysis; on the other hand, it may also serve
as matter for thought: "Les métaphores qui me viennent le
plus naturellement," he writes, "sont celles qui font 'con-

[9] *Cahiers*, IV, 881.
[10] "Mon Faust," *Œuvres*, II, 322; *Cahiers*, IV, 44.

templer' en choses sensibles des rapports intelligibles."[11]
The mind finds itself in objects, in a few favored images
that provide the analogical network of its own operations.

Of the metaphors most frequently used, none appear to
us to be more revealing than the serpent, the tree, and the
crystal. The first we encounter throughout the *Cahiers* as
the figure of the attempt by knowledge to go beyond the
limits of the body. "L'homme croit dépasser par l'esprit les
contacts et les connaissances de son corps. Mais l'esprit
s'arrête et le corps le rejoint."[12] Spontaneously the com-
parison emerges: the relationship of being to knowing is
like the progress of a reptile that pushes its head forward,
and whose tail then follows the head. Valéry will develop
the metaphor and speak of the tendency of knowledge to
change itself into self-knowledge like the legendary serpent
of the Gnostics, the ouroboros that discovers its own tail
and ends up having its head in its own mouth—the very
image, Valéry says, of a *theory* of knowledge.[13] Self-
contained, absolute, it is also the symbol of an impossible
eroticism, each of us seeking to be the other, to devour and
to absorb by way of the dialogue of love. Parallel to such
remarks he began to write his poetic monologue "Ebauche
d'un serpent," which develops these themes. Yet the poem
now introduces the Biblical associations of the fall, and the
scene of Eve and Satan is played out in terms of the sensi-
bility and the intellect. The conflict of being and knowing em-
braces the connotations of the Red Slayer, the Destructive
Element, Satan, the Principle that denies; and, from its
origin as a metaphor in the *Cahiers*, the image of the ser-
pent enables Valéry to invent a type of personal theogony,
offering his grandiose version of Eden as an internal drama
of the mind.

Such is the case of one image treated in a highly personal
way. When it comes to the metaphor of the tree, we are

[11] *Cahiers*, VI, 782.
[12] *Cahiers*, VI, 914.
[13] Cf. *Paul Valéry vivant* (Marseilles: Cahiers du Sud, 1946), p.
276.

struck by the visual immediacy of Valéry's treatment, its concrete detail.

O plante, arbre, répétition rayonnante,
Tu rayonnes ton âge par saisons et par germes
Tu répètes ton motif régulièrement à chaque angle
De chaque étage de ta croissante statue, et tu répètes
Ton essence en chaque graine, tu te produis, tu te jettes
Autour de toi périodiquement sous forme de chances—
                                          en tel nombre
Tu élimines tes similitudes.[14]

Yet the tree is also the symbol of man, his aspiration to grow in knowledge despite the roots that bind him to an earthly destiny; it is his vibrant unity and internal dynamism: "L'image de l'arbre ou de la plante qui me vient si souvent est image représentative de lois simples de la chose vivante élémentaire et fait ressentir des forces une continuité, des fonctions de forces un lien variable vectoriel, une *géométrie intrinsèque* d'un seul tenant où dimensions, tempo, masses, forces sont liés et s'expriment l'un par l'autre."[15] It is also, Valéry speculates, the image of the ideal act of meditation in which all growth is the symmetrical branching of elements that were present from the start, the development of an initial seed. "Vois comme l'Arbre aveugle aux membres divergents s'accroît autour de soi selon la Symétrie. La vie en lui calcule, exhausse une structure, et rayonne son nombre par branches et par brins, et chaque brin sa feuille, aux points mêmes marqués dans le naissant futur."[16] The image, it is clear, has become the parable of a balanced continuity of the intellect, like the wholly coherent poem, or the desirable unfolding of a sequence of abstract thought. In the fruit, meditation and poetic expression find a single image of magical power; in thought that has reached its sensuous maturity we hear the multitudinous resonance of the whole man, or, as it were, of the original

[14] "Motifs ou moments," *Œuvres*, I, 353.
[15] *Cahiers*, XI, 604.
[16] "Dialogue de l'arbre," *Œuvres*, II, 193.

tree: "L'inflexion, la plénitude, le timbre sans prix, le dessin miraculeux de la forme interne, à la fois désir et possession, regret, espoir, durée, mouvement, et ce qui meut et est mû, avec le plus haut et le plus bas, *arbre gigantesque de la voix,* arbre sacré, poussé dans la chair chargée des idées, poésie même."[17]

As for the image of the crystal, it takes us to the heart of Valéry's research. If the serpent is knowledge and the dream of self-containment, if the tree is the metaphor of ideal consistency, the crystal may be said to subsume them both and to contain Valéry's lifelong ambition of "pureté." *Pureté* is the name he gave to the central object of his pursuit, the substance to which language must reduce the world: "J'ai cherché sur toute chose *pureté* et *précision,* et pas un de ces . . . qui ont écrit sur moi ne l'a dit quoique je l'aie dit moi-même cent fois."[18] It is the impossible goal he imagined as a young man when he decided to dedicate himself to his *Cahiers* and discover the luminous form, the crystal that was to be his philosopher's stone. "J'aurais voulu te vouer à former le cristal de chaque chose, ma Tête, et que tu divises le désordre que présente l'espace et que développe le temps, pour en tirer les puretés qui te fassent ton monde propre, de manière que ta lumière dans cette structure réfringeante revienne et se ferme sur elle-même dans l'instant, substituant à l'espace l'ordre et au temps une éternité."[19] Should he reach a summit of exaltation, he will express his feelings by means of the same image of the crystal: "je me *suis,* je me réponds, je me reflète et me répercute, je frémis à l'infini des miroirs—je suis de verre."[20] But characteristically Valéry will also talk in his "Lettre sur Mallarmé" of the crystalline systems of poetry formed when thought and the image are not separate but are corresponding facets of a single diamond, or like the ray of light that is captured by transparency:

[17] *Cahiers,* VIII, 38.
[18] *Cahiers,* XVI, 31.
[19] *Cahiers,* XXIV, 3.
[20] "Extrait du log-book de Monsieur Teste," *Œuvres,* II, 44.

Une esclave aux longs yeux chargés de molles chaînes
Change l'eau de mes fleurs, plonge aux glaces prochaines,
Au lit mystérieux prodigue ses doigts purs;
Elle met une femme au milieu de ces murs
Qui dans ma rêverie errant avec décence,
Passe entre mes regards sans briser leur absence,
Comme passe le verre au travers du soleil,
Et de la raison pure épargne l'appareil.[21]

"Intérieur" and "extérieur" are wedded in the marriage ode of a radical order within the poet's mind. For him the language of poetry is gracious, bringing the delights of fresh womanhood, renewing his sense of wonder but leaving his powers of abstraction intact. The structural principle of the poem offers a balance between sensuousness and abstraction, an even division of labor reflected in the use of the epithet *pur* that denotes both the lyrical fingers of the woman and the austerity of reason.

LINKED one to the other like integral strands in the fabric of thought, these images recur in several of Valéry's major compositions and serve in particular as implicit models. No doubt to each case he gave fresh poetic action: no doubt each form had reasons that reason alone did not control; but latent in his sensibility, waiting for the lyrical movement to which they would apply, informing the substance of his meditation, the serpent, the tree, and the crystal suggest the native atmosphere of the poet-thinker.

It is therefore patently a false question for us to ask whether a given poem is in any simple way the translation of thought, or, conversely, an idea the development of a metaphor. We must divine a mental activity that was unable to divide, its intensity refusing to reduce analysis to logic, or poetry to the forces of common sentiment. On one occasion Valéry described the procedure of composing a poem in these terms: "Une abstraction s'exprimant en termes concrets—c'est de la poésie"; and again: "L'idéal,

[21] "Intérieur," *Œuvres*, I, 147.

c'est peut-être: un principe, une idée, un précepte bien vu par l'esprit clair et cristallin, puis à force d'être compris, se faisant ressentir, s'emparant de l'être—devenant peu à peu capable d'agir ou de produire, engendrant enfin l'application, l'acte, l'œuvre comme par une incarnation. C'est ainsi que parfois l'on finit par devenir ou par faire ce qu'on a désiré pendant des années, considéré comme son 'impossible'. Un jour vient. Une connaissance devient capable d'existence."[22] So acutely, he says, would thought be felt that it would be "conceived," take on life and a logic of its own. And yet if in so conceiving the poet could discover the key elements of his imagination, if he grasped anew their significance, how are we to say with any meaningfulness that principle, precept, or idea *produced* the poem? The "intellectual sensibility" may be a term that is difficult to define, but its operations and effects are written plainly in the *Cahiers* and the poetic compositions.

It is evident, however, that we should not confuse the ambition of the analyst with that of the author of poems. He constantly had recourse to theological terms when he wished to describe poetry, as we observe in the fragment just noted, in which the word "incarnation" conveys the transmutation of essence into existence, the potential into the actual. The poem is a "miracle," a "corps incorruptible," a complete system that of words makes a body, of polarities a magical reconciliation. It is also a language of a very special kind, since it does not address other men nor even the self, but invokes its own divinities, creates them by the timbre of its emotion. Nothing could more appropriately describe this form and this aspiration, this negation of the world in favor of the most necessary movements of the sensibility—attraction and repulsion, love and death—than that it should be called a "charm," an "enchantment," a "liturgy" of the feelings.[23] Like the palm branch it moves in

[22] *Cahiers*, VI, 209; *Cahiers*, VI, 510.
[23] One of the first drafts of a title page for *Charmes* reads: "Carmina—Chants magiques—Liturgia" (cf. my book *Lecture de Valéry: une étude de "Charmes,"* p. 12).

a time and space of its own, and is nurtured by an act of grace:

> Admire comme elle vibre,
> Et comme une lente fibre
> Qui divise le moment,
> Départage sans mystère
> L'attirance de la terre
> Et le poids du firmament![24]

A substantive oneness that is closed on itself and vibrant with movement and sound, it is in the likeness of the serpent of the sea:

> Hydre absolue, ivre de ta chair bleue,
> Qui te remords l'étincelante queue
> Dans un tumulte au silence pareil.[25]

Herein the self can contemplate its own dearest image that has surrendered every superficial concern and reached a supreme tension, a transparent projection of the purity that is the crystalline mask of Narcissus:

> Là, d'un reste du jour, se forme un fiancé
> Nu, sur la place pâle où m'attire l'eau triste,
> Délicieux démon désirable et glacé![26]

"Equinoxe," the poem I propose to examine, has not as yet, it would appear, been taken seriously by Valéry's critics, and no study, partial or complete, has been made of it. Nevertheless I believe it to be a truly remarkable composition which luminously captures a central pattern of his work. The movement is that of thought which pursues its own premises and finds at the peak of its awareness an unique relationship between the self and the world. Specifically we are told nothing about objects or the nature of the mind, but the poem demonstrates the inevitable transiency of consciousness, which at last comes to the realiza-

[24] "Palme," *Œuvres*, I, 154.
[25] "Le Cimetière marin," *Œuvres*, I, 151.
[26] "Fragments du Narcisse," *Œuvres*, I, 125.

194

tion that loss is gain, that absence is replenished by a new presence. Hesitating between death and beauty, the self follows the curve of its own thought, the birth, life, and death of a moment that is wrenched from banal preoccupations, until the rhythms of renewed physical activity bring meditation to a close. Thus the poet has delved once again into his crystal of reflection and discovered, with what we might take to be a fatal inevitability, the leafy trees of nature and the serpent that lingers darkly in the pool of self-consciousness. "Quel poème admirable," observed Valéry in his first notebook, "quel poème admirable que la contemplation se nourrissant d'elle-même. Répétition sans accoutumance, répétition qui excite le désir et provoque la conscience au lieu de s'en défaire peu à peu. Ce qui ne fait penser à nulle autre chose; et puis au lieu de s'éclairer par la pensée— l'éclaire, cela est beau, et par sa seule présence."[27]

It is in this regard important to observe the epigraph he added on the occasion of the poem's publication: "To look. . . ." He was following a practice he had established in his earlier collections, in one case modifying a passage from Corneille, in others quoting lines from the Vulgate, Virgil, Ovid, even the inscription on Narcissa Young's grave in the Montpellier Public Gardens. It was Latin he chose most often to provide a classical echo for his themes, to extend their mythological resonance. A signal exception is to be found in "Le Cimetière marin," where the celebrated words from the Third Pythian Ode introduce the poles of immortality and mortality between which the twenty-four stanzas will hesitate, before at last the protagonist conforms to the weight of Pindar's injunction to "exhaust the domain of the practical": thus Valéry's epigraph sets a philosophical tone, and provides a Mediterranean atmosphere in which man is the measure of the universe. Yet we must quite clearly seek elsewhere if we are to justify the phrase that introduces "Equinoxe." Why, indeed, should Valéry have chosen this plain English infinitive? If the answer is not obvious, one may be excused for adducing first of all a

[27] *Cahiers,* I, 524.

typically "Claudelian" answer: the phrase, one might say, constitutes an ideogram, the very image of alertness conjured up for us by this sequence of three open eyes followed by a sharp guttural (whereas the word *sleep* represents for Claudel "deux yeux fermés—la tête sur l'oreiller p"). It would be overhasty for us to reject out of hand such apparently fanciful considerations in Valéry, the more so when we recall that both he and Claudel were strongly influenced by a common source, Mallarmé's *Les Mots anglais*. We cannot, then, deny that he was possibly struck by the visual appropriateness of this word in a language that, despite his long acquaintance with it, remained for him largely exotic; he might also have considered that the English word managed to suggest his theme in a manner that was poetically rich, its linguistic strangeness lending enchantment. Perhaps it even recalls a literary source as well: although no self-evident reference comes to mind, we might be struck—and the French reader even more so— by its echo of Shakespeare's "To sleep, perchance. . . ," the ellipsis beckoning us toward philosophical speculation.

We must, however, immediately enlarge on such initial considerations by observing that nothing could more adequately serve to introduce this poem, as indeed the rest of his work, than the notion of precise and lyrical scrutiny. The method he developed in the *Cahiers* and illustrated in his compositions may be summed up in the ardor of his practice of contemplation. This it is he celebrates in "Profusion du soir" with a kind of mystical vigor as "l'Ange frais de l'œil nu" which brings with it a "lucide tendresse" —clear-eyed appraisal, impassioned incisiveness, voluptuous concern.[28] All things have to be considered from the same unswerving point of view so that their secrets can be violated—not only external phenomena, but consciousness itself as it strives to know and understand: "Si tu ne comprends pas quelque chose arrête-toi et regarde-toi ne pas comprendre."[29] The crisis of 1892 was essentially an

[28] "Profusion du soir," *Œuvres*, I, 86.
[29] *Cahiers*, XXIX, 247.

"affaire de regard"; once he conceived the ambition to melt down every idol in the crucible of intellectual penetration, his angel became a stern will to perceive: "Te rappelles-tu le temps où tu étais ange? Ange sans Christ, je me souviens. C'était une affaire de regard et de volonté, l'idée de tout traverser avec mes yeux. Je n'aimais que le feu. Je croyais que rien à la fin ne résisterait à mon regard et désir de regard—ou plutôt je croyais que quelqu'un pourrait être ainsi et que moi j'avais l'idée nette et absolue de celui-là. Tout me semblait si simple que la littérature devenait impossible. Plus d'objet."[30] What words could be more revealing of his compulsion to *look*. The glance was felt to possess an infinite power that would consume all things and reduce them to a single essence. In this respect we remember the summit of the poet's graveyard reflections, when thought and feeling willingly embrace the images of sacrificial fire:

> Ici venu, l'avenir est paresse.
> L'insecte net gratte la sécheresse;
> Tout est brûlé, défait, reçu dans l'air
> A je ne sais quelle sévère essence . . .
> La vie est vaste, étant ivre d'absence,
> Et l'amertume est douce, et l'esprit clair.[31]

Vaporized by the eye's analysis and having become the thinker's own, the world is subject to his lucid rigorousness. This is the process at the heart of Valéryan lyricism, that movingly espouses the designs of thought.

THE COMPOSITION of "Equinoxe" extended over a considerable period, the poet rewriting and revising his elegy intermittently, it would seem, for some twenty-five years as it developed from the narrow compass of five stanzas. Thus, although it was published for the first time among the *Pièces diverses* in 1942, it was begun at the same time as the main substance of *Charmes*. Two early versions ap-

---

[30] *Cahiers*, IV, 705.
[31] "Le Cimetière marin," *Œuvres*, I, 149.

pear in the notebook "Petits poèmes MCMXVII," while it is mentioned under the title "Pause" in a list of twenty-eight compositions Valéry drew up at about the same time with a view to publication. (The choice includes "L'Abeille," "Aurore," "La Ceinture," "Cantique des colonnes," "L'Insinuant," "Intérieur," "Le Cimetière marin," "Au Platane," "La Pythie," "Ode secrète," and "Le Rameur," which appear in *Charmes*; but also "La Caresse," "La Distraite," "Heure," and "Colloque pour deux flûtes," which, with "Equinoxe," were later collected in *Pièces diverses*.) One may think that "Equinoxe" would not indeed have been unworthy to figure in the company of the other poems of *Charmes*, although several reasons may have decided Valéry against its inclusion: quite obviously, for one thing, he was dissatisfied with the expression and felt the need to refashion it; then again, he may have been at pains to fit it into *Charmes* without disrupting the sequence, or echoing too clearly certain traits of other poems; even more directly, having once determined to make of *Charmes* an "ars poetica" that would illustrate—how magnificently, we know—a gamut of prosodic arrangements and literary kinds, he possibly did not wish to include a second elegy after "Au Platane."

Nevertheless, none of Valéry's other compositions has quite the same form. Here as elsewhere, once the seed of the future poem stirred in him, he worked from the conception to the expression, from pattern to pretext, his imagination seeking an individual language for the prosodic structure and motif he was to celebrate. In this case the swaying motion, the tender balance of alternate alexandrines and octosyllables, the long feminine lines followed by brief masculine ones (in contrast to "Au Platane") suggested to him the notion of a poem on the self turning upon a point of attraction, lovingly held in an unique moment of time. With constant changes in the rhythmic scheme and intonation, the twelve quatrains offer the development of this complete lyrical figure that brings us to the final rejection of an interrelationship which has been explored step by step. Yet the poetic unraveling does not take place on one level alone or in a single tone but rather, as we shall see, in four parts that we might resume under the headings of the self, the nymph, death, and life. To these divisions correspond stylistic variations brought about by self-description, the recourse to Greek myth, invocation, and a crowning excitement. Throughout the poem there is, then, a marked progression. By the repeated use of cumulative coordination, causality is avoided, a cycle of events being composed as they occur in the poet's thought and just as quickly are replaced: "*Et* je me sens vivant sous les ombres descendre," "*Et* ce cœur qui bat sans espoir," "Que je m'irrite *et* que j'existe!"

The poem recalls in its vocabulary characteristic traits of *Charmes*: the "sibylle" of "Palme," the "sable" and "pas" of "Aurore," the "flèche" and "vent" of "Le Cimetière marin," the "fuite" of the reflected image of Narcissus framed by leaves and a darkening nature, the Greek allusions of several pieces, especially "Au Platane," the "Psyché" who appears in one draft of "Les Pas," the serpent, the tree, and the crystal. Had we no other evidence, these details would suggest the organic connection between the poems collected in 1922 and "Equinoxe." Sternly abstract yet unflagging in its sensuous attention to the drama of the intellect, "Equinoxe" provides a fitting example of the intensity that makes of Valéry's finest work the matter of an intimate aspiration: "Rejoindre ce qu'on voudrait être devant soi, TEL QUEL —mais rendu *celui d'une fois pour toutes*."[32] Here as elsewhere he seeks to constitute the "perfect thought," in front of which he can at last fall silent and disappear.

Numerous drafts allow us to follow the gradual development of form and meaning from the narrow compass of five stanzas to the last refinements of phrasing in the late 1930's, at the time the collected edition of *Poésies* was being prepared. By the great courtesy of Madame Valéry I have been able to consult a total of eleven unpublished manuscripts which demonstrate as it were *in actu* the fine art

[32] *Cahiers*, XXVI, 366.

by which the poem was brought to fruition. The first of
these (we shall call its recto side MS A) bears the title
"Station," which, like the later "Pause," then "Equinoxe,"
sets the keynote for a climactic immobility, a privileged
moment of being. Already the rhythmical movement, the
scheme of metaphors, and the general outline of the poetic
action are firmly established.

> Mes secrets sont calmés . . . De feuilles immobiles
>   Est chargé (voilé) l'arbre que je vois.
> Ses bras ont achevé de bercer les sibylles:
>   Leur (Le) silence achève leurs voix.

Variant:

> Mes secrets sont calmés . . . Les feuilles immobiles
>   Accablent l'arbre que je vois
>
> Le songe, si le songe était une fontaine
>   Chantant les miracles des eaux,
> Se fait (s'apaise) une eau (vasque) profonde où
>   la pierre lointaine
>   Marque la tombe des oiseaux.
>
> Au lit sombre (simple) d'un (de) sable aussi fin
>   (mol) que la (qu'une) cendre
>   Repose mon but enchanté
> Mon (Le) plus secret désir à peine ose
>   (n'oserait pas) descendre
>
> .   .   .   .
>
> Tandis que je m'attache à ce regard (mon siècle)
>   (Mais tandis que j'habite un tel porche) de pierre
>   Dans le pur et profond pourquoi
> Un vent se dresse et glisse une mince paupière
>   Entre moi-même et moi.
>
> Hélas! mon corps se réveille assailli (au milieu)
>   d'une automne
>   Que soulève un vent rouge et triste

Flot (Dont il court des ..) de pourpre panique un
    vol de feuilles tonne (aux feuilles d'or étonne)
(Un cœur où) La solitude existe

Variant:

    Tant de pourpre panique et tant d'or pur m'étonne
      Que je me dresse et j'existe

In addition we find in the margin an advanced draft of
the future stanza 10.

    O quelle éternité d'absence spontanée
      Vient sous la faux de s'abréger
    Une feuille qui tombe a divisé l'année
      De son événement léger.

We note, then, that the pattern of the internal drama was
clearly present from the start, although much had to be
done in the way of improving the expression and develop-
ing the middle stanzas of the poem. On the back of the
same draft (MS B) Valéry pays special attention to the for-
mer of these tasks in a version entitled "Pause":

Mes secrets sont calmés . . . De feuilles immobiles
    Est chargé l'arbre que je vois.
Ses bras ont achevé de bercer les sibylles,
    Le silence achève leurs voix.

Le songe, si le songe était une fontaine,
    Chantant les miracles des eaux (Célébrant la
                 soif des hasards)
Se fait (s'apaise) une eau profonde (se change en
           paix liquide) où la pierre lointaine
Marque (Presse) la tombe des oiseaux (regards)

Au fond (lit) sombre de (d'un) sable aussi fin
               qu'une (que la) cendre
    Repose mon but enchanté
Et mon cœur se contemple et en vain veut descendre
    Et tout mon sort est aimanté (Redoute l'abîme
                    aimanté).

Tandis que je m'attache à mon regard de pierre
　　Dans le fixe (pur) et le pur (profond) pourquoi?
　　(le très pur, le même . . .)
Un air passe sur l'eau qui ferme (L'air qui passe
　　　　　　　　sur l'eau fait battre) une paupière
　　Entre moi-même et moi.

Et mon éternité (Brisant) d'absence spontanée
　　De son léger événement
Quand une feuille qui tombe a divisé l'année
　　. . . étonnement.

Et mon corps se réveille au milieu d'une automne
　　Où se lève un vent rouge et triste
D'une pourpre panique un vol de feuilles tonne
　　Et tourbillonne (et chasse) si j'existe
　　(La feuille morte seule existe).

I shall resume briefly the variants of the subsequent drafts:

Title: MS C: no title; MS E: "Elégie"; MS G: no title; MS H:
　　2 (Elégie); finally, MS J: "Elégie" ou ("Equinoxe")

Stanza 1: line 2: Oppriment . . . (MS E)
　　　　　　Oppriment l'arbre (changent/revêtent le
　　　　　　hêtre) (MS G)

　　　　　line 4: Mon silence achève leurs voix (MS G)

MS I, which consists solely of a late version of the first
stanza that is typed on the back of some stanzas for in-
clusion in the 1942 edition of *Poésies* such as "Vaine-
ment tonne aux cieux le dieu de la matière . . . ," des-
tined to become the sixth stanza of "Eté" in the *Album
de vers anciens* (*Œuvres*, I, 1566):

　　Mes transports abolis, ces feuilles immobiles
　　　　Accablent l'ombre que je vois:
　　Ses bras épais sont las de bercer mes sibylles,
　　　　Mon silence achève leurs voix.

Stanza 2: line 2: Qui chantait la gloire (fête) des vives
eaux (MS E)

Stanza 3:

> Au lit simple d'un sable aussi fin que la cendre
> Dorment les pas que j'ai perdus;
> L'âme même, si bas qu'elle peut descendre,
> Craint ces vestiges confondus. (MS C)

> line 2: Repose mon but (un regard) enchanté
> (MS G)
> Dorment les feux de mon soleil (MS G)

> line 3: L'espérance se sent sous les ombres des-
> cendre (MS E)
> Ma voix même, si bas qu'elle peut descen-
> dre (MS G)

> line 4: Craint ce désert (bonheur/moment/repos)
> diamanté (MS G)
> Craint de nommer (le nom de) ce som-
> meil (MS G)

Stanza 4:

> Je perds distinctement Psyché la somnambule
> Dans l'horreur (la paix) d'un désert si beau
> (pensif)
> Où (Dont) le temps rare à peine (immobile)
> est troublé d'une (compté par la) bulle
> Qui se défait de ce tombeau (MS C)

> line 2: Au bord de l'abîme (d'un voile) si beau
> (MS E)

Stanza 5: We find no variants of this stanza. It would appear
to have been incorporated into the poem at a late stage.

Stanza 6:

> Elle laisse à mon cœur (à ma chair) sa perte
> inexpliquée
> Et mon image sans espoir
>
> .   .   .   .
>
> Par le serpent (sort du) soir. (MS E)

Stanza 7:

> L'âme fuit l'or mourant de ses vaines annales
> A l'ombre elle cède le jour;
> L'invincible douceur des plages infernales
> L'appelle aux pentes sans retour. (MS D)

>> lines 1-2: Soleil! mourant témoin de mes vaines annales
>> Soleil! elle cède le jour (MS E)

>>> On the same MS, alongside the draft of this stanza, the words "Ses pas l'épousent."

>> line 2: Vois, Soleil, mourir notre amour (MS H)

Stanza 8:

> Hélas . . . Tristesse accrue
> . . . affreuse lucidité
> Toute chose m'est claire à peine disparue
> Je demeure seul (MS H)

Stanza 9: lines 3-4: Le frémissement noir d'une paupière
> Entre moi-même passe, et moi! (MS D)

>> Tandis qu'un dieu (sort) m'attache à mon
>> regard de pierre
>> Dans le fixe et le dur pourquoi
>> Un frémissement passe et (le frémissement
>> neuf/noir) plisse une paupière
>> Entre moi-même et moi! (MS G)

>> line 3: Un frémissement d'ombre (MS H)

Stanza 10: We read in MS G beside the final version of this stanza an octosyllable which was perhaps intended as the initial element of a new stanza but was later abandoned:

> Je vis au plus loin d'un corps

In MS I, one variant for the third line:

> Quelque feuille qui tombe a divisé l'année

Valéry's "Pureté"

Stanza 11: line 1: Sur moi (MS H)
Sur (Vers) moi (MS I)

line 2: Tombez de vos (MS H)
Tombez de vos sombres (frêles/hauts)
berceaux (MS I)

Stanza 12:

Fantôme de moi-même, investi d'une automne
Que soulève un vol rouge et triste,
Tant de pourpre panique aux trombes (souffles/fuites/
traînes/rages) d'or m'étonne
Que je m'arrache (Qu'elle m'ébranle/Qu'elle frissonne)
et que j'existe. (MS G)

line 1: Moi, je m'éveille, hélas! (enfin)
investi d'une (de cet/d'un âpre) au-
tomne (MS I)
Mais enfin je m'éveille, hélas! . . . (MS I)

line 4: Que je m'éveille (m'irrite/m'anime) et
que j'existe (MS I)

In addition to these variants we find two versions of a
stanza that was later abandoned. It first occurs separately in
MS C, then as a sequel to the future stanza 7 ("Sombre et
mourant témoin de nos tendres annales. . .") in MS E:

Et (Quand/Ame) de notre amour, (Ame/ombre), es-
tu donc si lasse
Ou curieuse de ces fleurs (partir)
Que tu vis un (l'autre) hiver sur les vitres la glace
Devant toi faire (former de) tes pleurs (MS C)

Ame de notre amour, âme, es-tu donc si lasse
Ou curieuse de ces fleurs
Que nous vîmes dans l'hiver sur les vitres (le verre)
la glace
Devant toi (nous) former de tes (nos) pleurs?
(MS E)

We should also note several lines, some well worthy of "Equinoxe," which the poet discarded. Thus in MS F one reads this alexandrine:

> Pâle commencement, chambre vide et nacrée

On the back of MS G we find:

> L'âme écoute sa voix évanouie

with its admirable variant that completes the alexandrine:

> J'écoute au bord de l'âme une heure évanouie

And again:

> Toute chose future s'ouvre l'extrême ouïe
> Il visite (explore) l'homme de l'ère évanouie
> Je visite l'homme d'une ère évanouie
> Impuissant dans la lucidité
> Toute chose m'est claire, et l'âme évanouie
> Est présente

The value of an analysis such as this, I take it, is to show in one particular instance the scrupulous art Valéry brought to the discovery of his language of the intellect. We have seen the way in which the prosodic and semantic elements were established from the first; the endeavor to perfect the initial stanzas while composing the central section of the poem; then the consideration of many variants, some of which introduced new details into the action and were therefore rejected, while others were thought to be gauche in their phrasing or inadequate with respect to the pattern of sound and rhythm. Of the changes, one significant aspect of "Equinoxe" was concerned with the variations of identity and difference between the self and the object of its pursuit, the convergence and divergence of reason and sensibility. Yet, I suppose, more than by any other thing, we are struck in the final instance by the exquisite patience of an act of composition that comprised so many drafts over some twenty-five years, that only discovered the expression of the first stanza at the end of many attempts, at a point

later than the eleven drafts I have examined. In the same
way each quatrain had to conform to the necessity of the
whole—like the coil and the serpent, the leaf, the branch,
and the tree, the facet and the diamond—so that, rather
than a cumbersome movement, the final version may in
fact be said to be simpler than the first, and to convey for
us the ultimate amenity of the mind.

> Je change . . . Qui me fuit? . . . Ses feuilles immobiles
>   Accablent l'arbre que je vois . . .
> Ses bras épais sont las de bercer mes sibylles:
>   Mon silence a perdu ses voix.[33]

THE SUDDEN realization on which the poem begins is that
the sensibility is subject to time. A nameless nymph has
been lost, a form which by its flight has destroyed the suf-
ficiency of the past. Consciousness is stirred, made aware of
its variation, for a virtue has pathetically left it. Like ob-
jects in the mirror of contemplation, leaves hang heavily
over the water; and although they are ordinarily the deli-
cate token of the tree's desire, they now overwhelm their
source and reduce it to silent immobility. The world has
become foreign to a mind meditating on its own proc-
esses: "La seule réalité est le changement qui ôte leur
réalité à toutes les autres choses."[34] Nevertheless, thrown
back on his own resources, the poet instinctively obeys
the rhythm of an idyllic moment when nature offered tender
care and cradled prophetic voices of inspiration.

> Mon âme, si son hymne était une fontaine
>   Qui chantait de toutes ses eaux,
> N'est plus qu'une eau profonde où la pierre lointaine
>   Marque la tombe des oiseaux.

The speaker contrasts past and present, fullness of
activity and death. To translate lost inspiration he calls on
the image of water, his memory of an exultant fountain

---

[33] "Equinoxe," *Œuvres*, I, 159.
[34] *Cahiers*, VI, 730.

within. For such a man there can be no doubt that the soul existed, since it was synonymous with his vital well-being ("*Ame*, personification de ce à quoi nous reconnaissons que nous vivons");[35] yet now the prodigal noise of waters has ceased, and sober analysis makes him look deeply into his heart. The element he finds is desperately pure, offering no reflections to comfort a mind that sees the consequences of its lucidity. Inscribed with fatal plainness in the pool of meditation is the idea of death: the past is this stone which poignantly conjures up the singing of birds and the self's former expansiveness.

> Au lit simple d'un sable aussi fin que la cendre
> Dorment les pas que j'ai perdus,
> Et je me sens vivant sous les ombres descendre
> Par leurs vestiges confondus.

As the monologue unfolds, remembrance loses its sway. Instead of to the past, the speaker tenderly turns to the images before his eyes; but if they draw him with the power of a spell, they lie ineluctably beyond. He knows indeed that the world he perceives signifies death ("cendre," "ombres"), the ultimate limits of thought; yet the presence he cherishes is not dead, and his words, in their alliteration and assonance, are gently attentive ("simple," "sable," "aussi," "cendre," "sens," "sous," "descendre"). The sensibility gravitates toward a pole of attraction, is moved to follow a path that will lead it knows not where, while consciousness alertly watches a descent into hell which love inspires, like that of some modern Orpheus. (We shall see that the mythical reference, here implicit, receives further development in the next lines.)

> Je perds distinctement Psyché la somnambule
> Dans les voiles trop purs de l'eau
> Dont le calme et le temps se troublent d'une bulle
> Qui se défait de ce tombeau.

[35] *Cahiers*, VI, 714.

Valéry's "Pureté"

Meditation is pursued in pitilessly clear light ("distincte-ment," "voiles trop purs") as a new section of the poem begins, and the unknown mistress finds substance and form. Walking through the realms of sleep, Psyche is the true object of the heart's desire, for she bears the name of the mind itself. Beyond life and yet on this side of death, at the calm center of reflection, a movement indicates her presence; but this beloved nymph the self cannot ravish, since desire and its object, the intellect and its image, have ceased to coincide.

> A soi-même, peut-être, Elle parle et pardonne,
>   Mais cédant à ses yeux fermés,
> Elle me fuit fidèle, et, tendre, m'abandonne
>   A mes destins inanimés.

The poet continues to look and wonder at the divine nymph dwelling in his thought. Although she is speaking, her words are a song of self-containment that refuses to unseal its secrets. Through the glass she is seen but un-heard. There has been no brutal rupture of relationship with this mythical presence that alone can interanimate the mind: the nymph remains faithful, affectionate, but all is in flight ("cédant," "fuit," "m'abandonne") and the verbs echo the plaintive movement of the first line of the poem. The source of life, like the source of poetry, is a mysterious language expressing a moment that has gone, an image of the intellectual sensibility at its purest and most obscure. Now Psyche walks with eyes closed, unresponsive to any gaze.

> Elle me laisse au cœur sa perte inexpliquée,
>   Et ce cœur qui bat sans espoir
> Dispute à Perséphone Eurydice piquée
>   Au sein pur par le serpent noir. . . .

The sense of loss becomes acute as the heart strives vainly to explain the disappearance of its nymph. Such change, of course, is essentially inexplicable, like time, like conscious-ness itself; but to know this is not to be reconciled to it.

Yet while the sensibility can nourish no hope to regain what has gone, it must of necessity create its future with every heartbeat, in the same way as the poem conforms to the meter it has once established. Inextricably bound to the image it desires, the self again adopts legendary terms to convey the struggle between earth and hell, poetry and silence; and a reference to Eurydice introduces the colors of the Orpheus myth, which Valéry had previously long explored in his poems and notebooks. His internal drama has become the image of the poet's will to look at death, both to possess and to understand. The black serpent claiming its own, holding beauty in its thrall, is opposed by the intellectual sensibility. But is not death the vital law of consciousness? Does not "self-variance" demand the loss of the present? The second half of the poem will make clear that loss signifies quite surely constant gain.

> Sombre et mourant témoin de nos tendres annales,
>> O soleil, comme notre amour,
> L'invincible douceur des plages infernales
>> T'appelle aux rives sans retour.

A new section indicates the continuous movement of the self as it revolves on the axis of time. Instead of seeking for the nymph, it looks away once more from Mind ("Esprit") and Body ("Corps") to the World ("Monde"), the third term of the Valéryan formula of existence. At this autumnal equinox the sun is undergoing a similar movement of flight, obeying the same attraction of death. It has been witness to a tender union which has now ended, and inexorably carries away this memory. Yet we find no tragic accent: we are far from the austere alexandrines of "Narcisse" that lead us forward to an inescapable dénouement, for the elegiac pattern realizes the reversal of death and the achievement of fresh energy. This is already apparent in the stanza we are now considering, which exorcizes hell by calling it an "invincible douceur," replacing one gentleness with another.

Automne, transparence! ô solitude accrue
    De tristesse et de liberté!
Toute chose m'est claire à peine disparue;
    Ce qui n'est plus se fait clarté.

The full awareness of time redeemed finds expression
in the eighth stanza. If no hope remains of arresting sum-
mer's warmth, no regret is felt; on the contrary, autumn's
coming is hailed by the speaker. Whereas previously the
water was "too pure" because of the irrecoverable image
it was seen to contain, this new limpidity makes the self
exult: time opens an unbridged distance between present
and past, but it allows of a point of view that is infinitely
precious. The poet knows with the knowledge that only
hindsight permits, and his eye of memory is clear. The
mind cannot analyze and simultaneously participate: alone
("solitude"), aware of being separated from what it loves
("tristesse"), capable of embracing all things with clear-
sighted vision ("liberté"), it discovers that to comprehend
it had first to be dispossessed; and this idea the last two
lines repeat with lyrical delight. For the speaker, as for the
Valéry of the *Cahiers,* autumn is par excellence the period of
perspicuous illumination: "Automne—tu donnes l'idée de
l'objet incorruptible que l'on voudrait être. Une chose d'or
dans un air froid, un achèvement aigu, le sentiment que la
lumière n'est pas ce que l'été l'avait fait croire—l'avenir
qui se sent souvenir, un grand changement comme statue
et figure de tous changements;—horripilent . . . —me
traversent."[36]

> Tandis que je m'attache à mon regard de pierre
>   Dans le fixe et le dur "Pourquoi?",
> Un noir frémissement, l'ombre d'une paupière
>   Palpite entre moi-même et moi. . . .

With the ninth stanza the poem attains an abstract
severity that takes the moment of self-analysis to a peak be-
yond which it cannot go. (The only possible sequel will be

[36] *Cahiers,* II, 714.

a sudden reaction such as we find in the last three stanzas.) The self has finally brought present and past face to face in a supreme tension of self-consciousness. Time is motionless ("regard de pierre," "fixe," "dur") as glance meets glance to create a temple of thought that excludes every other object. This is the climax of contemplation, of the act of *looking*: "je suis comme l'œil qui voit ce qu'il voit"[37] —an enduring instant, an activity that generates a corresponding capacity for renewal, an analysis that scrutinizes both subject and object, an excited interchange of values. But it takes its full preciousness from the fact that it is played out against the background of a mortal threat ("noir frémissement," "l'ombre d'une paupière") which corresponds to the rhythm of time and the heart, the very brevity of vision ("palpite") that is ready to destroy the self's sense of deific power. "Mystique sans Dieu," "Ange sans Christ," the poet experiences a moment sufficient unto itself that consciousness will lose as soon as it is gained.

> O quelle éternité d'absence spontanée
> Vient tout à coup de s'abréger? . . .
> Une feuille qui tombe a divisé l'année
> De son événement léger.

"Si nous pouvons quelquefois parvenir à nos antipodes," Valéry writes in his "Fragments des mémoires d'un poème," "nous ne pouvons guère ensuite qu'en revenir."[38] The poet has been momentarily absent as far as the world is concerned, given over to a contemplation that has been prepared by his own lucidity; but its summit, of a different character from anything that led toward it, was a bounty that escaped the coils of time ("absence spontanée"). The "eternal" moment must end, however, showing once more that consciousness traces out the notion of transiency from its own processes. It has fled as lightly as it came, like voices (line 4), birds (line 8), footsteps (line 10), Psyche, which each have woven the pattern of inevitable loss. Poised between

---

[37] *Cahiers*, VI, 153.
[38] "Fragments des mémoires d'un poème," *Œuvres*, I, 1488.

one period of time and another, between one hemisphere and another, the equinoctial balance, perfect and yet infinitely fragile, has passed. The most tenuous movement has imposed a wholly new face on things, like the leaf, heavy with consequences, that falls into the water, or the eyelid (stanza 9) that was about to close.

> Vers moi, restes ardents, feuilles faibles et sèches,
>   Roulez votre frêle rumeur,
> Et toi, pâle Soleil, de tes dernières flèches,
>   Perce-moi ce temps qui se meurt. . . .

Sound and sense are at last caught up in excited rejection of meditation. Just as in the concluding stanzas of "Le Cimetière marin," the imperative mood is called on to destroy the idol of consciousness and bring fresh activity and vigor. Summer's lingering fires that can be seen in the dry leaves must stir, disturb the calm, shower the speaker with number and noise. Splendidly, "frêle rumeur" conveys a multitudinous murmur. The sun also will become a heroic protagonist, no longer (stanza 7) a resigned witness. The moment of self-analysis, the instant of searching appraisal, must be wholly undone as autumn transfixes it with its shafts. Now comes the supreme flight, the loss of all things, which the self accepts without regret in an attitude that is essentially unreasoned, for it wells up from hidden springs of the heart.

> Oui, je m'éveille enfin, saisi d'un vent d'automne
>   Qui soulève un vol rouge et triste;
> Tant de pourpre panique aux trombes d'or m'étonne
>   Que je m'irrite et que j'existe!

The final section of "Le Cimetière marin" again echoes in these four lines that bring the poem to an unexpected close. The wind that "gets up" corresponds to the self's awakening and a vibrant resonance of the sensibility. Now the poet welcomes change, surrenders to its wild strength: nothing is more compulsive than such a summons. We may recall in this regard, a passage of similar lyricism from the

Cahiers: "Sens debout le vent neuf instantanément frais durcir. Il fait mouvoir l'ombre et les feuilles noires. Et jusque dans mon cœur il presse des forêts. Et je change!"[39] The flight of leaves is autumnal red and bears the rich token of summer, but rather than lulling the self, it points up a latent tension with the world. Signifying sadness ("vol rouge et triste"), it intermingles color and agitation, beauty and death in a rising crescendo. Yet, in accordance with its rhythm, the self is reborn; the seed of life emerges from a conflict in spite of and beyond reason. Through surprise, inner disquietude, and vital affirmation ("m'étonne," "m'irrite," "existe"), the last words describe the spontaneous escape from reflection's cycle of enchantment.

IN HIS first notebook Valéry speaks in suggestive terms of the "retentissement de l'être seul"[40]—the resonance within the self, or, more precisely, the varied murmur along the corridors of the mind. We might say that "Equinoxe" offers a masterly evocation of this ceaseless language, as one moment of consciousness reaches out to grasp the desirable fancy that bears its own mythological name. In so doing it is led to explore its secret architecture, the serpent, the tree, and the crystal of its fears and hopes, wonderment and attraction, and to come face to face with death. The constant rhythm, the simple balance of alexandrines and octosyllables, creates an atmosphere of suave charm to guide the intellectual sensibility; but it belies, and paradoxically plays across, the fatal drama which is here enacted, for it is finally life and not death that is discovered when consciousness returns to the acceptance of sensation and a direct relationship with the world.

Clearly this theme coincides with Valéry's research into the nature of consciousness, undertaken after the "crise de Gênes." From this point of view, "Equinoxe" can be described as offering an ideal model of mental functioning, a "system of transformations," a complete "circuit" of the self

---

[39] *Cahiers*, II, 915. [40] *Cahiers*, I, 809.

that in turn calls on the three modes by which we interpret the world—sensation, affectivity, abstraction. Consciousness is *flight*, that is to say, "self-variance" ("L'esprit est ce qui change et qui ne réside que dans le changement"),[41] although here we realize that pure meditation, freed from the claims of utility, is symmetrical, that loss is balanced by gain. The speaker moves fruitfully between the extremes of death and life and composes the portrait of a man beyond practical interests who has achieved his potential freedom. His time is redeemed, having reached a point of meaningful self-sufficiency ("Le temps est le changement dans la connaissance totale—irréversible. Pour supprimer le temps il n'y a qu'à supposer cette irréversibilité détruite").[42] Thus it is possible to place the work in the perspective of a lifetime's analysis and speculation, to see it as the end result of Valéry's theory of a total act of the mind. ("Il ne suffit pas d'expliquer le *texte*, il faut expliquer la *thèse*.")[43]

Yet "Equinoxe," far from being a formula, is for us first and foremost a highly successful poem which incarnates its abstract motif with consummate clarity of outline. In conformity with the sections we have indicated, it contains four equal angles of vision that alter their register and emotion as the extremes of thought are explored, and as they take the speaker to the "rives sans retour" from which he returns to the restlessness of action. By its discipline, by its imagery, by the breadth of its scheme, by its overall pattern of sensation leading to abstraction and abstraction to sensation, it bears comparison, as I have suggested, with "Le Cimetière marin." But instead of the gravity of a philosophical meditation, its law is elegiac and its meter one of surrender to lyrical movement. Here, in the sense and substance of the poem, on a knife-edge of time, reason meets feeling, and the "external" will to know, and to know what one knows, coincides with the intuitive desire for a

[41] *Cahiers*, VI, 892.   [42] *Cahiers*, I, 313.
[43] *Cahiers*, XXIV, 117.

wholly incorruptible body. "Mon sentiment," we read, "me donne le divin comme œuvre de la vie."[44]

Thus Valéry provides us with the example of a writer who develops the twin activities of analysis and lyricism and finds in practice that they are not hostile to one another but indeed complementary. If we look exclusively at his poetry, we are ready to agree with his contemporaries that his work takes its place as a culminating point in the Symbolist movement. In its richness of texture, its dignity of language and form, its combination of intellectuality and sensibility, it consummates the search for "perfection et pureté poétique"[45] that stems, by way of Mallarmé, from Baudelaire. On the other hand, his *Cahiers* reveal another Valéry, who must henceforth occupy an eminent position among the great French rationalists. In his thought there is a skepticism that submits everything to an extreme desire to decompose and define. Confidence is accorded the language of lucidity, but never, we should note, a complete and unreflecting faith, which experience shows to be unjustified. "Deux dangers," he observes, "ne cessent de menacer le monde: l'ordre et le désordre"; and again: "Il faut que notre pensée se développe et il faut qu'elle se conserve. Elle n'avance que par les extrêmes, mais elle n'existe que par les moyens."[46]

Yet despite appearances, poetry and analysis for Valéry are not isolated but intimately associated enterprises, as indivisible as thought itself, and he moves from one mode to another with the skill of a virtuoso. In both he gives evidence of the virtues of attention, precision, patience, determination, abnegation, and self-criticism that accompany his fascination with the object of his research, his sensuous desire to prolong it through his poems. Criticism and creation here find a ground on which one of the least vulnerable

[44] *Cahiers*, VI, 13.

[45] "Situation de Baudelaire," *Œuvres*, I, 613: "Tandis que Verlaine et Rimbaud ont continué Baudelaire dans l'ordre du sentiment et de la sensation, Mallarmé l'a prolongé dans le domaine de la perfection et de la pureté poétique."

[46] "La Crise de l'esprit," *Œuvres*, I, 993; *ibid.*, p. 1006.

of recent works has been built. His remarkable accomplishment, such as we find it in "Equinoxe" and his other major poems, is to have forged the instrument of self-conscious control, internal coherence, translucid precision: a language that permits him to encompass, and mythically to enclose, the exigencies of reason as well as poetic imagination, reason's errant but enriching companion.

Chapter VII

Music in Apollinaire

TODAY, fifty years after his death, Apollinaire is no doubt the most widely popular of the poets we have discussed. The new edition of his complete works in four handsome volumes has been hailed, the pocket *Alcools* has attained the status of a best seller, while scholarly studies grow more and more numerous. He flourished on the borders of Symbolism; yet although he did not frequent the circles of Claudel and Valéry, as one might have presumed from his less than bourgeois background and Bohemian tastes, he must be seen, I believe, as one of the leaders of the same Symbolist adventure, of the function it accorded poetry, its will to order, its need to transcend.[1] René Char, one of the outstanding figures of Surrealism and after, has underlined the clear distinction to be made between the poet of "La Chanson du Mal-aimé" and his successors: "Enfin Apollinaire, le poète Guillaume Apollinaire," he writes, "trouve en son temps la hauteur interdite à tout autre que lui, et trace la nouvelle voie lactée entre le bonheur, l'esprit et la liberté, triade en exil dans le ciel de la poésie de notre siècle tragique...."[2]

Like many another writer of his time he sought new avenues of expression under the sign of the correspondence of the arts. He became interested in painting, as we know, during his adolescence, published art criticism as early as

[1] Apollinaire praised the Symbolists on several occasions, in particular Mallarmé, whom he named among those he admired in his *Manifeste futuriste*. He valued the new freedoms that Symbolism had won: "C'est le propre et la grande louange du symbolisme que chacun d'eux se soit aussi complètement mis à part de ses contemporains" (*Vers et prose*, June 1908). On this subject, see Marie-Jeanne Durry, *Guillaume Apollinaire: "Alcools"* (3 vols.; Paris: S.E.D.E.S., 1956-1964), and S. I. Lockerbie, "*Alcools* et le symbolisme," *Revue des lettres modernes*, Nos. 85-86 (1963), pp. 5-40.

[2] "Pauvreté et privilège," *Recherche de la base et du sommet* (Paris: Gallimard, 1955), p. 86.

1902, and was later the leading exponent of Cubism. His poetry reflects this interest by his use—as constant and deliberate as Baudelaire's—of paintings as subject matter, and by the poem-drawings he composed and baptized "calligrammes." In addition, his manuscripts suggest that his verbal imagination worked concurrently with his sense of linear form, since we find innumerable sketches in the margins. On the other hand, if we are to believe the testimony of his friends, he would appear to have had very little musical sensitivity. Madame Faure-Favier has described his lack of enthusiasm for concerts (with the possible exception of a performance where an over-ardent pianist broke his instrument!); likewise, the well-known musician Georges Auric, in an article given over to the subject, concluded that this was "un art [. . .] auquel il était insensible."[3] But a writer's sense of music may on occasion be in inverse proportion to his capacity for enjoying concerts. In fact, as I wish to show, music had a central relevance to the creative process in Apollinaire. It was for him a point of reference both formal and conceptual, at the beginning, as it were, and at the end of artistic activity, indicating a method of composition as well as a spiritual ideal. In an endeavor to illustrate this attitude, I should like to examine the relationship of "music"—music as he interpreted it—to his prosody, images, and artistic theory, before proceeding to the analysis of one of his finest compositions.

For him, it is apparent, the creative process originates in song. Poetry becomes the verbal echo of a rhythm, a melody, a musical pattern, as it was for folk-poets or lyric-writers in general before the seventeenth century. Among his immediate forerunners one is tempted to recall similar tendencies in Paul Verlaine and Jules Laforgue: Laforgue, who called

[3] Cf. Madame Louise Faure-Favier, *Souvenirs sur Guillaume Apollinaire* (Paris: Grasset, 1945). At the "Journées Apollinaire" held in Stavelot in August 1965 the theme of the colloquium was "Apollinaire et la musique." See *Actes du colloque* (Stavelot: Editions "Les Amis de Guillaume Apollinaire," 1967; 108 pp.).

himself "the musician with his seemingly parasitic harmonies."

From time to time Apollinaire took his inspiration from folksongs with which everyone is familiar and which he called "peut-être les plus anciens monuments de la pensée poétique" and "la source la plus limpide où puisse s'étancher la soif lyrique."[4] "Veille,"[5] for example, is based on the old air "Malbrough," while "Le Tabac à priser"[6] employs the famous refrain "J'ai du bon tabac." In "Les Saisons" is to be found the adaptation of a traditional children's round I once heard near Grenoble—"Connaissais-tu Pipot, Pipot / Quand il était militaire / Connaissais-tu Pipot, Pipot / Quand il était matelot":

> As-tu connu Guy au galop
> Du temps qu'il était militaire
> As-tu connu Guy au galop
> Du temps qu'il était artiflot
> A la guerre[7]

Mario Roques in an excellent essay showed similar influences at work in "La Petite Auto," "La Loreley," and "Le Pont Mirabeau." Apollinaire did not, however, restrict his borrowings to traditional songs. "Le Cercle 'La Fougère' " was written to the popular tune "A Ménilmontant":

> On essaie d'poétiser
> La couq'l'lard les ch'veux frisés
> La cultur' des pomm's de terre
> A la fougère[8]

In the same way, a music-hall success of 1900, "Je n'ai jamais vu Carcassonne," was used in one of the poems addressed

---

[4] *Vers et prose*, June 1908. Again: "ces rondes aux paroles absurdes et lyriques qui sans doute sont les restes des plus anciens monuments poétiques de l'humanité" ("L'Obituaire," *Le Soleil*, 31 August 1907).

[5] *Œuvres poétiques*, ed. Marcel Adéma and Michel Décaudin (Paris: Gallimard, Pléiade, 1956), p. 216. This edition is henceforth designated *OPO*.

[6] *OPO*, p. 596.   [7] "Les Saisons," *OPO*, p. 240.

[8] *OPO*, p. 528.

to Linda; and the gay rhythms of the Caf' Conc' are easily heard in this amusing stanza which I discovered among the manuscript pages of the *Poète assassiné:*

> Mon père est à Paris
> Ma mère est à Versailles
> Et moi je suis ici
> Qui couche sur la paille
> > Avecque ma
> > Avecque mi
> Avecque ma marmotte en vie.

Yet comparatively few of Apollinaire's poems are based on the rhythms of popular or folk music. One needs to mention the considerable importance of religious harmonies and tones, which allow him to describe his poetry as "une litanie," "une oraison." He recaptures both the fervor and simplicity of traditional hymns of praise:

> C'est le beau lys que tous nous cultivons
> C'est la torche aux cheveux roux que n'éteint pas le vent
> C'est le fils pâle et vermeil de la douloureuse mère
> C'est l'arbre toujours touffu de toutes les prières[9]

Likewise, when he sings of Lou, a sequence of votive parallelisms links the erotic and the mystical:

> Je donne à mon espoir mes yeux ces pierreries
> Je donne à mon espoir mes mains palmes de victoire
> Je donne à mon espoir mes pieds chars de triomphe
> Je donne à mon espoir ma bouche ce baiser
> Je donne à mon espoir mes narines qu'embaument les
> > fleurs de la mi-mai
> Je donne à mon espoir mon cœur en ex-voto
> Je donne à mon espoir tout l'avenir qui tremble comme
> > une petite lueur au loin dans la forêt[10]

We are particularly impressed, in his verse written at the war front, at a time when he was least concerned with lit-

[9] "Zone," *OPO*, p. 40.
[10] "L'Amour, le dédain et l'espérance," *OPO*, p. 465.

erary effects, by the frequency with which he turned to such explicit echoes of liturgical patterns.

A third source of prosodic inspiration is contained in echoes of the rhythms and versification of his favorite authors, the most notable of whom are Villon, La Fontaine, Baudelaire, Rimbaud ("un naturaliste sans rival en poésie," as he called him), and Verlaine. At times the allusion is quite patent, and the poet no doubt expected it to be recognized by his readers; at others less so. In this regard we shall be able to appreciate what appears to me to be a subtle yet decisive influence on the part of another author, rather less expected, when we come to study "La Chanson du Mal-aimé."

Nevertheless, however strong the prosodic impulse may be that associates the poem with song, or religious intonations, or literary readings, the act of composition is most characteristically accompanied by other harmonies which Apollinaire hums in order to guide his words. In his letters and in the *Anecdotiques* we find him repeating several times what he wrote in 1913 to Henri Martineau: "Je compose généralement en marchant et en chantant sur deux ou trois airs qui me sont venus naturellement et qu'un de mes amis a notés."[11] Where else should we look to discover the nature of these harmonies than to his recording of three of his poems, made in 1914 at the Archives de la Parole? The poet read "Le Pont Mirabeau," "Le Voyageur," and "Marie," all lyrics which had appeared the previous year in his first collected book of verse, *Alcools*. And here we do in fact find that the poems are sung.

[11] Letter to Henri Martineau, published in *Le Divan*, March 1938. It is worth noting that Apollinaire referred in July 1914 to the recording of his voice that had been made at the Sorbonne. He wrote: "comme je fais mes poèmes en les chantant sur des rythmes qu'a notés mon ami Max Jacob, j'aurais dû les chanter comme René Ghil . . ." (*Anecdotiques* [Paris: Gallimard, 1955], p. 183). Was this a kind of coquetry, or else mystification, since the poems as we hear them today are indeed "sung"? Perhaps neither: it is possible that another recording was made subsequent to the performance at the Archives de la Parole in May 1914 and that, in addition to the two poems he mentions ("Le Pont Mirabeau" and "Marie"), he read "Le Voyageur."

Music in Apollinaire

Apollinaire's voice is deep, his articulation clear and un-embellished, although slight breaks in the diction suggest an underlying pathos. According to the theme the pace is varied: rapid in "Marie," and "Le Pont Mirabeau," it is slow at the beginning of "Le Voyageur" but faster at the end. A significant factor is the importance given to "e" mutes: thus in "Le Pont Mirabeau" one syllable in every five is mute, and the rhymes, which are all feminine, are pronounced by Apollinaire in contrast with normal practice, emphasizing the liquidity and gentleness of sound by what Valéry called "silences élémentaires."

The recitation consists in working over a complete scale between G and A, the first line of the poem being the highest point attained, the last line the lowest. At the beginning of each stanza there is a rise (sometimes slight) in pitch, but within the stanzas the movement consists of a descent by tones or halftones. This movement may be regular, line by line, or irregular, as when the poet pronounces two or three lines on the same note. Thus, in "Le Voyageur," the four lines that contain the most disparate images in the poem are all recited on the same note, as if to transcend the shock of the words.

> O vous chers compagnons
> Sonneries électriques des gares chant des moissonneuses
> Traîneau d'un boucher régiment des rues sans nombre
> Cavalerie des ponts nuits livides de l'alcool

As an example of this manner we can quote "Le Pont Mirabeau," in which one finds the following pattern:

G	Sous le pont Mirabeau coule la Seine	
	G	F♯
	Et nos amours	
	F	
	Faut-il qu'il m'en souvienne	
		E
E♭-D	La joie venait toujours après la peine	
	E♭	D

223

E   Vienne la nuit sonne l'heure
              E

D-*C*♯   Les jours s'en vont je demeure
             D   *C*♯

F   Les mains dans les mains restons face à face
          F   E

               Tandis que sous
               E♭

           Le pont de nos bras passe
                  D   *C*♯

C   Des éternels regards l'onde si lasse
       between C♯ *and C*

D   Vienne la nuit sonne l'heure
             D

B   Les jours s'en vont je demeure
             C♯   *C*-*B*

E   L'amour s'en va comme cette eau courante
       E

               L'amour s'en va
               E   *F*

           Comme la vie est lente
             F   *E*

E♭-*D*♭ Et comme l'espérance est violente
          E♭   *D*   *D*♭

D   Vienne la nuit sonne l'heure
             D

D♭   Les jours s'en vont je demeure
                          D♭

E   Passent les jours et passent les semaines
       E

               Ni temps passé
               E

Ni les amours reviennent
E

D   Sous le pont Mirabeau coule la Seine
        D

C   Vienne la nuit sonne l'heure
        C   C♯

A   Les jours s'en vont je demeure
        B   B♭-A

Let us emphasize that the recitation is not a simple automatic return to the same note at the beginning of each stanza, such as we might perhaps find in the elocution of a child. The movements I noted give every indication of being subtly concerted. Indeed, as we pursue our examination, it seems possible to describe these harmonies as being the adaptation of the psalmody which Apollinaire heard regularly at the Collège Saint-Charles in Monaco as a boy. A little-known statement by Max Jacob, one of the poet's intimate friends, appears to me of special relevance: "Il avait retenu des Pères de Monaco la psalmodie des Vêpres. C'est sur cette psalmodie qu'ont été composés presque tous ses poèmes. Il vaguait dans les rues de Paris répétant un mot puis un autre sur un air grégorien. Si le poème était sinistre, il psalmodiait d'un ton sinistre."[12]

The church intonation was not adopted unchanged. It became, as Apollinaire says elsewhere, "le rythme de [son] existence." The words were spoken, according to the emotion, in a lively or slow manner; the descent of the scale also became a personal adaptation of the chant. But the fact remains that here is a pattern whose harmony, like the chant, refuses declamatory effects, and where the words well up at the summons of this principle of form. Creation becomes the meeting place of the discontinuity of language

[12] Note by Max Jacob in *Présence d'Apollinaire*, a collection of homages published in 1944 by the Galerie Breteau on the occasion of the exhibition "Le Temps d'Apollinaire."

(that is, the outside world) with the continuity of an inner presence of music.

A natural and important consequence of this method of composition was the suppression of punctuation. There were, of course, numerous poets long before Apollinaire who seem to have disliked as much as he did any breaks in the poetic phrase. Among the Symbolists we may mention Tristan Corbière when he composed his "Cris d'aveugle" to a Breton folk song,[13] or Mallarmé, who believed that "les signes [. . .] ne serviraient qu'à diviser inutilement le tout,"[14] and practiced what he preached. From the very first poems of Apollinaire, punctuation was reduced to a minimum. The poems in his notebooks from his nineteenth year have only an occasional comma, although for publication purposes he added the conventional signs. Yet about October 1912, when *Alcools* was being printed, he finally decided to eliminate all punctuation. How did he justify himself? "La ponctuation courante ne s'appliquerait point à de telles chansons."[15]

The change in typography was not a mere example of wayward poetics. It came from a desire, as deeply rooted in Apollinaire as the poetic gift itself, to break with declamation, to substitute an intonation. The poem is born in a personal harmony, a continuity of sound which "has a dying fall" and suggests a gradual discovery of the poet's inner self.

I have described what I believe to be the underlying force of the movement which, like a ground swell, carries forward Apollinaire's poetry. We can now examine briefly the nature of the imaginative universe his images reveal. Symbolism, it is clear, oscillates between the poem whose every detail is precise and fitted into a whole, and the

[13] Cf. Tristan Tzara, "Geste, ponctuation et langage poétique," *Europe,* January 1953, pp. 59-78.

[14] Cf. Ch. Chassé, *Lueurs sur Mallarmé* (Paris: Editions de la Nouvelle Revue Critique, 1947), p. 74.

[15] Letter to Henri Martineau, quoted by André Rouveyre, "La poésie d'Apollinaire protégée par lui-même," *Le Divan,* March 1938, pp. 65-67.

poem of mood where each detail blurs and merges into the next so that the sequence of images forms a fleeting glissando. In the case of Apollinaire, all is "musicalized": there is no longer plastic reality but a state of flux, a set of references providing constant surprise. The complexity of texture that results suggests so many aspects of the poet's identity:

> Les brebis s'en vont dans la neige
> Flocons de laine et ceux d'argent
> Des soldats passent et que n'ai-je
> Un cœur à moi[16]

Object sparks object, a series of metamorphoses leads the poet on through this most subjective of worlds. Verbs are the focal points of contact; and changes in tense convey the instantaneous character of the notations:

> Un chien jappait l'obus miaule
> La lueur muette a jailli[17]

The absence of punctuation naturally increases the surprise effect of these unexpected juxtapositions.

Here is what we may call Apollinaire's music of the senses, or the rapid interweaving of themes. The only guiding principle of the poem is the poet himself, restlessly striving toward an ideal. He seeks his inner self and his dream of love and poetry. In this regard the symbolical representations he gives of himself are significant: he is first and foremost the "Voyageur," "flâneur," "tzigane," "baladin," "saltimbanque," "guerrier d'Epinal," crossing Europe and recrossing the memories of his life; he is also Merlin, Croniamantal, Orpheus, Que-vlo-ve, each of whom is unhappy in love, each the poet-prophet seeking an impossible ideal. "Et je cherche une divinité, mais je veux qu'elle me paraisse éternelle."[18] All are energetic explorers of the unknown and have the same restless haste that we

---

[16] "Marie," *OPO*, p. 81.
[17] "Chant de l'horizon en Champagne," *OPO*, p. 265.
[18] *Le poète assassiné* (Paris: Gallimard, 1945), p. 70.

find in the poet of *Alcools* and *Calligrammes* to reach across the succession of rapid images to a hidden goal. Apollinaire evokes the poetic sensibility in these terms: "Ses yeux dévoraient tout ce qu'ils regardaient et quand ses paupières se rapprochaient rapidement comme des mâchoires, elles engloutissaient l'univers qui se renouvelait sans cesse par l'opération de celui qui connaît en imaginant les moindres détails des mondes énormes dont il se repaissait"; and again: "il se réfugia dans sa mémoire et allait de l'avant, tandis que toutes les forces de sa destinée et de sa conscience écartaient le temps pour qu'apparût la vérité de ce qui est, de ce qui fut et de ce qui sera."[19]

His imagination bears, therefore, structurally, a likeness to that of a fleeting music and in translating it he makes constant reference to a world that is likewise seen in terms of music: thus the "chant des moissonneuses" ("Le Voyageur");[20] Paris "chante sa belle chanson" ("Les Collines");[21] the machine gun on the battlefield "joue un air à triples croches";[22] the noise of cannon is like "lourdes cymbales";[23] and "la terre tremble comme une mandoline."[24] But occasionally, as if by enchantment, another music is heard, definite and stated. At the end of "Un Fantôme de nuées," which describes a performance of tumblers on the Boulevard Saint-Germain, the grace of a little boy is such that it conjures up in the hearts of all the spectators an ideal past, a mythical beauty.

> Le petit saltimbanque fit la roue
> Avec tant d'harmonie
> Que l'orgue cessa de jouer
> Et que l'organiste se cacha le visage dans ses mains
> Aux doigts semblables aux descendants de son destin
> Fœtus minuscules qui lui sortaient de la barbe

[19] *Ibid.*, pp. 45-46.
[20] *OPO*, p. 79.
[21] *Ibid.*, p. 171.
[22] "La Nuit d'avril 1915," *OPO*, p. 243.
[23] "Fusées," *OPO*, p. 261.
[24] "La Mandoline, l'œillet et le bambou," *OPO*, p. 209.

Nouveaux cris de Peau-rouge
Musique angélique des arbres
Disparition de l'enfant[25]

Apollinaire brings us to a Bergsonian "durée," a time other than the rapid succession of impressions. Similarly, in "Le Musicien de Saint-Merry," the thought of past love is for the poet a continuum like flute music heard in the distance:

O nuit
Toi ma douleur et mon attente vaine
J'entends mourir le son d'une flûte lointaine[26]

Memory is "un chant lointain,"[27] a "chantante ronde" ("Adieu adieu chantante ronde / O mes années ô jeunes filles").[28] The love felt for Annie makes Apollinaire think of De Quincey's metaphor of the palimpsest; but his own image will be drawn from the realm of music:

Les souvenirs sont cors de chasse
Dont meurt le bruit parmi le vent[29]

It appears important to observe that all these references to an ideal past occur at the end of poems and are thus the central intuition which the poet attains by means of his creation.

At other times Apollinaire reaches a less tenuous music than memory in the "music" of poetic vision. He hears the future that appears to him, as to Rimbaud, "aussi simple qu'une phrase musicale." Rather than the sound of hunting horns and flutes, it is a chorus of praise: "L'hymne de

[25] *OPO*, p. 195.
[26] *Ibid.*, p. 191.
[27] "La Porte," *OPO*, p. 87.
[28] "A la Santé, I," *OPO*, p. 140.
[29] "Cors de chasse," *OPO*, p. 148. A history of this image would include Vigny, Baudelaire ("Le Cygne"), Verlaine, Laforgue. But Apollinaire's image has its own originality: its rapid statement bare of adjectives, its tone of a moral truth discovered and accepted. Cf. M.-J. Durry, "Cors de chasse," *Revue des Sciences humaines* (October-December 1956), pp. 391-399; Antoine Fongaro, "Cors de chasse," *Studi francesi*, I (1957), 88-89.

l'avenir est paradisiaque."[30] "Le Brasier" presents a poet
who is subject to the "tons charmants" of the Amphion, and
anxious to hear "le chant du pâtre toute la vie."[31] In "Les
Collines," published ten years later, he tells us that in order
to hear this music he has killed "le beau chef d'orchestre,"
and now to the divine poet alone is revealed the ideal:

> J'ai traversé le ciel splendide
> Où la vie est une musique
> Le sol est trop blanc pour mes yeux[32]

We may say, then, that Apollinaire introduces into his
images a giant counterpoint in which derivative melodies
are striving to become the principal one, fragmentary
themes to achieve an unbroken sequence. It is, as Mallarmé
would have put it, the attempt to transpose a brute fact
into the ideal. The very moving thing about Apollinaire's
art is that within the framework of the poem we are led to
experience and participate in this same aspiration. We may
compare it to the "voluntary" memory of Baudelaire, but
Apollinaire's paradise is not the memory of some exotic
Mauritius: it is, as against the immediate music of the
senses, an ideal creation of the mind. In one of those strik-
ing passages of self-revelation which we find in his corre-
spondence, he indicates the contrapuntal nature of his in-
spiration. "Rien ne détermine," he writes in a letter to Yves
Blanc, "plus de mélancolie chez moi que cette fuite du
temps. Elle est en désaccord si formel avec mon sentiment,
mon identité, qu'elle est la source même de ma poésie."[33]

What we have noted may be corroborated, moreover, by
a short analysis of his critical writings. In 1901 and 1902,
during his stay in Germany, he began to write alert articles
about painting and literature which were to continue to
come from his pen until his death. They made him the cham-

---

[30] "Le Chant d'avril 1915," *OPO*, p. 244.
[31] *OPO*, pp. 108-110.
[32] *Ibid.*, p. 175.
[33] *Lettres à sa marraine* (Paris: Gallimard, 1948), p. 72. "J'ai tou-
jours désiré que le présent quel qu'il fût perdurât" (*ibid.*).

pion of the young generation, the first and most penetrating critic of Picasso and Matisse, the defender of individualism in the arts. He realized that "l'art naît où il peut,"[34] but that did not prevent him from seeking its essence. It was for him the discovery of the self: "ce périlleux voyage à la découverte de la personnalité."[35] The poet, the painter returns to first principles, is "reborn," finds his own center, "l'idée divine qui est en nous si vivante et si vraie."[36] He appears to be a demiurge. His deepest intuitions, however, are only a rediscovery of some universal law. He is a god, might we say, but there is Moira. "Quelle saisissante image pour un artiste: les dieux, tout-puissants mais soumis au destin."[37] That is the destiny of art; the new discovery is an eternal truth. It reunites us with an absolute, an order, that Apollinaire expresses, as did the earlier Symbolists, by the image of music. "La musique," he says in his *Méditations esthétiques*, "est de la poésie pure." Elsewhere he affirms that the aim of art must be "finally to compose a persistent harmony, the most powerful that man has imagined."[38] But art for Apollinaire must be no flight into abstracts. Aware of the new slant he is giving to an aesthetic concept, he declared that poetry must be born in shock. There had been no clearer expression of the role of surprise in modern literature than the speech he gave in 1917 at the Vieux-Colombier. "La surprise est le plus grand ressort du nouveau. C'est par la surprise, par la place importante qu'il accorde à la surprise que l'esprit nouveau se distingue de tous les mouvements artistiques et littéraires qui l'ont précédé."[39] Surprise is the impact of the external world on the ideal, on the music that the apparent chaos must become. From it, consciously, the artist must "ordonner un chaos." "L'ordre et le métier sans quoi il n'y a point d'art."

[34] *Revue littéraire de Paris et de Champagne*, September 1906.
[35] *La Phalange*, December 1907.
[36] *L'Esprit nouveau et les poètes* (Paris: Haumont, 1946), p. 36.
[37] *La Phalange*, December 1907.
[38] *Les Peintres cubistes: méditations esthétiques* (Geneva: Cailler, 1950), p. 82.
[39] *L'Esprit nouveau et les poètes*, p. 17.

We see, then, that in the critical writings of Apollinaire art is regarded as a movement toward an inner reality, just as, in his own poetry, we traced the intuition of a spiritual music. From the contact of this harmony with the harmonies of the outer world was to come that surprise and tension which the poem alone could resolve.

We may, I think, conclude from the foregoing observations that in Apollinaire we find poetic creation constantly linked with music. Like the other Symbolists, he sought to "reprendre à la musique son bien." He did this, however, in no single, simple way. Poetry for him approximated music first of all by its genesis, which follows the dictates of an inner harmony, a truly lyrical movement. The sound invites the words. We, therefore, find in his poetry a refusal of a purely external security of form in favor of continuity from beginning to end.[40] Secondly, poetry approximates music by reproducing a glissando of images: Apollinaire experienced the world as a becoming where objects are in constant change. But this principle of change implied no tragic circle. For him it was dynamic and purposeful, working to attain an inner secret harmony. Music is the transitory world, but on a different level it is also the still center, the eternal where the self is found. Like Mallarmé, we might say, he believed in a poetic Eden: "toute âme est une mélodie qu'il s'agit de renouer" is a statement he would willingly have supported. Yet whereas it is possible to maintain that Mallarmé wanted salvation as if in spite of the world, Apollinaire sought the ideal music through his contact with outer reality. It is possible, then, to consider his attitude as a personal dialogue with Symbolism which continued the ambition of his predecessors to wed poetry and music but which rejected the temptation of angelism for the shock and tension of external phenomena. The images of the outside world thereby became his way to self-integration; and the poem, its prosody sustained by a chant,

[40] Hence, of course, the ease with which Apollinaire's poetry is learnt by heart—what Paul Valéry would call its high "mnemonic value."

could approach the inner continuity of its author's desire: "Les jours s'en vont je demeure."[41]

To STUDY in some detail one of his major compositions, together with the pervasive presence of a central image and ideal, I should like to turn to a critical moment in Apollinaire's development: thus, although his work written in Germany in 1901 and 1902 spelt out with authentic power the legendary atmosphere of the Rhineland, one must date the discovery of his true voice, and its fullness, from 1903. The sudden revelation of his talent in "La Chanson du Mal-aimé" was indeed surprising: the young poet used rhythms and expressions that already mark his earlier work, but there was now a new register, a deeper tonality. He told of an unhappy love, transformed a destiny into music, having realized once and for all that he belonged among those who "péniblement, amoureusement, génialement, peu à peu peuvent exprimer une chose nouvelle et meurent dans l'amour qui les inspirait."[42] At the age of twenty-three he had gauged the vital nature of his art.

Published in 1909 in the *Mercure de France*, his long poem did not reach any sizable audience until 1913, with the appearance of *Alcools*. Half a century later, one is struck by the feeble reaction of recognized critics of the time, most of whom spoke of the presumed antecedents of the collection and gave little prominence to "La Chanson du Mal-aimé." Alone, we feel, this poem would have been sufficient to reverse his reputation as a mystifier, or "second-hand dealer" as Georges Duhamel called him. Today the situation is different: "La Chanson du Mal-aimé" has made its way into our memories and sensibilities, and it is no exaggeration to say that it marks a significant point in the development of modern lyricism. Yet, however erudite some of his more recent critics may be, they have perhaps too often tended to study Apollinaire himself to the detriment of his

[41] "Le Pont Mirabeau," *OPO*, p. 45.
[42] Letter to André Rouveyre, quoted by A. Rouveyre, *Apollinaire* (Paris: Gallimard, 1945), p. 192.

work. So it is that one finds commentators who have little
hesitation in identifying his life with his verse, in taking his
theme to be that of sentimental confession ("des per-
sonnages de légende . . . créent de piquantes diversions
dans ce récit d'une déception," as one critic puts it),[43]
in substituting shadow for poetic reality. Within the limits
of this analysis I shall try to approach the meaning by
which on one occasion the poet made himself, as I take it,
other than the man he was, providing a sense and sign that
transcend the conditions of creation.

Nevertheless, I shall first of all describe the circumstances
of composition, for if the poet's life does not explain the
writings (nor, assuredly, the writings his life), he well knew
the dialectical relationship that exists between the two.
"Chacun de mes poèmes commémore un événement de ma
vie," he affirmed;[44] and with reference to "La Chanson du
Mal-aimé" he wrote: "(elle) commémore mon premier
amour à vingt ans."[45] Over the last ten to fifteen years we
have learnt much of Apollinaire's liaison with Annie Play-
den, the young woman whose image pervades the poem.
She was, as we know, the daughter of a London architect
of Puritan upbringing, and was born in 1880—the same year
as Apollinaire. At twenty she went to Paris as governess
in the house of the Viscountess von Milhau, and it was
there that, one day in 1901, Apollinaire presented himself
on a friend's recommendation to ask for a position as tutor.
"I remember," Annie wrote forty-five years later, "the day
he came to introduce himself, he smiled at me all the time
he was talking [. . .]. When he knew me he declared that his
friends had asked if the countess was charming—and he re-
plied: 'No, but the governess is, and that's what made me
decide to take the job!' "[46] And so he left for the Rhine-

---

[43] Jeannine Moulin, *Textes inédits* (Geneva: Droz, 1952), p. 13.
[44] Letter to Henri Martineau, cited above, note 15.
[45] Letter to Madeleine of 30 July 1915, *Tendre comme le souvenir*
(Paris: Gallimard, 1952), p. 70.
[46] Letter of 21 October 1946 to Robert Goffin, quoted by R. Goffin,
Entrer en poésie (Brussels: A l'enseigne du chat qui pêche, 1948),
p. 137 (my translation).

land in August 1901 and remained for a year. From the point of view of his poetry this was an eminently productive period, since he assimilated German folklore and the *Rhein-romantik* with amazing speed, and composed pieces of captivating charm that treat of the Rhenish countryside and its inhabitants—gypsies, Jews, brigands, children, lovers. But no poetry is less subject to realistic description, since Apollinaire's Rhineland is essentially the springboard for an imagination that is fascinated by the magic of legend, and the desire to weave a poetic enchantment.

He seems to have paid immediate court to the governess and was soon held by a domineering passion. One day he took Annie to the summit of the Drachenfels in the Seven Mountains and asked her to marry him. When she refused the fortune and noble name he offered, he threatened to kill her by pushing her over the cliff. The terrified girl accepted, but reneged when she was safely on level ground.[47]

> Le cher Amour je l'ai perdu
> Dans une forêt d'Allemagne
> Il gît sanglant le cou tordu
> Derrière les Sept Montagnes[48]

What was the nature of their love? It was believed for a long time that it had remained platonic. In his biography published in 1952 Marcel Adéma considered Apollinaire's claim in a letter to Jean Onimus,[49] in which the poet wrote "Je couche avec la gouvernante," to be nothing but a young man's boast. Yet what we learn from their correspondence and elsewhere leads us to suppose the contrary. Although the detail may indeed appear trivial, we can perhaps bet-

[47] Cf. Leroy C. Breunig, "Apollinaire et Annie Playden," *Mercure de France*, April 1952. I am indebted to Professor Breunig's articles, notably his penetrating study of the architecture of "La Chanson": "Le Roman du Mal-aimé," *La Table ronde*, September 1952, pp. 117-123.

[48] Rejected lines quoted by M. Décaudin, *Le Dossier d' "Alcools"* (Geneva: Droz, 1960), p. 103.

[49] *Guillaume Apollinaire le Mal-aimé* (Paris: Plon, 1952). The letter of Jean Onimus was published in *Les Lettres françaises* of 13 December 1951.

ter understand, once we admit their carnal relationship, the exasperation which from beginning to end underlies the poem. In like manner, it is not without relevance to the "Interlude des sept épées," which, as we shall suggest, contains a stylized sequence of the symbols of love.

In the spring of 1902 the young couple were in Munich. The poet was confused in the extreme: at one moment he would shake Annie by the shoulders and make her weep; a short time later he would send her flowers. Doubtless, too, this was the scene of some moments of happiness that find their expression in the naïve spontaneity of the Aubade, the song "à Laetare" in which the poet was inspired by the rejoicing in honor of the Virgin before Easter; but the nature he exalts is pagan, smiling and shameless. His love is a cult that spring has brought again with the green world and long-lost gods.

> C'est le printemps viens-t'en Pâquette
> Te promener au bois joli
> Les poules dans la cour caquètent
> L'aube au ciel fait de roses plis
> L'amour chemine à ta conquête[50]

Yet as his stay in Germany continued, Apollinaire felt he was more and more the pawn of love, and became madly jealous of the attention the local schoolteacher paid to Annie. He went so far as to write to a friend: "Si je n'obéis pas aux conseils de ma mère qui m'enjoint de revenir pour la fin du mois, je marche [. . .] à la désagrégation mentale."[51]

Thus, leaving the Milhaus in August 1902 at the end of his year's contract, he returned to Paris and found employment in a bank. He had decided to forget Annie. Yet they still exchanged letters and Apollinaire's imagination was haunted by his memories ("Rhin artère bleu d'un corps de femme Europe / Le corps d'Annie aux veines bleues"). In November 1903 he left for London, where she was once

---

[50] "La Chanson du Mal-aimé," *OPO*, p. 49.
[51] Letter to Jean Onimus, *Les Lettres françaises*, 13 December 1951.

more living with her family. Despite the poet's efforts to make a favorable impression on the Playdens, her father, Annie tells us, "did not at all approve of my friendship with a foreigner."[52] Returning to Paris, he seems to have begun composing "La Chanson du Mal-aimé." Yet a few months later he received urgent letters from Annie recalling him—"Now, *will* you *come* or *not*"; "Je serai gentil, chérie" (sic)—and he went once more to London in May 1904; this time his idea was that they should elope if her parents did not consent to their marriage. Annie was unable to make up her mind and finally announced that she had decided to leave for America, where a fiancé was waiting for her. For the second time Apollinaire left London, and never again saw her (she did indeed sail for the United States that same year to take up a position). The remaining portion of "La Chanson" was no doubt composed during the summer of 1904, after the poet's return to Paris.

I have retraced the evolution of this love affair since it not merely constitutes the pretext of the poem, but provides its very weft. The memory of the Rhineland is to be found in the Aubade, that of the first visit to London in stanzas 1 to 5, the winter and spring of 1904 in stanzas 10 and 38 to 40, the Paris summer in stanzas 55 to 59. It is nevertheless essential to note that "La Chanson du Mal-aimé" in no way constitutes a narrative; on the contrary, it constantly rejects precise chronology. Here the sequence is that of the artist who discovers a temporal sequence of his own. He seeks to fuse various moments of the past and present, to undo the succession of events as he lived them: in suffering and solitude the lover devotes himself to becoming time's magician.

To appreciate Apollinaire's art we must, then, leave the purely biographical level to enter upon the question of composition. A poet, as we know, owes less to events than to art itself, to the artists he admires and wishes to equal and surpass. We have seen the importance of melodies that lingered in Apollinaire's sensibility and, in particular, of a

[52] Letter to Robert Goffin, *Entrer en poésie*, p. 138.

personal incantation that commanded his diction, reducing it to a severe psalmody, guiding his quest for an inward accord. But this was no simple song: it had to constitute a grand symphony, the expression of the whole of love on a vast scale. In this regard many critics have insisted on a parallel between "La Chanson du Mal-aimé" and *Le Grand Testament*. They observe that certain imagery and the very architecture of the poem are reminiscent of Villon. The comparison is no doubt useful, for there is an affinity between the first poet of Paris and the "Flâneur des deux rives." Yet we must remind ourselves that such an affinity in no way implies parentage. The voice of Apollinaire is not that of Villon: more indirect, less familiar and amused, it is characterized by frequent identification with noble personages of the past. In addition, the use of stanzas of five octosyllabic lines gives the poem a new rhythm, a rapid movement that is suddenly interrupted, then taken up again. Although Apollinaire had begun to use the *quintil* in poems written at Stavelot in 1899 or perhaps even before, he had not attained the breadth and accent of "La Chanson du Mal-aimé."[53] Was there then perhaps a literary influence more decisive than Villon's which at least partly explains the adoption of this form, as well as the use of particular techniques? For my part I have been struck to find in a poem of Larmartine the same stanzaic form, the theme, the rhythms, even the metaphors of the modern poet. One can hardly be surprised, of course, that Apollinaire should turn to Lamartine, since he could not fail to perceive the closeness of their poetic sensitivity, their parallel taste for music, their tragic sense of the passing of time. The piece which I feel oriented Apollinaire's expression in "La Chanson du Mal-aimé" is to be found in the *Nouvelles méditations poétiques*, "that scamped work," M. Guyard recently wrote, which "merely exploits the formulas that brought its author

[53] Cf., among the pieces of *Le Guetteur mélancolique*, "L'Amour," "Or nous regardions les cygnes . . . ," "S'en est allée l'amante . . . ," "Je ne sais plus ni si je l'aime. . . ."

fame."[54] Yet the piece in question is, in my opinion, touching and worthy of the attention of Apollinaire. It is his "Adieux à la poésie," which, like Apollinaire's song, is "un poème de fin d'amour." The poet is alone, uncertain, hesitating between past and future. His memories are too close and bitter for him to feel anything but despair. Is there a chance of surviving to find consolation? Lamartine hopes for "cette seconde jeunesse / Qu'un doux oubli rend aux humains," while Apollinaire likewise exclaims: "Qu'un ciel d'oubli s'ouvre à mes vœux." One must forget; but death is waiting, and the poet may perish in some shipwreck. Here Apollinaire uses the same metaphor as Lamartine, envisaging the moment when he will come to sleep motionless on the shore. Only poetry will remain, that sad, melodious poetry written in memory of faithless women: "Mais toi, lyre mélodieuse / Surnageant sur les flots amers," says Lamartine; and Apollinaire acknowledges that his proud destiny is to change his despair into song:

> Moi qui sais des lais pour les reines
> Les complaintes de mes années
> Des hymnes d'esclave aux murènes
> La romance du mal-aimé
> Et des chansons pour les sirènes

We could pursue the comparison between the two poems, noting the presence of a whole series of analogous expressions, the importance given above all to images of the sea, even the use of references to mythical or historical figures whose circumstances contrast with the poet's present lot. So great a number of common points leaves me in little doubt: Apollinaire, I feel, knew Lamartine's poem, which served to crystallize his own experience, as well as the ambitions of a "poète inconnu parmi d'autres poètes inconnus." He found in it the five-line stanza, the concurrent themes of lost love and enduring poetry, metaphors, tones, inflections which, eighty years before, point to "La Chanson

[54] M.-F. Guyard, *Alphonse de Lamartine* (Paris: Editions Universitaires, 1956), p. 52.

du Mal-aimé." Naturally the objections might be raised that we have had to seek Lamartine's poem in a collection little read today and that, despite the influence it may well have exercised on Apollinaire, it is not among its author's masterpieces. This is indeed so: far be it from us to want to diminish Apollinaire's originality or to reduce "La Chanson" to a simple pastiche. The poet used a framework, a mode of expression, as Mallarmé and Verlaine when they refashioned Baudelaire or Valéry when he rewrote Mallarmé, but from this contact with another work, in this struggle with another vision and style, he discovered a language of his own which could not be assimilated to its formal origin. Thus, whereas "Adieux à la poésie" is stamped with the seal of its time and contains Lamartine's characteristically plangent voice, "La Chanson" turns a new page in French poetry.

How can we define the originality of the poem? We observe first of all the total refusal of the univocal style of the Romantics: here the poet does not take up a fixed stance in front of his audience. A single mask is no longer sufficient, since he knows that his identity is multiple and self-contradictory. He seeks to remember love, but also to forget; he insults his mistress, voices obscenities which suddenly become expressions of tenderness. He hates and loves a woman desirable and false, beautiful but impure:

> Regret des yeux de la putain
> Et belle comme une panthère
> Amour vos baisers florentins
> Avaient une saveur amère
> Qui a rebuté nos destins

The poet pronounces his lays, hymns, imprecations, moves across modern Paris and London, Homeric Greece, Kalidasa's India, the steppes, in a continual odyssey of the emotions to the most disparate places and times. But each allusion modifies those that precede and follow, so that we can well say that Apollinaire's procedure is ceaselessly ironical: obscenity and tenderness, faithfulness and revolt

mingle to translate the complex world of love. Besides, does
not the "mal-aimé" invite us in his epigraph to envisage his
whole song in an antiromantic perspective?

> Et je chantais cette romance
> En 1903 sans savoir
> Que l'amour à la ressemblance
> D'un beau Phénix s'il meurt un soir
> Le matin voit sa renaissance

He distances his emotions, exorcizes whatever might ap-
pear irremediable. Guarding himself against any criticism
that could mock the excesses of a love-lament, he is the first
to combat sentimentality by wielding irony and making it
the very principle of his expression.[55] There is in his poem
a great variety of tones, a psychological complexity such as
we find rarely in lyric poetry. "La Chanson" offers, as it
were, the complete range of sentimental reactions that love
may provoke, felt not in a logical order but as they fire each
other and intermingle. It is clear, moreover, that the ab-
sence of punctuation, which seemed to his early readers
to defy common sense, corresponded exactly to the need
to translate the continuity, the "music" of the emotional
surge of each development.[56]

This multiple self designates the lover of Annie Playden;
yet not him alone, for one cannot fail to recognize that it
is a *composed* self. Here we broach what is perhaps the
most delicate point for the comprehension of the poem: we
must, I believe, rid ourselves of the idea that the poet ex-
presses a state of emotional incoherence, remembers, re-
counts, translates a subjective disorder. This opinion neg-
lects the plan of the poem, and implicitly denies that Apol-
linaire was the artist of his own experience. On the con-

---

[55] On the importance of irony in Apollinaire, see the unpublished
thesis for the doctorat d'Université presented at the Sorbonne by
Margaret Davies, "L'Ironie de Guillaume Apollinaire" (1948).

[56] "Pour ce qui concerne la ponctuation je ne l'ai supprimée que
parce qu'elle m'a paru inutile et elle l'est en effet, le rythme même
et la coupe des vers voilà la véritable ponctuation et il n'en est point
besoin d'une autre" (Letter to Henri Martineau, cited above).

trary, I consider one of the most striking aspects of the poet's genius to be that he suggested so pertinently the confusion of love, created so diverse a poetic identity, and, at the same time, achieved a sequence that is other than temporal and possesses a structural necessity. We may note first of all an evident detail of formal balance: the nine stanzas at the beginning and end of the poem were conceived so as to constitute a symmetrical contrast. With the attention of a Parnassian, Apollinaire arranged his metaphors, compared the wintry atmosphere of London (stanzas 1 to 5) with the June of Paris (stanzas 55 to 59), called on (stanzas 6 to 9) the kings of the past who were fortunate in love, Ulysses for instance:

> Lorsqu'il fut de retour enfin
> Dans sa patrie le sage Ulysse
> Son vieux chien de lui se souvint
> Près d'un tapis de haute lisse
> Sa femme attendait qu'il revînt

Or else the Hindu prince Doushmanta, who unjustly rejected his wife but later realized her exemplary faithfulness:

> L'époux royal de Sacontale
> Las de vaincre se réjouit
> Quand il la retrouva plus pâle
> D'attente et d'amour yeux pâlis
> Caressant sa gazelle mâle

On the other hand, in the corresponding stanzas of the last section, Apollinaire designates those other kings who, like himself, suffered the madness of love:

> Destins destins impénétrables
> Rois secoués par la folie

In the same way the controlled use of two refrains underlines the solitude of the poet and his constant solicitude to sing of passing love ("Moi qui sais des lais pour les reines"), his uncertain hope in a love that will one day renew his life as the epigraph has already suggested:

Music in Apollinaire

Voie lactée ô sœur lumineuse
Des blancs ruisseaux de Chanaan
Et des corps blancs des amoureuses
Nageurs morts suivrons-nous d'ahan
Ton cours vers d'autres nébuleuses

These details are ample proof of a dominant design. One might also point to constant traits of the vocabulary, with its alliance of ideal beauty and harsh realism, its mixture of erudition (for instance, "ahan," "argyraspides," "dendrophores," "pyraustes") and vulgarity ("pet foireux," "putain," "voyou," "cul"), its insistence on certain key terms that are like so many charms (the most characteristic is "amour," found sixteen times, to which we must add "amoureux" [1], "amoureuses" [3], "aime" [1], "aimais" [1], "aimé" [2], "aimée" [2], "aimés" [1], "amant" [1], the exclamation "ô" [12], the words "femme" [6], "cœur" [6], "yeux" [9], "blancs" [6], and "mort" [10], together with "meurt" [1], "mourir" [1], "mourut" [1], "mourant" [1]). Similarly, the rhyme scheme shows a repetitiveness that increases the impression of emotional concentration. In nineteen of the fifty-nine stanzas we find the rhyme -ant: it is above all associated with the lover—"amant," "tremblant," "rampant," "surnageant"; in eleven others we find -é: the poet evokes memory and regret ("Avons-nous assez navigué / . . . Avons-nous assez divagué"); while eight stanzas with rhymes in -aine recall the presence of Annie—"inhumaine," "dame damascène," "châtelaine," "reine."

Yet does a reading of the poem as a whole bear out the presence of a controlled pattern? Let us consider the seven parts into which Apollinaire divided his work. The first, composed of fourteen stanzas, forcefully expresses the obsessive nature of love. No less than eight times the poet repeats the word "amour," while "amant" and "aimé" each occur twice. He wanders through the city, encounters the image of his love in debased forms that draw him irresistibly:

Un soir de demi-brume à Londres
Un voyou qui ressemblait à
Mon amour vint à ma rencontre
Et le regard qu'il me jeta
Me fit baisser les yeux de honte

From the first lines we enter into a nocturnal world, the uneasiness of which is conveyed in part by evanescent rhythms and impure rhymes. Apollinaire grapples with a dream that transforms a London street arab into an inner deity of shameful seductiveness. Held captive and humiliated, he is drawn by an imperious fascination, threatened by the roofs of London like the waves of a legendary ocean.

Je suivis ce mauvais garçon
Qui sifflotait mains dans les poches
Nous semblions entre les maisons
Onde ouverte de la mer Rouge
Lui les Hébreux moi Pharaon

Que tombent ces vagues de briques
Si tu ne fus pas bien aimée
Je suis le souverain d'Egypte
Sa sœur-épouse son armée
Si tu n'es pas l'amour unique

He sees himself as the actor in a Biblical scene whose end will be tragic, but then proceeds to turn the image inside out in a most extraordinary way: he is the Pharaoh, and his sister-wife, and his entire army, if this woman to whom he now directly speaks was not loved by him; that is to say, he adopts a mask before declaring that, were he to lie, he would assume wholly this very same mask. It is a striking illustration of the poetic self-awareness which will characterize "La Chanson du Mal-aimé."

The unfaithful woman is not a vague or clear image, but a mythical force ("la fausseté de l'amour," "le faux amour") surrounded by fire, blood, lamentation, however debased its form ("Sortit saoule d'une taverne"). Emotion reaches its peak in stanza 5, which forces the self to take refuge in an idealized past and evoke with intentional naïveté a picture-book Hellas that is the consoling image of fidelity. The poet has just begun his search along the ways of memory, but Ulysses has ended his; London was peopled with fleeting forms, but the scene he now imagines is as immobile as an Epinal engraving. A second image of happy love is Shakuntala's enduring fidelity despite her lord's repudiation: the vignette of princely lovers who rediscover happiness is a sunny one, and the details are imbued with a suggestive Orientalism. But after these two "illuminations," which recall those given over to Homer and Milton in the "Adieux à la poésie," the poet returns to his own situation and speaks of the obscure world of the emotions in which "false love" and "she whom I still love" form a two-headed divinity. His present anguish goes beyond reason and is expressed by the extravagant hyperbole of more than mortal martyrdom ("les quarante de Sébaste / Moins que ma vie martyrisés"). The forces of destiny prescribe this round of memories, the suffering which awaits him and leads him on as irresistibly as the urchin of London; but in an intuitive way he also knows that the movement of his song, however painful, is his only resource against despair:

> Mon beau navire ô ma mémoire
> Avons-nous assez navigué
> Dans une onde mauvaise à boire
> Avons-nous assez divagué
> De la belle aube au triste soir

If he is one of those swimmers who die of love, their faces turned toward the stars which are so many cold and distant women ("ces grelottantes étoiles / De fausses femmes"), he yet can place his trust in a rebirth which will mean love transcended. (Similarly, in a critical article, Apollinaire wrote in 1908: "Le poète chassera, à cor et à cri, les ourses étincelantes et les autres constellations bestiales, jusqu'à l'heure où pour dernière féerie il créera encore lyriquement les astres de sa propre transformation.")[57] Thus at last, in

[57] *Vers et prose*, June 1908.

stanza 14, he abandons himself to the cycle of remembrance: "Je me souviens d'une autre année"; now the whole bittersweet thread of memories must be unwound. Fleeing the present, he finds his former voice, which was far from shadowy and ambiguous, but he does not realize that the context already predetermines the coloring of his Aubade and that, by dint of rediscovering the past, he will deepen his despair. The introductory section has, then, established the emotional tension of the self torn between love as the poet consciously judges it and the enchanting image of the loved one, the alcohol of life and that of the poem, the reality of experience and the "nouvelle réalité" of the poem that must be written.

As we have had occasion to observe, the three stanzas of the Aubade that follows are the Eastertide exaltation of nature untouched by Christianity, when love "n'était pas, comme maintenant, une statue de petit dieu nu et malade, à l'arc débandé, un honteux objet de curiosité, un sujet d'observations médicales et rétrospectives."[58]

C'est le printemps viens-t'en Pâquette
Te promener au bois joli
Les poules dans la cour caquètent
L'aube au ciel fait de roses plis
L'amour chemine à ta conquête

Mars et Vénus sont revenus
Ils s'embrassent à bouches folles
Devant les sites ingénus
Où sous les roses qui feuillolent
De beaux dieux roses dansent nus

Viens ma tendresse est la régente
De la floraison qui paraît
La nature est belle et touchante
Pan sifflote dans la forêt
Les grenouilles humides chantent

[58] Introduction to *L'Œuvre du Chevalier Andréa de Nerciat* (Paris: Bibliothèque des Curieux, 1910), p. 5.

Once again the object of his fascination is evoked, but in tender terms. The brightness, gaiety, concrete simplicity are no doubt less inspired by Victor Hugo's *Chansons des rues et des bois* than by medieval poetry, to which Apollinaire freely admitted his debt: "Mes maîtres sont loin dans le passé, ils vont des auteurs du cycle breton à Villon."[59] In these lines the use of the unfamiliar word "feuilloler" is one token of this influence, since Apollinaire came across it in 1899 in the *Roman d'Alexandre* (thirteenth century) by Durmart, where it means "voler en l'air et retomber comme les feuilles."[60] Yet the whole Aubade is typical of many developments in medieval romances like the following:

> La terre meismes s'orgueille
> Pour la rosée qui la meuille
> Et oublie la povreté
> Où elle a tout l'hiver esté
>
> .   .   .   .
>
> Lors se déduit et lors s'envoise
> Li papaguez et la calandre;
> Lors estuet jeunes gens entendre
> A estre gais et amoureus
> Pour le temps bel et doucereus[61]

Apollinaire had a remarkable gift for expressing a similar candor. The comical precision of his images ("Les poules dans la cour caquètent," "Les grenouilles humides chantent") breaks with the atmosphere of the first section and takes us from the pathos of memory to a confident invitation to love. His naïveté is manifestly not spontaneous: the poet consciously delights in his song and images, and

[59] Letter of 11 May 1908 to Toussaint Luca, quoted by Toussaint Luca, *Guillaume Apollinaire: souvenirs d'un ami* (Monaco: Editions du Rocher, 1954), p. 83. My interpretation differs from that of Margaret Davies in her *Apollinaire* (London: Arnold, 1961), where she describes the Aubade as "a precious, superficial conceit" (p. 108).

[60] Cf. M. Décaudin, *op.cit.*, p. 16.

[61] Guillaume de Loris, *Le Roman de la Rose*, in *Poètes et romanciers du moyen âge*, ed. Albert Pauphilet (Paris: Gallimard, Pléiade, 1952), p. 548.

the adjective "ingénus" ("Devant des sites ingénus") shows a detachment that is foreign to medieval lyricism.

With the third section, spring and its joyful gods, both pagan and Christian, have disappeared; love that flowered so tenderly is dead. The self finds another object for its cult in the idols of memory. For the first time the speaker becomes aware of himself as a poet:

> Moi qui sais des lais pour les reines
> Les complaintes de mes années
> Des hymnes d'esclave aux murènes
> La romance du mal-aimé
> Et des chansons pour les sirènes

Alone, abandoned by happiness, he can but remain faithful to untouchable queens, to heartless seductresses, to the past. He is a galley slave of olden times who sings of the fish that surround him, free and yet deadly, wishing his death like faithless women. But his patient fidelity is transformed: he knows it is his destiny to celebrate his sorrow and, like a feudal minstrel, the words he uses to describe his songs suggest the stylized atmosphere which is that of "La Chanson" as a whole, composed of lays, laments, and hymns. The poet makes a myth of his experience, one of the comparisons he uses being drawn from Greek legend: "Comme la femme de Mausole / Je reste fidèle et dolent." Sorrow and fidelity mingle in his mourning as in that of Artemis, who built a marvelous tomb to honour Mausolus. Apollinaire, too, trembling before the void the present opens up to him, consoles himself by building his own mausoleum of song that he dedicates to the memory of love.

Yet his plaintive expression of constancy is followed by quite another atmosphere in stanzas 24 to 26: plagiarizing a Polish text of the false letters from the Zaporogue Cossacks to the Sultan, the poet links together a series of coarse insults, refers to Barrabas, to the prince of demons, reveals cruelty, shame, and obscenity. Which of us has not had reservations on reading these stanzas for the first time? One of the admirers of the poem and its dedicatee, Paul Léau-

taud, could not refrain from condemning them: "La pre-
mière version était plus belle que la seconde. [Apollinaire]
y a fourré ensuite les Cosaques Zaporogues qui n'y fi-
guraient pas."[62] Indeed, only the first stanza appeared in
the version published in 1909; the two others, which are
much more violent, are not found until the publication of
the poem in book form. But one may consider that the
technique adopted has an astonishing ambivalence which
suggests the feelings of the "mal-aimé" regarding his love.
He must on the one hand free himself from his obsession,
reject it with all the strength of impersonalized speech: on
the other hand he will proclaim fidelity to his idols, his re-
fusal to exchange them for others. In this Interlude with
its psychological ambiguity we reach, then, a further peak
of emotion.

Now, after two sections expressing the tensions of fidelity,
two sections affirm its pain. The first (stanzas 27 to 41) con-
tains the cry of the self which cannot and will not abandon
its memories. For the first time the poet details the fetishes
that are inseparable from his fascination: the glance, the
kisses. Yet the idea of beauty is not divorced from that of
infidelity, so that he reviles at the same time as he appeals:
"Regret des yeux de la putain / Et belle comme une
panthère." With tender melancholy he forges the naïve
name of the bridge where he waits ("le pont des Reviens-
t'en"), whose arch crosses life, time, memory, like the Pont
Mirabeau. His feeble hope in love's return is expressed with
childlike artlessness:

> Et sur le pont des Reviens-t'en
> Si jamais revient cette femme
> Je lui dirai Je suis content

Yet the tone changes completely to express the return of
sadness. Instead of the entreating accent of the preceding
lines, the image offers a radical violence: suffering is like
an exhaustion of the heart and brain, a rain of tears that

[62] Paul Léautaud, *Entretiens avec Robert Mallet* (Paris: Gallimard, 1952), p. 113.

drowns sensitivity and reason. To turn away from his an-
guish the poet has recourse to a litany celebrating the mem-
ory of the woman and enumerates seven images which
constitute, as it were, a magical portrait from which all
shadows are excluded. The voice we heard in the Aubade
momentarily allows him to compose a form as captivating
as nature itself. The self takes pleasure in recalling the very
simple proof that it was loved, this "exfoliated daisy"—
"Marguerite, Fleur petite, Rouge au bord, Verte autour, Dis
le secret de mes amours."

> Je ne veux jamais l'oublier
> Ma colombe ma blanche rade
> O marguerite exfoliée
> Mon île au loin ma Désirade
> Ma rose mon giroflier

Nevertheless, there is nothing stable for the suffering con-
sciousness in which the images of love aggravate those of
sorrow:

> Les satyres et les pyraustes
> Les égypans les feux follets
> Et les destins damnés ou faustes
> La corde au cou comme à Calais
> Sur ma douleur quel holocauste

Here is another litany, a succession that shows in profile the
fleeting divinities of the past—imps of the woods and fields,
wondrous monsters, fire spirits, will-o'-the-wisps. They are
ambiguous images, for we know not if they signify ill-
fortune or happiness, if they are redeemed or damned: all
cross the imagination of the poet, the pyre of sorrow on
which the entire past must be burned. From it there may
arise another life, a renewed destiny; but though he is aware
of this chance, the fabulous unicorn of his soul and the
capricorn of his body still hesitate to abandon themselves
to the fire of forgetfulness and its rite in honor of the god
Sorrow. We have reached the most somber point of the
poem and, for the hallucinated eyes of the poet, his

shadow is a serpent of fatality that measures implacably the fragile limits of his being.

> Et toi qui me suis en rampant
> Dieu de mes dieux morts en automne
>
> Tes victimes en robe noire
> Ont-elles vainement pleuré
> Malheur dieu qu'il ne faut pas croire

He tries to conjure away death by envisaging the origin of their union as a marriage ceremony to which he affectionately brought his loved one: the self, he affirms, led forth a faithful form from night, and created the god of its past: it is the act of the poet that gives form and significance to his memories, annexing them ("Tu es à moi en n'étant rien") at the very moment when they threaten to destroy him.

> Au soleil parce que tu l'aimes
> Je t'ai menée souviens-t'en bien
> Ténébreuse épouse que j'aime
> Tu es à moi en n'étant rien
> O mon ombre en deuil de moi-même

However, the charm of this atmosphere is suddenly broken; we rediscover the substantial world of nature and another death—not black Sorrow nor the serpent-shadow, but the whiteness of a snowy winter. The farmers have performed their familiar rites in burning the hives and preparing for the new season, and nothing is less like the consecration of the mad priests of Sorrow than these traditional chores. Now death is resolved into life according to the unchanging order of the seasons, as birds sing the praises of spring and lighthearted April. Content in the thought of such seasonal transformation, the poet uses learned words that convey the vigorous beauty of nature (the "argyraspides" are Alexander the Great's stouthearted warriors; the "dendrophores," the bearers of symbolic trees at the spring rites). Winter is a god who must eternally die and be reborn,

whose silver bucklers are the immense shining shields of
the snowy landscape which melt today to reappear afresh—
immortal like love (although the poet cannot yet accept
this). Everything in nature and in the city has its appointed
place to ensure that happiness emerges from the wheel of
time.

> L'hiver est mort tout enneigé
> On a brûlé les ruches blanches
> Dans les jardins et les vergers
> Les oiseaux chantent sur les branches
> Le printemps clair l'avril léger
>
> Mort d'immortels argyraspides
> La neige aux boucliers d'argent
> Fuit les dendrophores livides
> Du printemps cher aux pauvres gens
> Qui resourient les yeux humides

In the midst of this rejoicing the self suddenly declares
its solitude: "Et moi j'ai le cœur aussi gros / Qu'un cul
de dame damascène." The poet's emotion overflows in an
exclamation of coarse humour which serves as his safety
valve, as it did in the "Réponse des Cosaques Zaporogues."
Now he proposes the traditional image of the Seven Swords
which sums up a personal suffering that is mythical, like
the passion of the Virgin. He knows he is twisting the
knife in the wound, the swords in his heart, but cannot help
contemplating the "claires douleurs" of memory: "Comment
voulez-vous que j'oublie?"

The Interlude of the Seven Swords contains a mysterious
and original series of illuminations that enshrine the mem-
ories of love. It is a splendid movement, without doubt
the most captivating of the poem, offering us experience
transformed and ritualized to form the prism, or magically
complete representation, of love's ambiguity—both beauti-
ful and deadly, severe and sentimental. Each stanza pre-
sents an immobile attitude that is wrenched from time and

contingency.[63] First there is the virginal beauty of the girl "toute d'argent," whose name is "Pâline"—"pâle" (pale) and "câline" (coaxing). The shining white of purity and frigidity attracts the poet with a fatal charm:

> La première est toute d'argent
> Et son nom tremblant c'est Pâline
> Sa lame un ciel d'hiver neigeant
> Son destin sanglant gibeline
> Vulcain mourut en la forgeant

Blood accompanies this beauty—the blood of menstruation and defloration that is woman's destiny and haunts Apollinaire ("Aujourd'hui tu marches dans Paris les femmes sont ensanglantées," we read in "Zone"). The blade is "Ghibelline," no doubt because Apollinaire assimilates love to an antireligion by recalling that the Ghibellines were those who opposed the Pope (moreover, the first version of the third stanza referred to an "anti-papesse"). It may also refer to Mount Gibel, as has been suggested, and therefore be associated with the wiles of the fairy Morgan, who is the subtle enchantress of men. The fascinating whiteness of womanhood is such that a god died to create it: "Vulcain mourut en la forgeant."

[63] I broached this question in an article published in *Le Flâneur des deux rives*, No. 3 (September 1954), pp. 10-13. Since then it has been discussed several times, most notably by Margaret Davies, (*op.cit.*, pp. 113ff.); by Pol-P. Grossiaux ("Recherches sur 'Les sept épées,'" *Revue des lettres modernes*, Nos. 146-149 [1966], pp. 41-83), who makes several penetrating comments within a framework that perhaps fails to convince us ("La séquence des 'sept épées' apparaît comme une quête existentialiste de soi-même . . ." [pp. 73-74]); and by Lionel Follet ("Images et thèmes de l'amour malheureux dans 'Les sept épées,'" *Europe*, special number devoted to Apollinaire [1967], pp. 206-240). This essay, admirably clear and precise, and written in the light of a close reading of the whole of Apollinaire, calls the sequence "une série de charades, dont chacune doit évoquer, à la fois, concrètement, l'image d'une épée, et, symboliquement, une souffrance amoureuse—le second terme étant évidemment le plus important" (p. 207), "une espèce d'*Il n'y a pas d'amour heureux* systématique" (p. 208), "le douloureux décompte des souffrances que [l'amour] engendre" (p. 235).

La seconde nommée Noubosse
Est un bel arc-en-ciel joyeux
Les dieux s'en servent à leurs noces
Elle a tué trente Bé-Rieux
Et fut douée par Carabosse

The wicked fairy Carabosse grants a magical force to love, an enchantment that has been tragic for a host of gay fellows ("Bé-Rieux" is doubtless the Walloon form of "beaux-rieurs"). A recent commentator, Pol-P. Grossiaux, has given evidence from another poem of Apollinaire for interpreting the "bel arc-en-ciel joyeux" as a girdle, and "Noubosse" as a portmanteau word "Noue-bosses."

Le troisième bleu féminin
N'en est pas moins un chibriape
Appelé Lul de Faltenin
Et que porte sur une nappe
L'Hermès Ernest devenu nain

The phallic image, surrounded in mystery, is offered as a sacred grail. Corresponding to Carabosse, it is Hermes, god of magic, who bears the "chibriape" as the lover approaches his mistress.

La quatrième Malourène
Est un fleuve vert et doré
C'est le soir quand les riveraines
Y baignent leurs corps adorés
Et des chants de rameurs s'y traînent

The poet depicts the happiness of lovers in some idyllic riverside festival that charms both eyes and ears. It is the image of sirens and Ulysses, the bewitching of men by beauty, which is no doubt also suggested by the name "Malourène": the woman is queen ("reine") but also ill-chance ("malour" in Old French).

La cinquième Sainte-Fabeau
C'est la plus belle des quenouilles
C'est un cyprès sur un tombeau

Music in Apollinaire

Où les quatre vents s'agenouillent
Et chaque nuit c'est un flambeau

Like the third sword, the fifth presents, I take it, the phallic image of the lover: distaff, cypress, flame. It is his activity; the solemn homage of his tenderness and respect; his vital ardor.

La sixième métal de gloire
C'est l'ami aux si douces mains
Dont chaque matin nous sépare
Adieu voilà votre chemin
Les coqs s'épuisaient en fanfares

Morning brings a happy awakening: the beloved farewells and tenderly guides her lover as cocks crow triumphantly, and "Le jour" (as Hugo wrote) "sort de la nuit comme d'une victoire."

Et la septième s'exténue
Une femme une rose morte
Merci que le dernier venu
Sur mon amour ferme la porte
Je ne vous ai jamais connue

The seventh sword designates the death of love which bitterly slams the door of idyllic remembrance. The poet cries "Je ne vous ai jamais connue," like Laforgue: "Vrai, je ne l'ai jamais connue," like Apollinaire at the age of thirty-four after his liaison with Lou: "J'ai cru prendre tout cela, ce n'était qu'un prestige [. . .]. O toi que je n'ai possédée que morte." The destinies of men and women are forever different.

Thus, by evoking the murderous nature of memory through these seven swords of sorrow, Apollinaire detaches them from time and space. Their place is now in poetry, that is, in enchantment, just as in Nerval the charm of lyricism transmutes despair—"Modulant tour à tour sur la lyre d'Orphée / Les soupirs de la sainte et les cris de la fée." The pains and pleasures of love are held in quasi-mystical emblems that reflect in small the pattern of the poem as a whole, of grief become music.

We have still to consider the eleven stanzas of the last section of "La Chanson," its finale, where all is set under the sign of madness: the wild dance of the human race, the clamorous intoxication of Paris:

> Les démons du hasard selon
> Le chant du firmament nous mènent
> A sons perdus leurs violons
> Font danser notre race humaine
> Sur la descente à reculons

The poet enunciates a general truth, a "philosophy": man's fate is revealed by his own unhappy love with its vain efforts and threatened hopes. Resignedly, he turns to the music of the spheres that obliges us to conform to its devilish rhythms. The song of the firmament is the inexorable passage of time, leading us "de la belle aube au triste soir," from spring to winter, to begin again ceaselessly; it is also the distant, treacherous seduction of feminine beauty ("Ses regards laissaient une traîne / D'étoiles"). As though standing apart, the self contemplates this senseless movement to the music of violins while men pursue their fate blindly to death through the act of remembrance ("sur la descente à reculons"). In a series of exasperated exclamations Apollinaire raises his voice to tell the enigma of the human condition, the pathos of individual destinies. The images of kings, introduced in stanzas 7, 8, and 9, here find a symmetrical echo, but madness, not happiness, now distinguishes them. Moreover, the "shivering stars" recall the numerous parallel references throughout the poem to woman's coldness, winter, whiteness, dead love. Our destinies lead us from the presence of false love ("de fausses femmes dans vos lits") to its absence ("aux déserts que l'histoire accable")—those empty spaces dominated by the eye of irreversible time.

The theme of madness also brings back a precise memory. During his stay in Germany, on the occasion of one of his

long voyages, Apollinaire saw in Bavaria the tutor of the
two mad kings, Louis and Othon. Later he was to make
several allusions to this meeting in his prose writings, the
most detailed being found in one of his "anecdotiques" of
1911: "J'ai eu l'occasion de voir ce tuteur de deux rois fous.
Il a l'air d'un maître à danser du XVIIIe siècle. Petit, il
trépigne et il semble que ce soit en mesure. Il était, une
fois où je le vis, en costume de l'ordre de Saint Georges
et coiffé d'une toque empanachée [. . .]. Le prince Luitpold
faisait encore remuer ses pieds en mesure sous la table et
son visage spirituel portait encore les signes d'une gaieté
pleine d'insouciance. . . ."[64] The poet naturally associates
this image with his German love. He is himself like this
regent with the unconcerned air whose destiny is so inti-
mately linked with madness, who sobs when the fireflies
shine in the heart of summer, for they recall the wild vacil-
lating flames of the mind—either "les larmes d'un regret
ardent comme une flamme"[65] or "des regards de blâme /
Aux épouses de chair qui laissent en leur âme / Des voiles
d'amour vibrer le dernier son."[66] Fluid images express the
return of spring and an enchanting movement ("La barque
aux barcarols chantants," "sous l'haleine / Des vents qui
tremblent au printemps"), but whiteness ("lac blanc,"
"cygne") merges details into a beauty that is touched by
despair and death. The woman has left the castle and
abandoned her lover, while dead love is a siren, the swan
that sings as it dies. In search of love the king, like the poet,
can only drown in the image that fascinates him. And yet,
beyond death, his desire becomes legendary and is seen
again in his face turned toward the "ciel changeant," which
here as before represents perfidious beauty. He is like
Icarus, that other mythical personage we find in Apollinaire,
whose eyes remain fixed on the sun though it means his
death: "Au semblant des noyés, il ira sur une île / Pourrir
face tournée vers le soleil splendide."[67] Thus, objectivizing

[64] "La Vie anecdotique," *Mercure de France*, 15 April 1911.
[65] *OPO*, p. 588.   [66] *Ibid.*, p. 1134.
[67] *Ibid.*, p. 345.

his state of mind, the poet shows its final consequences
of fatal madness and pathetic survival in legend.

> Juin ton soleil ardente lyre
> Brûle mes doigts endoloris
> Triste et mélodieux délire
> J'erre à travers mon beau Paris
> Sans avoir le cœur d'y mourir
>
> Les dimanches s'y éternisent
> Et les orgues de Barbarie
> Y sanglotent dans les cours grises
> Les fleurs aux balcons de Paris
> Penchent comme la tour de Pise
>
> Soirs de Paris ivres du gin
> Flambant de l'électricité
> Les tramways feux verts sur l'échine
> Musiquent au long des portées
> De rails leur folie de machines
>
> Les cafés gonflés de fumée
> Crient tout l'amour de leurs tziganes
> De tous leurs siphons enrhumés
> De leurs garçons vêtus d'un pagne
> Vers toi toi que j'ai tant aimée

In the last stanzas the ideal atmosphere is replaced by a
noisy modernity (one thinks of the *silence* of London),
each stanza presenting the auditory images of love-cries,
lays, laments, hymns, songs. Whereas at the beginning of
the poem the poet's dreams carried him toward a London
of nightmare, he now describes the Paris he knows well.
The images of sun and fire denote the return of summer,
and complete the round of the seasons; yet it is a warmth
that only brings sharper pain. The present moment is suf-
fering, a fire which, like the pyre of grief, could burn the
poet alive, but still furnishes the very substance of his
song. Madness, sorrow, and melancholy are reconciled
("Triste et mélodieux délire") and make up the wandering

self which suffers from remembrance even if it fears forgetfulness still more. Once again we recognize the bond that inextricably unites poetry and sorrow in Apollinaire, as the rhymes and assonance, the irregular rhythms, the images translate a fretful monotony. Sundays drag on, empty like men's destiny. As for the "triste et mélodieux délire" of the preceding stanza, it merges in the sobbing refrains that echo the ill-loved poet. The flowers that lean down from the balconies and recall the Tower of Pisa convey languor and fatal decline.[68] The city is the Paris of 1900 with its din, its electricity, its intoxication, where green lights flash like obscurely sinister symbols, while the metallic clatter of trams figures the demented music of the poet's loneliness. In 1915, in one of the poems to Lou, Apollinaire again used the metaphor of these lines:

> Chaque jour
> Mon amour
> Va vers toi ma chérie
> Comme un tramway
> Il grince et crie
> Sur les rails où je vais[69]

The song of love has become an immense cry that emanates from the heart of the city; but in describing it the poet mocks himself, his emotions, his poetry. Ironically, he finds the language of his love in gypsy songs, in the sneezing of siphons, in waiters oddly dressed in loincloths. All this agitation, at once fervent and comical, is the image of his heart and song, addressed to lost love as a final offering. Once more the refrain is heard:

---

[68] "Nuit pisane" (*ibid.*, p. 588) captures a similar feeling by the same comparison:

> Alors sur les perrons en écoutant mourir
> La source qui languit les Pisanes penchées
> Comme leur Tour et par la mort effarouchées
> Attendent cependant l'amour qui va venir

[69] *Ibid.*, p. 387.

Moi qui sais des lais pour les reines
Les complaintes de mes années
Des hymnes d'esclave aux murènes
La romance du mal-aimé
Et des chansons pour les sirènes

In these last words Apollinaire breaks away from the noisy atmosphere to bring back again the stylized world of medieval poetry. Yet here the refrain takes on increased significance as it recapitulates the diverse images of the last section of "La Chanson." It constitutes the expression of the solitary self that creates an artistic present, at the same time as it summates the poem's essential ambiguity: the remembrance of the sorrow of love and its sufferings is at the same time the affirmation of poetry's triumph, the achievement of the "song" that was the implicit goal of song.[70]

Thus the poet has chosen to speak of his madness, his fascination, his vain faithfulness, his sorrow, in order to control them. Love, pain, and death may seem to have triumphed but he expresses them, gives them form: he it is who is their master. He has conquered a world that henceforth is his own:

Monde souffrant de mon orgueil
Vous n'avez une vie qu'en moi[71]

WITH HIS own experience as the matter of his art, he sought the language for what he feared the most. "La Chanson du Mal-aimé" declares the death of love, the gods, the self; yet this poet of exile changes his misfortune into a magic cycle: the harmony of his versification, the careful balance of open-

[70] It is clear that I am departing here from the interpretation proposed by Scott Bates in his excellent unpublished thesis, "The Aesthetics of Guillaume Apollinaire" (Madison, University of Wisconsin, 1955): "the last and gravest crisis of despair has spent itself and a passive melancholy takes its place," he writes of the last stanzas of "La Chanson."

[71] These lines are found in a draft of "La Chanson" which has been reproduced by M. Décaudin in his *Dossier d' "Alcools,"* p. 106.

ing and closing themes, the development in *seven* sections, the Interlude of the *Seven* Swords, the encyclopedic system of temporal and spatial references. "*L'univers* pleure par ma voix," we read in one draft.[72] If he is concerned with death, he also treats of resurrection; autumn and winter are followed by spring and summer. He knows the morning of rebirth, although he must first travel "de la belle aube au triste soir"; while love will be recognized as a legendary phoenix that dies only to be reborn. From the depth of his experience he will declare to Yves Blanc: "Ceux qui sont raisonnables, c'est-à-dire, les poètes, mettent à profit les souffrances de l'amour en les chantant."[73]

At the beginning, then, was the meeting with Annie Playden and an omnivorous passion that lasted three years. We witnessed his struggle to make for himself, in order to exorcize this spell, a style in the wake of the harmonies and motifs of Lamartine. As for the poetic structure, he found a model in the episodic development of certain medieval romances, in particular no doubt those of Villon; but rejecting the traditional lyric self in favor of a multiple persona, his poem took on the accents of what we might call an ironic romance in the sense that the élan is constantly modified and broken, and just as constantly renewed, according to the mode of a personal diction and rhythm. His deliberate search led to the fifty-nine stanzas of "La Chanson du Mal-aimé," in which the artist, by "an all-powerful will," "alters the order of things, contradicts cause and effect, annihilates the remembrance and the very truth of that which existed the previous day," so as to make "a succession of events establishing a new reality." "Chaque jour peut-être une volonté toute puissante change l'ordre des choses, contrarie les causes et les effets et anéantit le souvenir et la vérité même de ce qui existait la veille, pour créer une succession d'événements établissant une nouvelle réalité. Et ces nouveautés sont le mensonge de l'ancienne vérité. Tel est l'ouvrage poétique: la fausseté d'une réalité

[72] M. Décaudin, *op.cit.*, p. 106.
[73] *Lettres à sa marraine*, p. 44.

anéantie."[74] As the creator of just such a new reality—a language that imposes form and a vibrant coherence on the emotions it contains—he could not but seem to the Surrealists, despite the affinities they still felt with him, "le dernier poète."[75]

[74] *La Phalange,* August 1908.

[75] The term was applied to Apollinaire by André Breton in a lecture he gave in 1922, "Caractères de l'évolution poétique et ce qui en participe," later collected in *Les Pas perdus* (Paris: Gallimard, 1924), p. 203.

Index

Index

Index

Index

Index

Index